# Going Performative in Intercultural Education

## LANGUAGES FOR INTERCULTURAL COMMUNICATION AND EDUCATION

***Series Editors***: **Michael Byram**, *University of Durham, UK* and **Anthony J. Liddicoat**, *University of Warwick, UK*

The overall aim of this series is to publish books which will ultimately inform learning and teaching, but whose primary focus is on the analysis of intercultural relationships, whether in textual form or in people's experience. There will also be books which deal directly with pedagogy, with the relationships between language learning and cultural learning, between processes inside the classroom and beyond. They will all have in common a concern with the relationship between language and culture, and the development of intercultural communicative competence.

Full details of all the books in this series and of all our other publications can be found on http://www.multilingual-matters.com, or by writing to Multilingual Matters, St Nicholas House, 31-34 High Street, Bristol BS1 2AW, UK.

LANGUAGES FOR INTERCULTURAL COMMUNICATION AND EDUCATION: 31

# Going Performative in Intercultural Education

## International Contexts, Theoretical Perspectives and Models of Practice

Edited by

**John Crutchfield and Manfred Schewe**

MULTILINGUAL MATTERS
Bristol • Blue Ridge Summit

DOI 10.21832/CRUTCH8545
**Library of Congress Cataloging in Publication Data**
A catalog record for this book is available from the Library of Congress.
Names: Crutchfield, John, 1971- editor. | Schewe, Manfred, editor.
Title: Going Performative in Intercultural Education: International Contexts, Theoretical Perspectives and Models of Practice/Edited by John Crutchfield and Manfred Schewe.
Description: Bristol, England; Blue Ridge Summit, PA: Multilingual Matters, [2017] | Series: Languages for Intercultural Communication and Education: 31 | Includes bibliographical references and index.
Identifiers: LCCN 2017013367 | ISBN 9781783098545 (hardcover: acid-free paper) | ISBN 9781783098569 (epub) | ISBN 9781783098576 (kindle)
Subjects: LCSH: Multicultural education–Cross-cultural studies. | Intercultural communication–Cross-cultural studies. | Cultural pluralism.
Classification: LCC LC1099 .G66 2017 | DDC 370.117–dc23 LC record available at https://lccn.loc.gov/2017013367

**British Library Cataloguing in Publication Data**
A catalogue entry for this book is available from the British Library.

ISBN-13: 978-1-78309-854-5 (hbk)

**Multilingual Matters**
UK: St Nicholas House, 31-34 High Street, Bristol BS1 2AW, UK.
USA: NBN, Blue Ridge Summit, PA, USA.

Website: www.multilingual-matters.com
Twitter: Multi_Ling_Mat
Facebook: https://www.facebook.com/multilingualmatters
Blog: www.channelviewpublications.wordpress.com



The policy of Multilingual Matters/Channel View Publications is to use papers that are natural, renewable and recyclable products, made from wood grown in sustainable forests. In the manufacturing process of our books, and to further support our policy, preference is given to printers that have FSC and PEFC Chain of Custody certification. The FSC and/or PEFC logos will appear on those books where full certification has been granted to the printer concerned.

Typeset by Deanta Global Publishing Services Limited.
Printed and bound in the UK by the CPI Books Group.
Printed and bound in the US by Edwards Brothers Malloy, Inc.

# Contents

# Contributors

**Joelle Aden** is Professor in the School of Education at Paris-Est Creteil University (France), where she teaches research methodology in language education to students at Master's level and directs doctoral theses exploring the links between the arts and language learning. Her research interests include the impact of empathy on language interaction. Her most recent work investigates theatre activities from the point of view of enaction theory (Varela) to open new perspectives on the potential role of arts education in developing empathetic skills, which she considers essential for transcultural competence.

**Jane Arnfield** is an Associate Professor of Theatre and Performance and Subject Head Northumbria Performing Arts (NPA) Film and TV at Northumbria University (UK). A theatre practitioner and actor since graduating from Dartington College of Arts (UK) in 1988, Jane has been a member of three ensembles: Mike Alfreds' Method and Madness; David Glass Ensemble, facilitating and leading Lost Child Projects (South East Asia, South America, and Europe); and Alan Lyddiard Northern Stage Ensemble. Her research is focused on theatre of the real, adapting and performing solo auto/biographical performances sourced from testimony and researching survival mechanisms deployed by humans in extraordinary circumstances.

**John Crutchfield** is a US writer and theatre artist currently based in Berlin (Germany). His plays and performance pieces have been produced at independent theatres and festivals in the US, Ireland and Germany, and his poems, essays, stories, translations and reviews have appeared in a variety of international publications. At present, he also teaches and conducts empirical research in the Department of English Didactics, Freie Universität Berlin, where his courses include creative writing and theatre for future teachers of English as a Foreign Language. See www.johncrutchfield.com.

**Eucharia Donnery** is Lecturer in Intercultural Communication Studies in the Department of Applied Computer Sciences, Shonan Institute of Technology, Japan. Her main research and supervisory areas are intercultural communicative competence, drama in second language acquisition (SLA), computer assisted language learning (CALL), as well as colonial and feminist discourses in literature.

**Daniel Feldhendler** was Senior Lecturer at the Goethe University in Frankfurt on Main (Germany) from 1976 to 2014. He continues to teach at other European universities and in Canada. He is also actively involved in continuing and adult education with a focus on action methods, playback theatre, psychodrama and life stories. He is the co-founder of the Centre de Psychodramaturgie in Mainz (Germany), as well as a co-founder and board member of the German-speaking playback theater Netzwerk e.V. (PTN). He is the author of many publications on learning and teaching for adults using relational, drama and psychodrama approaches.

**Micha Fleiner** works as a lecturer in the College of Foreign Languages and Cultures at Xiamen University, China. He holds a PhD in Performative Foreign Language Didactics, an MA in German as a Foreign Language and an MA in Europe-oriented Bilingual Teaching. His current academic research focuses on the integration of performing arts into the area of linguistic, literary and intercultural education.

**Katja Frimberger** is Research Associate on the multisited AHRC/UK-funded project Researching Multilingually at the Borders of Language, the Body, Law and the State. She is based at the School of Education, University of Glasgow (UK), where she explores the role of arts-based pedagogy in 'post-method' intercultural and multilingual research contexts. She is interested in Brechtian theatre pedagogy, new materialism, filmmaking as a migratory aesthetic and feminist views on validity.

**Magdalena Haftner** is an Austrian actress, theatremaker and teacher. She studied Theatre Pedagogy and Education at the University of Vienna and Physical and Devising Theatre in Berlin and at the London International School of Performing Arts (LISPA) London. As co-founder of the improv collective *artig*, her professional teaching and acting practice investigates the potential of improvisational theatre for language learning as well as for challenging intercultural, business-related, social environments worldwide. See www.artiges.org.

**Evi Kompiadou** is a preschool educator and a PhD candidate at the School of Early Childhood Education, Faculty of Education, Aristotle University of Thessaloniki (Greece). Her research interests involve the use of multilingual material and identity texts for the promotion of intercultural education in preschool. Since 2011, she has been responsible for the educational section of the group Polydromo on bilingualism and multiculturalism in education and society. See www.polydromo.gr and www.facebook.com/polydromo.

**Almut Küppers** is an Educational Scientist and Foreign Language Specialist for English, German and Turkish. She earned her qualified teacher status at Birmingham University (PGCE) (UK), and her doctorate from Goethe University in Frankfurt on Main (Germany). She is currently affiliated with Sabancı University through Istanbul Policy Center, a think tank for which she carried out a research project on multilingualism in post-national immigrant societies. She also teaches at Marmara University in Istanbul, and has taught previously in the UK, the US and Germany. Her research focuses on diversity, language and identity issues.

**Antonis Lenakakis** is Assistant Professor of Drama/Theatre Pedagogy at the School of Early Childhood Education, Faculty of Education, Aristotle University of Thessaloniki (Greece). His research and teaching interests include drama/theatre pedagogy and teacher training, puppet and object theatre, and multicultural, intercultural and aesthetic education. Since 2011, he has been responsible for the theatre pedagogical activities of the group Polydromo on bilingualism and multiculturalism in education and society. See www.polydromo.gr and www.facebook.com/polydromo.

**Erika Piazzoli** is Assistant Professor in Arts Education at Trinity College, University of Dublin (Ireland), as well as Research Fellow at Griffith University, Brisbane (Australia). Her research interests are embodiment, teacher education, aesthetic learning and languages education. Her research focuses on the aesthetics of drama-based second language teaching.

**Alexander Riedmüller** studied Music and Movement Education/Rhythmics as well as Musicology in Vienna (Austria). In 2009, he co-founded the improv collective *artig* to investigate performative and pedagogical approaches to the technique of improvisational theater. Since 2011, he has lived in Buenos Aires (Argentina). He works at home and abroad as an actor, teacher and teacher-trainer in the interdisciplinary integration of German as a Foreign Language with music, movement and theatre.

**Julia Rothwell** works as a project and research officer in a culturally diverse, not-for-profit community organisation in Brisbane, Australia. She is a languages teacher with an ongoing interest in using drama in languages education in schools and in the workplace. Her doctoral research focused on the outcomes, from student and teacher perspectives, of using process drama as a multimodal, reflective means to intercultural language learning in middle school. She has taught languages in schools in the UK and Australia and lectured in Languages Curriculum at Queensland University of Technology.

**Michaela Sambanis** is Professor and Chair of English Didactics at the Freie Universität Berlin (Germany), a position she has held since 2011. From 2008 to 2011, she was researcher and head of an interdisciplinary research unit at the Transfer Center for Neuroscience and Learning at the University of Ulm (Germany). Her most recent major scientific publication is *Sprachen lernen in der Pubertät* (2017) co-edited with Heiner Böttger, with whom she also hosts the Focus on Evidence - Foreign Language Didactics Meets Neuroscience conferences in Eichstätt (2015) and, forthcoming, in Berlin (Germany).

**Manfred Schewe** is Professor at University College Cork (Ireland), where he served as Head of Department of German from 2005 to 2014. His teaching and interdisciplinary research activities focus on Applied Drama and Theatre, especially on performative approaches to language, literature and culture, and are closely linked to the SCENARIO PROJECT (http://scenario.ucc.ie). Since 2016 he has been Head of UCC's Department of Drama and Theatre Studies. As guest lecturer and workshop facilitator for associations and institutions worldwide, he continues to be a strong advocate of a new, performative teaching and learning culture. Further details at: http://research.ucc.ie/profiles/A016/mschewe.

**Roula Tsokalidou** is Associate Professor of Sociolinguistics at the School of Early Childhood Education, Faculty of Education, Aristotle University of Thessaloniki (Greece). Her research and teaching experience and interests lie in the areas of language contact, sociolinguistics, language and gender, bilingualism, translanguaging and education. Since 2009, she has coordinated the group Polydromo on bilingualism and multiculturalism in education and society, and is editor-in-chief of the multilingual periodical *Polydromo*. See www.polydromo.gr and www.facebook.com/polydromo.

# Introduction Going Performative in Intercultural Education: International Contexts – Theoretical Perspectives – Models of Practice

John Crutchfield and Manfred Schewe

## Acute Challenges for Intercultural Education

As we started work on this volume in early 2015, the full effects of the massive displacement of human beings due to violence and economic hardship in Syria, Iraq, Afghanistan and North Africa were just beginning to be felt in the countries toward which these refugees had made (and were still making) their way. As of this writing, in the spring of 2016, the long-term social, economic and cultural consequences of this ongoing 'migration' – particularly for Europe, where a great many of the refugees have sought asylum – can still only be guessed. In the short-term, however, one has become accustomed to speaking of a 'refugee crisis', and Europe is not the only place where this crisis has produced political upheavals that three years ago would scarcely have been imaginable: Above all, a powerful resurgence of nationalist political parties, sentiments and rhetoric. One thing has become clear: *integration* will be perhaps the single most urgent question facing European and other Western host societies in the near and foreseeable future. To a large degree, the course of Europe and the West, and certainly of the European Union itself as a political and economic body, will be determined by how that question is answered. Thus, a scholarly volume focusing on performative approaches to intercultural education arrives, albeit unintentionally, at a portentous moment.

Though refugees leave much behind – their homes and possessions, their jobs and daily routines, their friends and often their families – they bring their cultures with them. For many, this is all they have left. They may arrive disoriented, exhausted and penniless, but they retain the inexhaustible wealth of their languages and arts, their values and customs, their religious beliefs and practices. Clearly, it would amount to a further inhumanity to insist that refugees surrender these things too; and yet, given the specific cultures in question here, it is by no means obvious whether, to what degree or in what cases these cultural factors – for example, the view of gender roles and of sexuality – are suited or adaptable to life in a modern, secular, Western democracy. Can the democratic state 'guarantee' the rights of sub-cultures that do not, or do not in all respects, recognize its authority? In other words, is integration even possible? And if so, are we sure that it is desirable for all parties? And what exactly is meant by the term 'integration' in the first place?

Various solutions have been proposed. The 'monocultural' (or rather: 'colonial') solution, in which one group is simply treated as second-class citizens, has long ceased to be acceptable, and for good reason; but likewise the 'multicultural' solution, in which different groups coexist in the legal/ethical form of mutual respect, but without the content of mutual understanding, seems hardly less unsatisfactory due to its constant tendency toward 'identity politics' and social 'Balkanization'. More recently, an 'intercultural' approach to the issue of cultural difference has gained legitimacy: A solution that would fill the form of mutual respect with the content of dialogue and understanding between and among the various cultures represented in a given group or area. (And beyond this, as will be seen in several of the contributions to the present volume, there are even calls now for a 'transcultural' approach, in which cultures themselves become hybrid, porous, improvisational, subject to recombination and revision – a set of overlapping options for the individual to put on or cast off at will.)

It is worth noting, however, that the hermeneutic emphasis in 'interculturality', i.e. its emphasis on dialogic processes, roots it firmly in the question of communication and hence, of *language* broadly understood. The role of language in culture (and of culture in language) is extremely complex; but it is safe to say that the *struggle to communicate* is itself one of the chief means by which cultures, no less than individuals, begin to understand each other. Or to put it differently: *understanding* is not a state but a dynamic and open-ended process, in which *misunderstanding* constantly intervenes as catalyst, and in which both communicants are ultimately transformed. Thus, interculturality depends upon all participant cultures daring to embrace the possibility of change.

This has consequences for the question of integration. Obviously, if integration is understood in its traditional organic/metabolic sense as the 'absorption' of new arrivals by a native majority (literally 'drawing together the parts of a whole', from L. *integrare*), then interculturality cannot be made to serve as guiding principle. For an intercultural approach, the root metaphor is not organic but commercial: One seeks an exchange, an interaction, in which all parties benefit and learn from each other while maintaining a certain autonomy. This is where language comes in as currency, medium of exchange or middle ground. To the degree that, in the modern West, the foreign language (FL) classroom represents the most important zone for 'rehearsing' these exchanges, interculturality depends upon the quality of FL teaching and learning. Such, in any event, is the insight at the heart of Michael Byram's important work on *intercultural communicative competence* (ICC): FL classrooms are the indispensable laboratories for its development and ought to be structured accordingly (Byram, 1997).

Moreover, what's true in this respect of the *foreign* language classroom gains a special urgency in the *second* language (SL) classroom. Australian schoolchildren learning German as a foreign language (GFL) in Australia, for instance, have an opportunity to learn not only the German language but also a little of the culture of which that language is an expression. At the very least, this process will benefit them by both enabling them to communicate competently with actual Germans and encouraging them to reflect upon their own language and culture. For Iraqi, Afghan or Syrian refugee children learning German as a second language (GSL) (i.e. in Germany), the benefits are of a more existential nature: they are learning about their new home, about the way of life of their new neighbors, friends and future employers and co-workers. To a large extent, their success in negotiating these relations will depend upon the quality of their experience in the language classroom.

But the important point for interculturality is that this experience is a two-way street. The German men and women teaching these GSL classes, to say nothing of the other pupils (in the case of a multilingual classroom), are also, for their part, learning about the cultures of the refugee children in front of and among them. This dialogue has the potential to be mutually transformative. And if recent empirical research at the intersection of education and the neurosciences is to be credited, then the depth of this transformation is directly proportional to the degree to which the pedagogical approach addresses the *whole person* of the pupil: Not just his/her cognitive faculties, but also, and perhaps more importantly, the body and the emotions (Sambanis, 2016).

## Approaches to Intercultural Education within a Performative Foreign and Second Language Didactics

In our view, this is where the concept of *performance* proves decisive. The justification for the present volume rests on the now significant accumulation of empirical evidence to suggest that the holistic aims of interculturality are powerfully served by a *performative* FL/SL didactics, that is to say, by an approach to language teaching and learning that emphasizes *embodied action*, and that makes use of techniques, forms and aesthetic processes adapted from the performing arts – particularly from theater.

While theatrical or dramatic techniques have been put to pedagogical use since ancient times, the field of performative FL didactics is actually a quite recent innovation, and in many ways it is still emerging. (The chief scholarly organ of the field, the online journal *Scenario* [http://scenario.ucc.ie], was founded 10 years ago.) There continues to be vigorous debate around key concepts, such as the nature of 'the performative' itself; its relation to language, culture and the aesthetic; and its claim to be 'holistic'. Nor is this all, for the parallel development of performative approaches in various national and institutional contexts beginning in the latter third of the 20th century has led to a certain diversity in both theory and practice. The concept of 'drama in education', for instance, has existed for many years in the United Kingdom, but is not to be confused with 'theater in education', much less with 'theater education', as practiced in the United States, nor yet (heaven forbid) with 'Theater' as a school subject, also sometimes known as 'Drama' or, as it is called in Germany, 'Darstellendes Spiel' ['Representational Play']. In the German context, matters are further confused by the simultaneous currency of the terms 'Theaterpädagogik' and 'Dramapädagogik', which though theoretically distinct (one corresponds to the US 'theater education', i.e. the training of theater teachers, while the other corresponds roughly to the UK's 'drama in education', i.e. a pedagogical approach to any subject) are in practice often indistinguishable. In the end, one is tempted to say that the field of performative FL didactics is itself a study in intercultural (mis)communication.[1]

Nor is the apparent privileging of drama over other forms of theater and of theater over other performing arts entirely unproblematic. Our use of the term 'performative' here represents an attempt to circumvent this terminological confusion for the time being and to establish an umbrella term covering any and all pedagogical approaches that make conscious use of performance – *embodied action before witnesses* – as an essential tool for learning: in this case, FL/SL learning. Despite the broad spectrum of specific institutional and cultural contexts and, accordingly, the wide range of different theoretical perspectives and models of practice presented by the contributors to this volume, all of them advocate for the innovative role that performative pedagogies have to play in intercultural education.

The conceptual and practical diversity noted above, however, should alert us to the fact that 'performance' itself is by no means a culturally neutral or innocent term. Cultures understand performance in different ways, and the understanding that has gained legitimacy in much of the West – in no small part as a result of the mid-20th century anthropological work of Victor Turner (1957), Erving Goffman (1959) and Clifford Geertz (1973) – reflects a thoroughly Western, scientific epistemology. Suffice it to say, this is hardly the only way to understand performance; nor in terms of pedagogical praxis can it be assumed that, for example, a German language learner from Iraq will respond to 'performative' approaches in exactly the same way as someone from the United States, Papua New Guinea or Kenya will – to say nothing of cultural differentiation within these national groupings. To some learners, such performative 'basics' as eye-contact and physical touch may not be basic at all, but may constitute painful violations of cultural or religious codes of conduct. In short, we must proceed with extreme caution both in the way we speak of performance in theoretical discussions and in the way we apply it in praxis, lest a kind of cultural imperialism slip in through the back door in precisely the place where we are most at pains to avoid it: in intercultural education.

Through a careful perusal of the following chapters, the reader will of course form his/her own critical view of 'going performative' in relation to the specific intercultural contexts and pedagogical settings represented by the authors. Nevertheless, it will perhaps be helpful here at the outset – particularly for readers who are new to this discussion – to offer a brief overview of *the performative* in the field of education.[2]

In recent years, there have been increasing signs of a 'performative shift' in education similar to earlier developments in the social sciences. Wulf and Zirfas (2007) in their publication *Pädagogik des Performativen* [*Pedagogy of the Performative*] locate the performative as a new focus of educational research:

> Whoever refers to the Performative today is part of a discourse being established within the social sciences. This discourse brings together the terms 'performative' and 'performance' from linguistics, the term 'performance' from arts and theatre science, and the term 'performativity' from gender studies. Common to all these terms is that they examine occurrences and events on a phenomenological level rather than in terms of their hidden, deeper meaning; they focus on the process rather than on structures and function and, concentrating to a lesser extent on text and symbols, pursue the construction of actuality. The perspective of the performative foregrounds directing and acting practices of social and pedagogical behaviour, their reality-constituting processes, and the correlation of body and language, power and creativity. (Wulf & Zirfas, 2007: 10, trans. by eds)

Wulf and Zirfas' complex theoretical deliberations cannot be dealt with in detail here; noteworthy, however, is the proposed shift from *what* to *how*. Indeed, exactly *how*, i.e. through which (physical and verbal) processes, is knowledge being generated? And what kind of knowledge is it? This perspective opens up space for the perception of aspects that have long flown under the pedagogical radar – most importantly, perhaps, the connection of language and body in the processes of meaning-making and communication.

In many respects concurrent with this 'performative' turn, the last few decades have also seen a very lively and fruitful subject debate in the field of intercultural education, as evidenced by the volumes in this book series, Languages for Intercultural Communication and Education, a debate focusing, for example, on key concepts of *intercultural competence* (Witte & Harden, 2011) and *intercultural understanding* (Harden & Witte, 2000). In general, however, there seems to have been relatively little emphasis on forms of 'embodied teaching and learning' in intercultural education. An important exception is the volume *Foreign Language Learning in Intercultural Perspective: Approaches through Drama and Ethnography*, edited by Byram and Fleming (1998; see also Fleming, 2003), which represents a first attempt to relate the subject debate to the field of drama in education. This link was further strengthened by a volume which drew the attention of scholars, teachers and practitioners to the body as an integral element of the teaching and learning process: *Body and Language: Intercultural Learning Through Drama*, edited by Gert Bräuer (2002). In the introduction, the editor states that the volume

> … is designed to be an introduction to the use of drama in the foreign- and second language classroom. It highlights the bridging character of drama-based teaching for intercultural learning and, therefore, fosters a better understanding of the significance drama has also for first-language instruction in today's multicultural world, where transculturation […] is a growing individual and social necessity. Following the position of Norah Morgan and Juliana Saxton (1987), drama here is not limited to artistic work or pedagogical use, but rather it means the interplay between body and language in general that leads to doubts, questions, and insights for learners interacting with themselves and others and their linguistic and cultural identity. (Bräuer, 2002: ix–x)

Contributors to the volume give various examples of how this kind of interplay and interaction can be facilitated; but especially noteworthy is the perspective of Lynn Fels and Lynne McGivern (2002: 19–35), who introduce readers to the concept of 'performative inquiry' as

> … a research methodology and mode of learning that invites students to explore the imaginary worlds within which space-moments of interstanding and intercultural recognitions are possible. Performative

> inquiry explores creative actions and interactions through performance. Performative inquiry recognizes performance as an action-site of learning, thereby opening up opportunities for research and teaching investigations. (Fels & McGivern, 2002: 23)

Their notion of 'interstanding' is a provocative one, and they link it explicitly to the idea of a 'third space':

> Our ambition then is to engage our students in dramatic explorations that recognize the experiences, heritage, values, and stories embodied within individual students. Performative inquiry in the language classroom provides an opportunity to open up a 'third space' of presence and exploration, where intercultural interactions and possible negotiations and recognitions emerge. A third space or performative space is a creative interactive space within which participants negotiate multiple possibilities of action and, through shared participation and reflection, learn from each other both within and outside the drama. (Fels & McGivern, 2002: 21)

The authors consider the imaginary world created in the classroom as the 'third space' brought to life through the embodied presence of the students. The spatial metaphor here recalls the subject debate focusing on the concept of hybridity, including the perspective of Witte and Harden (2011):

> *This third space is the locus of intercultural competence*. The spatial metaphor indicates that it is neither completely subjective nor social. Space in this context does not refer to something like territoriality or a stock of traditions but rather the collective *production* of spaces as a multilayered and occasionally contradictory social process, of a specific social and psychological location of cultural practices, of a dynamic of social relations which implies the dynamism and fragility of space. (Witte & Harden, 2011: 5, emphasis by eds)

In this context, Benedikt Kessler's (2008) publication *Interkulturelle Dramapädagogik* springs to mind. Similar to some authors in the present volume, he uses Byram's (1997) influential ICC model as a point of departure for the development of his own innovative concept, which explicitly draws on 'drama in education' as a reference discipline for intercultural education. It could be argued that Kessler's 'Intercultural Drama Pedagogy' is an organic extension of Byram's concept, and that, by adding the dimension of body awareness (Kessler, 2008: 54–56) to the affective dimension in Byram's ICC model, it paves the way for the articulation of an intercultural performative competence. Kessler's concept cannot be discussed in full detail here, but in the context of the reflections above, his summary (in sub-chapter 7.3, entitled 'Interkulturelle Dramapädagogik als Realisierung des *dritten Ortes*' ['Intercultural Drama-Pedagogy as Realisation of the *Third Space*']) is worth noting:

> As has become clear through the previous discussion, the realization of such a place can be seen as one – if not *the* – primary goal of dramatic work. This is because the main business in dramatic interaction or dialogue involves entering into a process of mediation between the familiar and the foreign. A mediating process of this kind is directly and necessarily initiated through drama, since the articulation, the discussion and the reconciliation of cultural difference constitute the premises of a communally constructed dramatic world. Furthermore, students learn that the phenomena of foreignness and difference are less frightening than inspiring and stimulating; in the end only a productive interaction with difference leads in drama to successful and satisfactory results. Decisions about dramatic plot elements and representations are never made exclusively from one's own perspective, but also involve the perspective of the other, such that all participants are forced to adopt a multi-perspectival gaze with respect to the (dramatic) world. Because of this, drama is a truly intercultural medium, a 'medium of the third place'. (Kessler, 2008: 90–91, trans. by eds)

By now, 'drama pedagogy' ['Dramapädagogik'] has become an important reference discipline for FL/SL.[3] In more general terms, as outlined in an overview article in which Schewe (2013) proposes the model of a *Performative Foreign Language Didactics*, drama pedagogy can be considered as a gateway to a performative teaching and learning culture (Even & Schewe, 2016).

Against this backdrop, the present volume offers a range of examples of performative approaches which require learners to become physically active and experience the dynamic, fragile space of interculturality. This kind of experience, we would argue, is qualitatively different from – and leads to 'deeper learning' than is possible in – primarily verbal/intellectual approaches to intercultural education.[4] The rich potential of the performative arts for the area of FL/SL teaching is increasingly recognized, and there are now encouraging signs for 'going performative' in teacher training as well (Crutchfield, 2016; Fleiner, 2016).

## Overview of the Contributions in this Volume

**This volume is intended for professionals in all sectors of intercultural education**, including policymakers, scholars, educators, teacher trainers, artists, social workers, drama and theater practitioners and, especially, teachers of foreign and second languages. In putting together the contents, we invited contributions from theoreticians, researchers and practitioners worldwide – from Tokyo to Glasgow, Newcastle and Dublin; from Brisbane to Istanbul and Thessaloniki; from Buenos Aires to Vienna, Paris, Freiburg, Frankfurt and Berlin. Our contributors have done and are doing significant work in a variety of institutional contexts at this exciting point of intersection between performative pedagogy and interculturality in FL/SL education. We were delighted to discover not only many important areas of overlap, but also many notable fissures and areas of disagreement – signs of a vibrant and contested field of inquiry.

We've arranged the chapters in a way that we hope will enable readers to zero-in on their particular areas of interest. We begin, however, with a piece we feel conveys in refreshingly concrete terms many of the central motifs and challenges of a performative approach to FL/SL teaching, while at the same time illustrating the fundamental dialogic principle of interculturality: **Magdalena Haftner** and **Alexander Riedmüller** are co-founders of the international performance group *artig*, which has adapted Keith Johnstone's now canonical improvisational theater techniques for purposes of teaching GSL throughout the world. Their contribution, 'The Intercultural Surprise', will be of particular interest to practicing FL teachers, as it is rich in concrete examples from their experience as a company and in practical tips for how to begin using theatrical improvisation in an educational setting.

A common practice in volumes similar to this one is to divide the contents between theory and practice. From the beginning, we decided to take a different tack and invited our contributors both to theorize their practice and to offer practical examples of their theory. Though the proportions vary, each chapter thus contains a little of both. This more accurately reflects, we feel, the reality of the way work is being done in the area of performative FL/SL teaching and research. It also frees us up to arrange the chapters into sections according to broader thematic clusters.

In Part 2, the focus falls on specific projects developed for and with refugee and immigrant children in the schools. Taking as her reference point a project involving refugee students in a multilingual English as a second language (ESL) classroom at Glasgow College (Scotland), **Katja Frimberger** questions the universalizing claims of some intercultural pedagogies, according to which refugees are often pigeonholed as 'disadvantaged'. By rejecting this concept of 'refugee subjectivity' in favor of a concept that would allow for the full particularity of individual experience, Frimberger moves toward a theory of performative intercultural pedagogy as 'ethical praxis'.

**Evi Kompiadou, Antonis Lenakakis** and **Roula Tsokalidou** describe in detail an innovative drama-pedagogical project called *Diadrasis*, which was recently undertaken at a multicultural school in

Thessaloniki (Greece). Using performative techniques, 'multimodal' texts and 'identity' texts, the project staged multicultural and cross-generational interactions between families with Greek backgrounds and families with migrant backgrounds. Although learning the Greek language was an important goal of the curriculum, the immediate purpose of the project, as the authors write, was to 'activate the linguistic and cultural capital of students and their families and establish a context of communication, cooperation and trust'.

In her contribution, **Joelle Aden** summarizes her extensive work on the key role of *empathy* in intercultural communication and on the specific ways in which theatrical experiences are seen to strengthen it. Drawing on recent neuroscientific findings, she points to the need for a 'paradigm shift' in the way we conceive of the FL/SL classroom, especially in the context of the now 'unprecedented levels of mobility and migration' across the globe. As compelling concrete examples of what a new 'transcultural' pedagogy might look like, she describes in detail *The Gaza Monologues* and *September 11th 2001*, two intercultural theater projects in which professional artists worked directly with young people.

Though almost all of our contributors mention the important question of FL/SL teacher education, we felt that its importance warranted its own section. Part 3, therefore, contains three contributions which in different ways treat the issue of teacher training directly. In his contribution, **Micha Fleiner** (2016), whose recent dissertation comprises an exhaustively researched report on the state of performative approaches in FL teacher training within the German-speaking countries, draws on an impressive breadth of sources to explore the role interculturality might play in a performative teacher training, and follows up with a description of an exciting international project in which students at the University of Education Freiburg (Germany) and the Université Lumière Lyon 2 (France) were brought together in a bicultural performing arts collaboration.

By addressing the question of how to respond to national 'stereotyping' in FL teacher training, **Almut Küppers** elucidates an important aspect of the mutually transformative potential inherent in intercultural communication, which in her view might best be understood as 'identity negotiation'. FL/SL teacher education programs, she argues, are the necessary place to begin training this form of negotiation, and she offers as examples, first, a drama unit offered at Frankfurt University (Germany), in which GFL teachers-in-training, who are preparing for assignment to one of the partner schools in England for a one-year practicum/study-abroad, are brought together with older students who have just returned; and second, a similar unit offered to GFL teachers-in-training at Marmara University in Istanbul (Turkey).

In their contribution, 'Staging Otherness', **John Crutchfield** and **Michaela Sambanis** report on innovative 'translational' research recently conducted in the Department of English Didactics at the Freie Universität Berlin (Germany). Three recent masters theses based on empirical research into performative approaches for teaching English as a foreign language (EFL) are shown to have relevance for intercultural learning. As their report emphasizes, these projects hold interest of a different kind as well: They exemplify an approach to teacher training that could be of great advantage for promoting a 'performative teaching and learning culture': teachers-in-training are not only exposed to performative techniques in their coursework, but are also encouraged to test them in practice as part of their own academic research.

Part 4 offers readers a closer look at specific performative approaches in action. **Julia Rothwell** notes the phenomenon of increased learner engagement in connection with 'process drama'. In her contribution, she describes in concrete detail how she adapted various process drama techniques to encourage beginning learners of GFL at an urban public secondary school in Brisbane (Australia) to learn 'interculturally'. Drawing on Mikhail Baktin's theory of dialogic texts, she shows how students can be empowered to take on a more active, improvisatory role in co-creating dramatic performances in class, even (as is frequently the case in Australia, she notes), where students do not all share a first language.

Likewise restricting her focus to the techniques of process drama, **Erika Piazzoli** draws on an action research project she conducted over a period of five years at a public university and at two adult language schools in Milan (Italy), in which she investigated the connection between 'dramatic tension' and 'active participation' for intermediate students of Italian as a second language. Based on her analysis of these findings, she develops the concept of 'intercultural dramatic tension' as an explanation for the way well-managed process drama can lead to increased 'intercultural engagement', in which cognitive, emotional and social aspects of the learners are brought actively into play.

In certain respects, Part 5 is a continuation of Part 4: Here, the focus is on performative approaches that make important use of personal biography. In 'Enacting Life', **Daniel Feldhendler** introduces readers to what he calls 'relational dramaturgy', a theatrical method combining various forms of improvisational theater (such as Jonathan Fox's playback theater and Augusto Boal's forum theater), personal biography and the therapeutic technique known as 'psychodrama' and offers a succinct history of his own practice over the course of many years in the context of FL/SL teaching and learning and intercultural education.

Biographical/autobiographical texts and the techniques of playback theater and forum theater are also, *mutatis mutandis*, important tools for **Jane Arnfield**, who presents three case studies centered on a 'theater-in-education' curriculum project in which a dramatic adaptation of *The Tin Ring*, a memoir by the Holocaust survivor Zdenka Fantlová, was performed in tandem with *Suitcase of Survival*, a participatory educational program especially developed to accompany the performance and to foster dialogue on the play's themes of human rights, human resilience and well-being. Having conducted the project at several schools in England, Arnfield offers a compelling example of how theatrical performance focusing on intercultural learning can be integrated into a regular school curriculum.

We 'book-end' the collection with a contribution by **Eucharia Donnery**, 'The Intercultural Journey', in which she offers readers an overview in diptych of practitioners and programs experimenting with performative approaches to both Japanese as a foreign language in the USA and EFL in Japan. Along the way, she offers insights into the particular challenges these approaches face – as well as their particular advantages – with respect to Japanese culture.

Let us return for a moment to the issue of FL/SL teacher education. It will be noticed that, among our contributors, while all are experienced FL/SL teaching practitioners who use performative approaches, only half (Arnfield, Crutchfield, Feldhendler, Fleiner, Haftner and Riedmüller) have formal training and/or professional experience in the performing arts, and not always in theater. In our view, this is significant, as it raises the question of the teacher as mediator between the world of education and the world of the fine or performing arts. Should formal artistic training in performance be a part of a 'performative' teacher education? If so, then how could such training be 'delivered' in practice, short of sending education students to acting school? These questions are far from idle. In most university teacher training programs known to us, students are exposed only briefly, if at all, to performative approaches, which tend to be presented as 'tools' for the pedagogical 'toolbox'. Perhaps this suffices for teachers who wish only to enliven their classrooms from time to time. As will be seen from the following chapters, however, realizing the most profound intercultural potential of performative techniques requires both a fundamental orientation toward performance and a more sustained engagement in the classroom. This in turn requires that teachers themselves be well-versed in performative processes and aesthetic processes in general. Our call for a 'performative teaching and learning culture' is thus first and foremost a call for embracing performance as a core principle of teacher education and 'in-service' training: not just because it would enable teachers to more effectively adapt, design and implement performative techniques in their own classes, but because teaching is itself, finally, a performative art.

## In (Lieu of a) Conclusion

To what extent 'going performative' in FL teaching can impact the area of intercultural education, especially in the context of the aforementioned challenges of increasing global migration, remains uncertain. But there is a clear urgency to the question. As Schröder (2016) notes in his critical perspective on education systems in the EU:

> An important component of the linguistic/political negative development in Europe was certainly also the fact that Brussels had not taken into consideration the ubiquitous existence of migrant languages in the EU-countries of Western and Central Europe. Only the regional and minority languages existed; the languages of the migrants (with respect to Germany in the 1990's, above all Turkish and Russian, neither of them community languages) were in the eyes of the technocrats merely temporary phenomena, limited by acculturation or by return to the homeland. Thus the linguistic/political daydreams of the EU, founded upon mobility and the equality of community languages, drifted ever farther from the actual state of affairs. (Schröder, 2016: 9, trans. by eds)

With reference to developments in Germany and the EU, he points out that

> … non-European languages in our education and training systems are virtually non-existent. At the same time, Germany and Europe see themselves confronted, through the massive migration of non-Europeans, with a till now hardly imaginable multilinguality, in which the EU languages play a rather marginal role. The contemporary flood of migration, assuming the necessary linguistic and cultural assistance measures embracing the languages of origin, could turn out in the long run to be a blessing for Germany; but they could also, in the absence of such measures, become a curse, if concepts of integration are linguistically/politically under-supported by expertise and financial means, or are not ambitiously pursued. (Schröder, 2016: 10, trans. by eds)

Examples in the present volume demonstrate that performative approaches are ideally suited to creating 'third spaces' and thus opportunities for experiencing a sensory and in-the-flesh exploration leading to deeper understanding of intercultural encounter.[5] We hope that the authors' theoretical perspectives and models of practice will persuade readers that 'going performative' could break new ground in intercultural education. There are obviously no guarantees, but we are convinced that the stronger the commitment from policymakers, scholars, social workers and teachers, the greater the chances of developments in education proving to be a blessing for us all.

## Notes

(1) In this context, note Even and Schewe (2016: 175): 'Intercultural dialogue is also the focus of the *Scenario Correspondents* initiative. Correspondents in different parts

of the world report on forms of performative teaching and learning within their local educational systems, particularly in second and foreign language education. We assume that awareness of cultural-specific contexts and traditions will result in a more in-depth exchange about core concepts and terms, and that *Scenario* will make a considerable contribution to the development of an international glossary of performative pedagogy'.

(2) For a somewhat fuller, though by no means exhaustive genealogy, see Crutchfield (2016).

(3) In this context, note the journal *Scenario* (http://scenario.ucc.ie), founded in 2007. It focuses on performative teaching, learning and research, with a special emphasis on the role of drama and theater in FL/SL education.

(4) cf. especially Chapters 4 and 7 in this volume, which deal specifically with the neuroscientific point of view on the role of emotions in learning.

(5) The familiar term 'integration', with its aforementioned connotations of organic wholeness, might not be best suited to capture what happens in these spaces. We would like to propose instead the provisional term 'inte(r)gration' as a way of suggesting the intercultural values of mediation, communication, mutual exchange and mutual benefit. As this is complex conceptual territory, however, it cannot be pursued any further here.

## References


Bräuer, G. (ed.) (2002) *Body and Language: Intercultural Learning Through Drama.* Westport, CT: Ablex Publishing.

Byram, M. (1997) *Teaching and Assessing Intercultural Communicative Competence.* Clevedon: Multilingual Matters.

Byram, M. and Fleming, M. (eds) (1998) *Foreign Language Learning in Intercultural Perspective: Approaches through Drama and Ethnography.* Cambridge: Cambridge University Press.

Crutchfield, J. (2016) Brief encounters: Reflections on the performative integration of creative writing in the foreign language classroom (with a workshop for teachers). In O. Metz and M. Fleiner (eds) (in preparation) *The Arts in Language Teaching: International Perspectives: Performative – Aesthetic – Transversal.* Berlin: LIT Verlag.

Even, S. and Schewe, M. (eds) (2016) *Performatives Lehren, Lernen, Forschen – Performative Teaching, Learning, Research.* Berlin: Schibri.

Fels, L. and McGivern, L. (2002) Intercultural recognitions through performative inquiry. In Bräuer, G. (ed.) *Body and Language: Intercultural Learning through Drama.* Westport, CT: Ablex Publishing.

Fleiner, M. (2016) *Performancekünste im Hochschulstudium. Transversale Sprach-, Literatur- und Kulturerfahrungen in der fremdsprachlichen Lehrerbildung.* Berlin: Schibri.

Fleming, M. (2003) Intercultural experience and drama. In G. Alred, M Byram and M. Fleming (eds) *Intercultural Experience and Education* (pp. 87–100). Clevedon: Multilingual Matters.

Geertz, C. (1973) *The Interpretation of Cultures.* New York: Basic Books.

Goffman, E. (1959) *The Presentation of Self in Everyday Life.* New York: Anchor Books.

Harden, T. and Witte, A. (eds) (2000) *The Notion of Intercultural Understanding in the Context of German as a Foreign Language.* Bern: Peter Lang.

Kessler, B. (2008) *Interkulturelle Dramapädagogik. Dramatische Arbeit als Vehikel des interkulturellen Lernens im Fremdsprachenunterricht.* Frankfurt am Main: Peter Lang.

Sambanis, M. (2016) Dramapädagogik in Fremdsprachenunterricht – Überlegungen aus didaktischer und neurowissenschaftlicher Sicht. In S. Even and M. Schewe (eds) *Performatives Lehren Lernen Forschen/Performative Teaching Learning Research* (pp. 47–66). Berlin: Schibri Verlag.

Schewe, M. (2013) Taking stock and looking ahead: Drama pedagogy as a gateway to a performative teaching and learning culture. *Scenario* VII (1), 5–23.

Schröder, K. (2016) Einleitung des Herausgebers. In *Jahrbuch (4/2013) des Gesamtverbandes Moderne Fremdsprachen* (pp. 7–12). Braunschweig: Bildungshaus Schulbuchverlage.

Turner, V. (1957) *Schism and Continuity in African Society: A Study of Ndembu Village Life.* Manchester: Manchester University Press.

Witte, A. and Harden, T. (eds) (2011) *Intercultural Competence: Concepts, Challenges, Evaluations.* Bern: Peter Lang.

Wulf, C. and Zirfas, J. (2007) *Pädagogik des Performativen. Theorien, Methoden, Perspektiven.* Weinheim/Basel: Beltz.

# Part 1

# First Impressions

# 1 The Intercultural Surprise: Teaching Improvisational Theatre in Different Cultural Contexts

Magdalena Haftner and Alexander Riedmüller

## Introduction

Was it one or two kisses on the cheek we were supposed to give the participants before the workshop in the Argentinean province of San Juan? And do we have to repeat this protocol afterwards? Should we shake hands with our students in Yekaterinburg, or do Russians not expect that? Is it acceptable for me as an Austrian-born theater and language teacher, that for the second time in this class, when one of the students starts to improvise a scene, the German character has a blond beard and drinks too much beer? And should we encourage the scene in which the Austrian woman is always well-organized and tidying up in contrast to her Indian colleagues?

Questions like these have accompanied us, the German-speaking improv group *artig*, over the past years of teaching and performing in many places around the world. The group was founded in Vienna, Austria, in 2009 by four former students of diverse academic disciplines: Magdalena Haftner (Educational Studies, Theatre Pedagogy, Physical and Devising Theatre), Lino Kleingarn (Theatre, Film and Media Studies), Anne-Marie Kuhfuß (Romance Studies and German as a Foreign Language) and Alexander Riedmüller (Music and Movement Education/Rhythmics). After finishing our studies, and after some years of experimentation in stage projects with different types of improvisational theater, we started to use the knowledge of our respective professional fields to develop a strategy linking improv theater to German language training and education. We called this program 'spielend deutsch' which in German has the double meaning of 'acting in German' and 'easy, playful German'. During the past five years of improvisation and language teaching in more than 20 countries – in places like Buenos Aires (Argentina), Yekaterinburg (Russia), Chennai (India), Teheran (Iran), Addis Ababa (Ethiopia) or Portland (USA), to name a few – we have had a large number of intercultural encounters. Because our group teaches German language abroad, our work is mainly based on intercultural contact between the culture of the place we are visiting and the cultures of the German-speaking countries, Austria, Germany and Switzerland, from which we ourselves come.

Teaching through improv theater is almost synonymous with a spontaneous way of leading a group. This requires special preparation for the teacher, even more so in an intercultural context. How does one deal with the clichés about the German-speaking world or about the students' home countries? When and how does one correct the students in improvisational and language learning issues? In teaching improv, it is of fundamental importance that the teacher creates a safe environment to allow free associative acting. This can be achieved, for example, by playing with status while teaching, and in this way dismantling a hierarchical structure, especially in countries where this kind of relationship is common between students and teachers. Other questions continually confronting the members of *artig* include: How much physical contact is appropriate or even expected? How does body language allow for a different (inter)cultural layer of communication and a different relationship between pedagogue and pupils?

As one can probably imagine, the group has a great deal to tell about their experiences over the past years of itinerant teaching and acting around the globe. In this chapter, we give a short insight into our practice and the intercultural surprises we have experienced.

## Improvisational Theater

The methodological foundation of the workshops given by *artig* is improvisational theater. Before moving on to concrete examples from the workshops, it is important to give a short overview of improv theater in general, its pedagogical approach (based upon the work of Keith Johnstone), its potential in the context of foreign language learning and its method for dealing with stereotypes and clichés so as to enable good storytelling.

### Let us swim and sink together! How improv works on stage and the basics of its pedagogical approach

Improvisation is a form of live theater, in which the plot, characters and dialogue of a certain game, scene or story are made up spontaneously by the actors on stage. Often, improvisers request a suggestion from the audience, or draw on some other source of inspiration to get started, so the performance also has an interactive component. It is thus a non-scripted theater form, in which the actors must possess a high degree of flexibility and cooperation. They have to work together to define the actions and parameters of a scene. In short, it is as a process of co-creation that occurs live on stage and right in front of the audience. Besides its artistic value, improvisation training has a high pedagogical impact, as we will illustrate in what follows.

The contemporary understanding of improvisational theater was strongly influenced by Keith Johnstone. His concern as a teacher and later as a theater director, playwright and author, was to awaken the imagination and spontaneity in his students by developing exercises and strategies that are intended to take away their fear of failure and of making mistakes. In this approach, it is fundamental to connect the students with their own imagination in a playful way. Johnstone understands the job of the teacher as giving support to students in creative processes. In this imaginative play, they liberate their learning processes without the fear of failing (Johnstone, 2006a: 46). Accordingly, a good teacher never lets his/her students experience disappointing or discouraging failure, but makes them understand that failure is a necessary part of the learning process, which facilitates positive results by finding ways to overcome it and including it in the learning process (Johnstone, 2006a: 26). The moment of struggle should not lead to an experience of being unable to do something, but to recognizing it, being kind to oneself and finding another way of solving the task. Johnstone (2013) says: 'You can't learn without failing so we should welcome failure and laugh because we are on the right track'. Elsewhere, he refers to his art teacher, a man named Stirling, who suggests that if a child has trouble drawing a tree, the child should be permitted to go outside, touch it, feel it or try to model it in clay instead (Johnstone, 2015: 20). We assume that one of the most important principles of learning is pleasure, pleasure of experimenting. Experiments always include failure: it is part of the process of discovery with the tools one can use in the present moment. The teacher's task is to create spaces where the student feels safe and to allow him/her to experiment, to associate, to improvise – to learn.

For this reason, Johnstone developed exercises and games intended for the players to feel safe on stage. By not succumbing to the pressure of having to plan ahead how the scene will end, they can engage straight away and act freely. Likewise, positivity offers the key point for the progression of scenes. This means that the actor tries to pick up any type of scenic or spoken expressions without evaluating them in a negative way, as this is called 'blocking' in improvisational theater terms. Furthermore, Johnstone encourages the participants to offer and accept both their own ideas and ideas from their partner(s) on stage. The elements Johnstone (2006b: 174) calls 'game offers' are ideas that keep the story going and are alternately brought in by the actors, so that a story can be put together. In order to make the scenic play succeed, the willingness to change one's own ideas and conceptions and create the story in cooperation with a partner is a basic and necessary attitude. Johnstone (2006b: 89) describes the process on stage metaphorically as collective swimming and sinking. This means that while one is improvising, he/she has to be open to let go of his/her own assumptions if the partner does not share them. More than ever, the attitude of 'Yes!' becomes an important part of making a collaborative, improvised story happen. After the 'Yes!', new information follows, adding an 'and'. Unless we add something new, an improvised scene can't move forward.

The most important rules of improv theater can thus be summarized as follows:

(1) The first idea counts! Accept your own ideas and the ideas of your partners by saying 'Yes!'
(2) Add new information to keep the play going by saying 'and...'
(3) There are no mistakes! If you fail, it is an opportunity to create something new.
(4) We want to see cooperation and teamwork on stage! Make your partner look good, so you will also look good working together on the story.

## What if I say something that is not 'right'?: Advantages of improv theater in language teaching

Reading these four basic rules carefully as a teacher of a foreign language, one can see that they are also very suitable for language teaching. In the following subsections, we will focus on three useful advantages of improv theater in language teaching.

### *Courage of allowing 'mistakes' to appear*

The first parallel can be drawn with the learning process itself, as remarked by Huber (2003: 63, transl. by Haftner/Riedmüller): "The courage to be embarrassed is an essential feature of a good language learner." In improv, this becomes obvious, since in the performance, not only the learning process but also the development of the scene is enabled by courage. The fear of making mistakes blocks this process. Therefore, spontaneity and creativity, which are important both in theater and language acquisition, can only happen when an actor is being courageous in performing and speaking. Specific exercises that help improv actors open up and not be led by their fears of failing also help foreign language learners overcome their fears of making mistakes and allow them to speak more freely.

The prerequisite for a theatrical experience lies in establishing a theatrical reality that – like any form of fiction – is an agreement between audience and performers. As Göhmann (2004: 100) states, the boundary between these two areas of reality, 'as' and 'as if', allows the performers and the audience to perform and witness different actions, behaviors, attitudes, perceptions and expressions. In the course of this, the performers/learners create a secondary, theatrical reality with the role they play, which enables them to move between the realities of the imaginary world and their daily lives. Here, they can experiment scenically and in terms of the use of the foreign language. Looking at it in a sociological way, theater presents a specific form of social interaction. Therefore, theatrical learning always involves social, interactive and aesthetic learning processes.

In the scenic representation of improv theater, one has free choice in defining the details of the scene, including, among other things of course, the main characters. Their properties and behavior are entirely fictitious, creating a distance between the real-life person of the actor and the character in the scene. This means that learners withdraw from their personal reality and enter into the fictional realm. Using the theatrical reality, the performers/learners can communicate at the level of their respective linguistic abilities while 'hiding behind' a fictional character. Huber (2003: 330) sees the foreign language as providing a 'mask' (a so-called 'language-mask'), behind which the language learner's self can be hidden, thus enabling him/her to act as freely and safely as possible. As Huber puts it (2003: 332), 'Whoever wears masks does not need to save face!'

In improv-based foreign language teaching, learners have complete freedom of choice when choosing their role and can try out a variety of roles. This gives them an experimental flexibility that allows them to distance themselves from their own personal and perceived language skills. In this context, the focus is put on the skills of improvisation, not on the production of perfect language expression. During the dramatic process, we don't use any speech correction. If the students are experiencing a limitation of their linguistic options, it is up to them to find strategies to express themselves so that their partners can understand them, or conversely, to help their partners find an alternate means of expression. This is an important step towards cooperative learning, in which the students support each other. Talking about linguistic errors should be handled in a separate teaching phase, apart from the theater exercises.

### *Authenticity of speech production*

Another potential of the use of improv theater in language learning processes is its creation of an authentic, action-oriented and learner-centered space. As improv theater demands spontaneous play and impulsive speech production, the students become engaged with the proposed situations and develop them in an authentic, lifelike context, as Bach and Timm (2003: 11–12) suggest. In the context of improvised theater, the language is the consequence of performed actions. It is not forced, but appears naturally, almost as a second layer behind the actions and the story. In performance, the action triggers language use, not the other way round. By letting the learners decide about the content of the play, the speech intention comes

**Figure 1.1** Seeing the world through a character's eyes. German teachers in a workshop in Chennai, India

from the learners and corresponds to the concept of learner orientation as outlined by Huber (2003: 61). Improv theater opens up a space where the language learners can use their already known vocabulary and find a linguistic expression. It enables an experience where they can try out their language skills in a safe and playful context.

*A shift of the teacher–student relationship*

As a teacher, the image Johnstone uses of swimming in the same ocean with the learners is highly suggestive. This approach is particularly important, because on the one hand, it means being yourself as a person, and on the other hand, being on the same level with the students. The teachers' task is to support their pupils and to give them hints when they block their own or each other's ideas. This is a very interesting issue in looking at improvising in intercultural contexts, because there you might be confronted with unfamiliar ways of telling stories, of creating characters, or of seeing the world, or with preconceived ideas about the culture that lies behind the foreign language you are teaching. This last point leads us to another important topic for improv: stereotypes and how to work with them on stage and in the classroom (Figure 1.1).

## Finding the unusual with the usual: Expectations and surprises when playing with stereotypes

When faced with a new and different culture, one is always confronted with stereotypes in one's mind. Stereotypes help us to simplify the social world, especially when we meet new people, by creating a common idea of people's behaviors, appearances and beliefs. An advantage of stereotypes can be that they enable us to respond quickly to present situations we might have experienced or have heard of before. Of course, there is also the disadvantage of ignoring the actual differences between individuals and of generalizing an entire group of people.

As mentioned above, improvisational theater lives from the first associations and ideas that come to one's mind. When improvisers start to create a scene, it is very helpful to build on other people's ideas. It is necessary to refer to a common 'circle of expectation', which not only the improvisers on stage but also the audience members share. It is the circle of possible things that might happen. Staying within that circle nurtures the scene, the characters and the action and gives it a common direction. Johnstone (1999: 79) describes the emergence of this circle as follows: 'The spectators create a "shadow story" that exists alongside the improviser's story. Storytelling goes well when there's a close match between the players' stories and the spectators' shadow stories'. It is only to be expected that stereotypes and clichés might appear in order to create a common idea of the story as quickly as possible and to connect to the audience's expectations. This is especially true when the story is played in a certain genre, like a gangster movie, telenovela or love story, in which we actually want to see the stereotypical characters, for example the pregnant teenager, the father having an affair or the main character suffering from a severe disease. What storytelling needs, however, is to go beyond the expected to avoid getting lost in clichés. Johnstone (2013) has suggested that it is necessary both to fulfill the expectations of the audience and to surprise them by playing the irrational, the unexpected.

Therefore, we might say that good storytelling, including good improvisation, needs both the rational/expected and the irrational/unexpected. Apart from making a story more interesting, it is also good training for an improviser to stay alert and open to new offers and story twists. For this purpose, irrational 'tilts' are an effective way to provoke a change where you do not expect it. So what happens, for example, when the typical German beer drinker at the Oktoberfest meets a frog who can talk? What are his thoughts, how would he behave? Or when the correct and always-on-time Austrian bank lady falls in love with a clock which has stopped working? Will she be able to leave her paradigm because of love? Improvisational theater opens up the space to re-imagine stereotypes. It needs to be open for the actor to put himself/herself in the position of another character and to ask what would be the biggest challenge for him/her to make the story and the character's change most interesting. It is, in fact, the starting point for the deconstruction of the image we give, with the option to put it in an irrational context and bring it alive from a different angle. Stereotypes are therefore necessary to create a common ground from which to build a story, to open up a space where everyone is able to connect immediately. But interesting storytelling has the power to surprise the audience by bringing up something new in the already known landscape and showing different sides of a cliché character. It seems that for this reason improv lends itself in an ideal way to dealing with both language and intercultural issues. Improvised theater uses stereotypes and at the same time enables learners to manifest, break and recreate those stereotypes in a spontaneous, theatrical space.

The confrontation with people of different cultural backgrounds always brings you into more conscious contact with the stereotypes about the other as well as one's own cultural background. Questions like What shapes me? What is normal for me? What do I take for granted? What feels strange for me? inevitably appear. They can be seen from a different perspective and consciously manipulated in the collective play.

## Practical Examples

To clarify how the principles mentioned above can work in teaching improv in language classes, the following paragraphs give some examples of concrete moments in which intercultural surprises took place in the 'spielend deutsch' workshops. They also describe how the improv teachers actually reacted, given their background as actors and actresses of this specific type of theater.

### Intercultural contexts in teaching improv: A school workshop in Ethiopia

One of the two teachers is giving instructions in German: 'And now, all together, as fast as you can, without speaking, without demonstrating or telling others what to do: Be a tree!' You see happy concentrated faces, hear giggling and see the students get together in the center of the room, putting their arms up high and standing as close as possible. 'Well done. Now: Be the same tree, but in winter!' This time you can observe insecure-looking faces, some of the children start to talk quietly in their mother tongue, Amharic, while others look at the teacher with big eyes and do not move a bit. 'Try to do it without speaking!' says one of the teachers, reconfirming the initial order. As a result, the children stop talking, some start to lower their arms. The rest follow them, until the whole group is looking puzzled towards the teachers in silence with glimpses of helplessness and even slight frustration on their faces. And also on the teachers face you can observe a questioning look: 'Did I talk too fast? Was the order too complicated? Was the game going on for too long and have they lost concentration? What do I have to change, so that the game can work?' The answer, in this case, is simple: Let them experience winter first!

We are in Addis Ababa, the capital of Ethiopia in North East Africa. Here, so close to the Equator, the annual seasonal cycle commonly known in all countries of the world that are farther north or south of this line does not mean anything to the children of the local German Church School. There might be times with more or less rain during the year, but the sun rises and sets every day at the same time and, therefore, the four seasons do not play any role in these children's lives. This is an example of a situation in which a simple warm-up game, one that was only meant to encourage the spirit of the group and, initially, to get the students' bodies into action, starts to be an intercultural challenge. After a short reflection, a well-trained teacher can get out of this situation, for example, with the help of a game in which one student after another gets into the middle of the circle and poses to the theme 'winter' or 'frozen world' or 'Antarctica'. Surely, the children will have a lot of ideas about what these environments look like, and in this way, we can even imagine what a tree looks like in one of those places. Afterwards, the teacher could prepare the theme of the changing seasons and see what happens to the autumn leaves and what, as a result of them falling, the tree could look like in winter. All of this preparation would be necessary to form an image of a tree in winter that could be reproduced the next time we are playing the all-together game mentioned above. Another option would be (and actually this was the one spontaneously chosen by the two teachers of the group *artig* in this workshop for the Goethe-Institute in Addis Ababa) to react to what they see and encourage them to use it: 'Don't give up. Make your own version of the tree "in winter". It's going to be fine whichever way you do it. Make the craziest version of this tree you can imagine!' The frustration disappears and you might get the funniest looking winter tree you could possibly think of.

As suggested above, improv theater is a technique that requires a high degree of flexibility, not only while performing on stage, but also when used by a teacher during workshops. Linked to teaching a foreign language, its basic principles of 'follow your first idea' and 'there are no mistakes' reach another dimension. Especially here, where the aim is to deepen the understanding of a foreign language, it is even more important never to let the students' enthusiasm down by giving them the feeling of, for example, not having achieved a certain grammatical goal or not having fulfilled a verbal expectation. In the example of the 'tree in winter', these two worlds of scenic aims (create a 'convincing' tree in winter) and linguistic aims (understanding the meaning of the words) intertwine. For the students, these two goals are not perceived separately. Failing in the achievement of one is also failing in the other. Therefore, in order not to frustrate them, it is even more important to accept their idea and not to impose an outcome you as a teacher want to achieve. By teaching with improv theater techniques, this challenge might be even more important, because instructions have to be addressed instantly and without having too much time for thinking

**Figure 1.2** Let's jump into the unlimited world of imagination! German students at the Lycee Francais in Djibouti, Djibouti

about a solution for these (let us call them) 'intercultural bloopers', like the requested image of a tree in winter in Ethiopia. Johnstone's image of swimming and sinking together even gains an intercultural dimension for the teacher here, requiring a high ability for spontaneous adaptation of the exercises and games used in class (Figure 1.2).

## As intercultural as it can get: A youth summer camp in Portland

Mexico City is the base of the local project PASCH, which created a network between high schools in North America and the Caribbean that teach German as a second language. Once a year, this project gives a special scholarship to students who stand out because of their performance and interest in German. At the beginning of the summer holidays, a camp is organized. In the first session in July 2014 on a college campus in Portland (USA), a German improv workshop also took place. In this setting, around 60 teenage secondary school students from seven different countries from Panama to Canada came together to do different activities. All of these activities had topics dealing with Germany and they were all held in the German language by a team of the six workshop leaders, who were all German citizens but who lived in such diverse places as Berlin, London, New York and Buenos Aires. Given a scenario like this, it is obvious that this improv workshop had to deal with lots of intercultural questions both beforehand in planning and while it happened. The aim of using the German language as the lingua franca at the camp was a challenge because of the diversity of the participants' mother tongues: Spanish, English and French. These languages in turn were often the first foreign language for other participants, for example, English was the first foreign language of the Costa Rican students, French the first language of the English-speaking Canadian students. So for almost all students, German was the third language. In the improv workshop, however, this rich basis of cultural backgrounds was used by the students themselves as a vehicle for understanding this diverse patchwork and knitting it together.

In four days of workshops with improv techniques, the students were to learn some of the basic improv games to be able to create short scenes, which were filmed afterwards to gain lasting impressions of their experiences in the workshop. These stories were all developed by the students themselves. The teacher's role was to encourage them to create and give them tools that they could use for these original creations. One of the stories was given the title *Alexia liebt Tacos* ['Alexia loves tacos']. It starts with a family of four daughters and their father sitting at a table. The student in the role of the father, a boy from Mexico, painted himself a big moustache, underlining, in his understanding, the image of a Latino father of a big family. His daughter Alexia, also played by a girl from Mexico, angrily jumps up from the table and is frustrated to have to eat potatoes every day. Here it should be noted that the word *Kartoffel* ['potato'] accompanied lots of the workshop's improv scenes during the week, because it seemed to be a funny word for some of the students and also because evidently the variety of different potato dishes in German cuisine was an important anecdote for them. In the story, Alexia wanted instead to eat tacos. This was an idea brought in from a student from the US, after a trip that all the camp crew had made one day to the city of Portland, which is famous for its street stalls with food from different countries. The story continues with Alexia buying tacos at a food stall. Her father sees her there and tells her off because they have no money for such escapades. At the same moment he looks at the taco seller, who caught his attention, and asks her for her name. The seller, played by a girl from Nicaragua, tells him that she is called *Seekuh* ['manatee', or literally: 'sea cow'], a word that was elected in the category 'my favorite word in German' the previous day by all camp members. The sound of this word lets the father instantly fall in love with the seller so passionately, that they get engaged straight away. The scene finishes with a parody of Hamlet's opening question: *'Sein oder Nichtsein, das ist die Frage hier!'* ['To be, or not to be, that is the question!'] made by Alexia with tacos in her hands and a dance, with everybody in the scene encouraging her to dance by clapping and shouting: 'Go! Go!' (in English!)

This brief sketch gives an idea of how different cultural aspects can be easily linked in the work with theater techniques. The reality of diverse cultural backgrounds of this nationally very heterogeneous group did not interfere at all either with the aim of playing with German stereotypes and acting in a foreign language, or with finding a topic for their scene and creating it together as a group. The mix of these culturally diverse elements is also a good example of how several stereotypes can come together and help to add an interesting twist to a story. It can be observed that German was just one of many vehicles that encouraged the creation of the story, but in the end, it was an important part of the result, as all the scenes were acted out in German. The only exception was the group shouting: 'Go!' in the end. In any event, this can easily be interpreted as reminiscent of similar scenes in TV series that are well known in all of the students' home countries and thus should be allowed as a part of their reality and, even more important, as their own idea. The previous work with improv in the workshop was important to open the students' minds and allow them to freely associate different pieces of information with each other. Without this preparation, a story like the one described would hardly have been possible. Playing improv in the foreign language (German) mediated the use of words such as *Kartoffel* and *Seekuh*, apart from being important to encourage free expression in the target language.

The scene was also filmed and edited as the short movie *So ein Theater* by the team of Glocal Films (2014), who led a movie workshop at the youth camp in Portland.

## Playing with the unknown: Teaching improv in Teheran

As a final example of how intercultural experiences can provide surprises in teaching, let us describe how improv can work in an environment in which public opinion is subject to severe restrictions, in a country that has an ambiguous reputation internationally and evokes a lot of prejudices abroad: Iran.

When the four members of *artig* were invited to the Austrian Cultural Forum (ÖKF) in Teheran in 2012, the European Union had just agreed to an oil embargo against Iran a few months earlier. For that reason, many direct flights from European cities to Teheran had been cancelled, as the aircrafts had to have a sufficiently sized tank to be able to do a round trip, since it was not permissible to buy fuel in Iran. The European media also created the image that it was only a matter of weeks before an armed conflict between NATO and Iran would break out. These circumstances made the *artig* members reconsider whether they should accept the invitation. Fortunately, they decided to accept. Given that, from an Austrian point of view, Iran was perceived as a strict Muslim society, they prepared their workshop for various eventualities: 'What if the men and women can't work together in the workshop? Will it be possible for the women to do all the exercises with a headscarf? Hopefully the participants will not feel offended by spontaneous scenes concerning the topics of religion, women's rights, sexuality! Maybe it would be good to prevent acting of such contents right from the beginning'. In order not to commit too many 'cultural mistakes', they decided to start the workshop with a short round, in which everyone should present himself/herself and talk about their expectations. All of these earlier doubts were blown away after the first minutes of meeting their students. The workshop participants were a group of about 15 young Iranians between 20 and 30 years old who all studied German at the ÖKF and who some years earlier had formed a German-speaking theater group there. Straight from the beginning of the improv workshop, which lasted three intensive days, *artig* members discovered that none of their doubts or fears were of any importance at all. Teaching in Teheran under the roof of the ÖKF with its students offered just as much fun and surprises as it did in any other context where they had taught before. Intercultural challenges, when they occurred, were more likely due to such things as imaginary newspapers that were read from right to left, because the Farsi language is written in Arabic letters which are read this way, or because waving a hand with the palm facing down meant 'Come here!' instead of 'Go away!' as it means in Austria. Teaching in cultural contexts in which one is not familiar with some of the gestural expressions can lead to some interesting moments of misunderstanding. Following the 'Yes and...' attitude, the play with a different kind of gestural interpretation can open up new 'game offers' and train the students to be open to changes. Faced with the fact that reading a newspaper the 'wrong way round' can be the right way to do it, sharpens the teacher's eye and surely underlines the importance of always being as flexible as possible in teaching (Figure 1.3).

**Figure 1.3** Overcoming linguistic and cultural borders. Improv workshop in German at the ÖKF in Teheran, Iran

## Conclusion

Putting drama teaching into an intercultural context, it can be a challenge to handle topics that come up spontaneously and involve stereotypes or unwanted representations of any of the respective cultures. Encounters with people from different backgrounds and varied first languages are mostly a meeting of the unknown combined with pre-existing cultural assumptions or even prejudices. Teaching a foreign language through drama techniques is definitely an intercultural challenge. In our view, the basic tools for improvised storytelling, such as the attitude of saying 'Yes and...', are very helpful in generating a cooperative group process, especially when it comes to the intercultural encounters mentioned. These principles open up a theatrical space where the aim is to make your partner 'look good' by accepting his/her offers and putting a story together. Moreover, in the world of improvised theater, there are no mistakes. Every (intercultural) misunderstanding leads to a new situation, as we have seen in the example of the tree in winter in Ethiopia. It is of utmost importance to create an atmosphere where every association is welcome and to maintain an openness as a teacher. Only the ability to stay flexible at all times, to say 'yes' and allow both yourself as a teacher and the students to change constantly, makes it possible to swim together. Therefore, it is necessary first to have personal experience with improvisation to get an idea of how to teach it to a group. The training in coping with the unexpected, being open to the unknown, being attentive and listening to your partner(s), accepting ideas of others in a positive way and adding something new to continue the play is very useful to understand what makes improvisation work and which tools it offers for teaching practice. The school curriculum mostly doesn't allow for spontaneous acting in the classroom. On the one hand, it is obligatory to follow a curriculum, while on the other hand, the outside world demands being able to deal with a lot of changes, requiring spontaneity and fast adaptation every day. In this contradiction, we can find the big challenge of teaching nowadays, even more when it is carried out in an institutional frame. The school system seems to forget that learning is not a mechanical procedure that one can plan and execute precisely, as every learner, every group works in a different way. There is always the need for improvisation and openness to connect with the individuals one wants to make something accessible to. Every new thing we learn is something unknown. In order to open up the students' minds and perception without being afraid of the unknown, the facilitator needs a specific training that incorporates these skills. Improv trains one to stay open, even in the moments when one does not know what will happen next. This demands staying positive and moving forward. Thus, it could be an effective tool for developing a convincing and flexible teaching personality for teachers of any subject or content. As demonstrated above, it especially helps to prepare for intercultural encounters by training for an openness towards the unknown, which can be the other with his/her cultural background, but can also be the relationship to one's own culture by seeing it through the other's eyes.

## References

Bach, G. and Timm, J.P. (2003) Handlungsorientierung als Ziel und Methode. In G. Bach and J.P. Timm (eds) *Englischunterricht. Grundlagen und Methoden einer handlungsorientierten Unterrichtspraxis* (pp. 1–21). Tübingen/Basel: Francke.

Glocal Films (2014) So ein Theater. See www.vimeo.com/102375315 (accessed 30 March 2016).

Göhmann, L. (2004) *Theatrale Wirklichkeiten. Möglichkeiten und Grenzen einer systemisch-konstruktivistischen Theaterpädagogik im Kontext ästhetischer Bildung*. Aachen: Mainz-Verlag.

Huber, R. (2003) *Im Haus der Sprache wohnen. Wahrnehmung und Theater im Fremdsprachenunterricht*. Tübingen: Niemeyer.

Johnstone, K. (1999) *Impro for Storytellers*. New York: Routledge.

Johnstone, K. (2006a) *Improvisation und Theater*. Berlin: Alexander.

Johnstone, K. (2006b) *Theaterspiele. Spontaneität, Improvisation und Theatersport*. Berlin: Alexander.

Johnstone, K. (2013) 10 day workshop in Nykøbing in cooperation with Odsherred Theatre School, Denmark. See http://www.nyscenekunst.dk/ (accessed 2 April 2016).

Johnstone, K. (2015) *Impro. Improvisation and the Theatre*. London/New York: Routledge.

# Part 2

# Focus on Schools (Immigrant/Refugee Children)

# 2 The Ethics of Performative Approaches in Intercultural Education

Katja Frimberger

## Introduction

The following chapter is an exploration of whether the use of performative approaches in intercultural (language) education can contribute to the adoption of a more ethically sound critical pedagogy and the avoidance of universal assumptions and essentialism. My investigation was triggered by an unexpected 'story of hope' written by Nam Ha and Yun, two young people who have recently arrived in the UK as asylum seekers and refugees. Their story hints at the myriad of diverse life situations and identity positions concealed under the descriptive (and sometimes reductive) rubric 'refugee'. Nam Ha and Yun's story in particular resonates with the vibrant hopes for a good life brought to our classrooms (Figure 2.1). How do our intercultural pedagogies respond to such a story of hope? With the aim to critically examine the conceptual underpinnings of our performative pedagogies, I pursue two objectives. Firstly, before discussing drama pedagogy, I provide a detailed critical discussion of what we have achieved in intercultural language education so far, especially with regard to conceptualising critical intercultural pedagogies which avoid universal moral claims and encourage active stances of inquiry into difference. Secondly, I review drama pedagogy in light of the critical literature to discuss its role as ethical praxis. Do performative approaches stand as *critical* intercultural pedagogies?

> This is an egg – a baby animal – it hatches into a good world, from darkness to light, with small black eyes and little feet. Its heart is beating fast – everything is new and scary. He wants to find somewhere safe. So he goes to Scotland. Everything is different. It's very hard to find love. He finds peace and freedom. He sees wonderful things – they are soft and lovely colours. He feels relaxed and comfortable. He feels hope for the future. A rainbow! He finds love, friendship, someone to

**Figure 2.1** Hatching into a good world, from darkness to light (Nam Ha and Yun's story)

> hold hands, someone to help, to be together, to look after each other. To make a beautiful sound together. Together they are happy, they laugh and play like family. They are full, altogether complete. (Nam Ha and Yun)

I introduce this chapter with a short creative writing piece by Nam Ha and Yun, two 16-year-old English for speakers of other languages (ESOL) college students in Scotland, UK. Their story emerged as part of a creative writing workshop during a residential weekend and was later performed in a drama workshop. Objects and music were used as stimuli for the creation of what Cummins (2001) calls a performance-based 'identity text'. Such identity texts can 'symbolise, explicitly and implicitly, critical issues at stake in students' lives and can be representative of political, social, and economic life conditions' (Ntelioglou, 2011: 602). Nam Ha and Yun's story cannot be easily linked to specific 'issues' in their lives, much less to a singular identity position. Their creative production is fictional – it is a short, poetic story about a little animal that ventures out into a scary world to find love. It is not a literal narrative or testimony which mirrors factual events, in 'authentic' documentary style, about Nam Ha and Yun's personal lives. Their fictional story had a powerful effect on us, the listening teachers and researchers who attended the residential weekend with the students and facilitated the creative workshops. There was an attentive silence when the story was read again among us in the evening, after the day workshops were over. On the part of the teachers there was an enormous pride that students had communicated their story in English, a language they had just started to learn.

Nam Ha and Yun's story spoke beyond our fixed ideas of 'refugee subjectivity'. Their story resonated of not so much a trauma of the past, for example, but a relentless hope for the future. In the story, such hope is symbolised by the animal's quest for a home place where it will be surrounded by love and a caring community. The home metaphor is of course a significant symbol of hope when evoked in contexts marked by the complete loss of home. Writing about the dynamics of individual and social healing in countries that have suffered unspeakable violence and trauma, peace scholars Lederach and Lederach (2010) link the experience of the loss of home to the feeling of internal uncertainty and the loss of a sense of self (Figure 2.2).

> Violence destroys what was understood and known. What was assumed, taken for granted as 'normal' on a daily basis, has disappeared and people suspend, or outright lose the capacity to feel *at home*. Home often serves as a relational metaphor of feeling *surrounded* by love, a sense of well-being, shelter and unconditional acceptance. Violence destroys this feeling and the capacity to be oneself without mistrust or pretension; it destroys a sense of *at-homeness*. (Lederach & Lederach, 2010: 63)

The home metaphor poignantly reveals the significant link between the process of regaining a sense of trust, in oneself and in others, and the presence of social surroundings that foster a sense of 'at-homeness'. Through Nam Ha and Yun's fictional story, we, the listening teachers and researchers, were confronted with this home metaphor and the symbol

**Figure 2.2** What was taken for granted as 'normal' has disappeared

of hope it stands for. Nam Ha and Yun's story provokes us to position ourselves, not in the face of a single, personal story, but in the face of 'hope': How do our educational concepts and practices speak to this story of hope and 'at-homeness'?

## Background

Nam Ha and Yun are part of a group of 19 ESOL students at a Glasgow college, whom I got to know through my work as a postdoctoral researcher on the UK-funded, Arts and Humanities Research Council (AHRC) large grant project 'Researching Multilingually at the Borders of Language, the Body, Law and the State' (RM Borders). The RM Borders project sets out to investigate intercultural and multilingual practices in contexts where the subject of the encounter, and his/her languages, are under different forms of 'pain' and 'pressure' – psychologically, socially and politically. As part of a team which comprises community artists and researchers, I explore the role that performative approaches can play within such 'contested' intercultural and multilingual encounters.

The Glasgow ESOL classroom, which Nam Ha and Yun belong to, is a highly intercultural and multilingual environment. During break time, I hear the sounds of Kinda, Arabic, Farsi, Vietnamese, Mandarin, Dutch, French, Pushto, Borgow, Tigrinya and Amharic. English, for all of these young people, is an additional language, sometimes a second language (L2) but often a third (L3) or fourth (L4) language. Students are between 16 and 20 years old and have left, and often lost, parents and relatives to escape countries that, because of the escalations of war, political conflict and/or repressive state actions against citizens, made normal and peaceful lives impossible for them.

ESOL teachers at the college developed a unique course programme, called 16+, which takes students' specific psychological needs as well as their rich, acquired life skills – emotionally, practically, intellectually – as the starting point for pedagogical conceptualisations and activities. The 16+ programme integrates creative arts pedagogies, outdoor learning programmes, extensive personal guidance provision and sustained collaborations with local counselling and mental health services into the 'traditional' ESOL curriculum. The residential weekend, during which Nam Ha and Yun wrote their story of hope, is a fixed event in their school year. We (teachers, researchers, students) spent a weekend at the Allanton Peace Centre in Dumfries (Scotland) to enjoy the centre's beautiful location, eat home-cooked food and engage in outdoor learning activities and creative arts workshops.

My encounter with the students brings to mind the very *different* 'intercultural journeys' that lie behind us. It inevitably raises questions about the inequity and power dynamics that are built into our relationship.

**Figure 2.3** There are many narratives of being and belonging

Unlike the students, I enjoy the privileges of a European Union (EU) citizen with the right to work in the UK. In light of my position of power as a white, educated female researcher, with a secure political status and 'home place', and confronted with students' own hopes for 'at-homeness', how can we learn and work together? This necessarily triggers wider theoretical questions around the ways our educational conceptualisations respond to the structural inequalities experienced by students like Nam Ha and Yun. Anthropologist Malkki (1995) reminds us, however, to be cautious. The legal term 'refugee' functions 'as a broad legal or descriptive rubric that includes within it a world of different socioeconomic statuses, personal histories and psychological and spiritual situations' (Malkki, 1995: 496, quoted in Dennis, 2008: 212).

What happens to intercultural language education when it takes up the cause of 'humanity', in the face of this multiplicity of narratives of being and belonging, but without making those essentialising judgements, on who is a 'good' and 'bad' refugee, which pervade some political discussions at present? This question leads us into the realm of critical pedagogy (Figure 2.3).

## Critical Intercultural Language Pedagogy

> I celebrate teaching that enables transgressions – a movement against and beyond boundaries. It is that movement which makes education the practice of freedom. (hooks, 1994: 12)

Critical educators and scholars in the field of intercultural language education (e.g. Guilherme, 2006; Levine & Phipps, 2012; Phipps, 2014; Phipps & Gonzalez, 2004; Phipps & Guilherme, 2004) have long advocated for intercultural language pedagogies and educational concepts that take into account learners' complex, lived experiences. They call for pedagogical approaches that not only 'transgress' boundaries, but aid in establishing the broader conditions in which students can develop their full potential, individually and in wider society. These critical educators remind us to read competency not solely as open-ended potentiality, located within the individual and dependent on best efforts and harder work. We are instead asked to consider how educational environments, and the wider societal structures that hold these in place, enable and nurture, or equally often, disable the individual's disposition to become 'competent' in the first place (see e.g. Levine & Phipps, 2012). 'How people use language is strongly influenced by the situation in which they find themselves' (Blommaert *et al.*, 2005: 9), sociolinguists remind us. In an ecological view of language learning (Levine & Phipps, 2012), the speaker's inability to communicate, learn or 'flourish' in an educational environment is not solely caused by a position of lack or deficit located within the individual. It is rather considered a 'spatial' problem *for* the speaker, embedded in the communicative conditions and educational requirements produced by the environment (Blommaert *et al.*, 2005). Static and individualised notions of competence, in which the frameworks that construct the individual as having an (educational) deficit remain hidden from view, can especially disadvantage learners like our Glasgow ESOL class. Students bring a vast range of rich life and language experiences to the classroom, which, however, are often not validated within existing educational structures. Sociolinguists term this an institutionally produced 'deficit orientation' towards students; one which implicates them in a position of lack (e.g. of English language fluency) rather than capability (Grainger, 2013; Grainger & Jones, 2013).

A critical education, so Freire (1973, 1995) believes, starts when we think from within these contested relationships and struggles with our environment. Here, education is not seen as the mere consumption of classic canons, things worth knowing and languages worth learning. Instead, critical education positions the student, with his/her past life experiences and future hopes, at the centre of the educational encounter. Entrusted to act as a responsible subject, the student enters a dialogic educational space. Here, he/she does not just 'receive' knowledge from an expert educator, but plays an active role in setting the educational agenda as well as educating others by drawing on his/her past experiences and capabilities. In other words, the student–teacher relationship is democratised. Within this democratic orientation, difference and conflict is not played down or denied but is ultimately seen as an asset for critical pedagogy. An active engagement with difference allows the wider realities of social contestation that affect students' lives to become visible. This opens a space for reflection on how educational practices might hold them in place or equally 'transgress' them. In this way, critical educator bell hooks (1994: 31) cautions against the liberal educational ideal of a 'harmonious diversity', in which multiculturalism does *not* upset any social relations or the educational status quo, but is imagined to flow smoothly 'within cultural forms of uninterrupted accords'. Turner (1994) describes this as a 'difference multiculturalism' which prescribes difference for political aims (exemplified in the 'melting pot' idea or the 'rainbow coalition') but limits the individual's ability to negotiate his/her identity or even reject his/her inherited culture. In its extreme form, Prato (2009: 2) suggests, difference multiculturalism can 'exacerbate ethnic differences, essentialising them and limiting the individual's scope for the definition of self-identity'. An undisturbed intercultural education space in which difference doesn't lead to wider, critical reflection but can be easily 'consumed', can then run the danger of exoticising otherness in a form of cultural determinism.

In an interview with Giroux, a leading figure in radical education theory, Guilherme (2006) explains how intercultural competency models in the field of language and intercultural education (e.g. Byram, 1997) should in this respect not just aim to produce undisturbed intercultural educational spaces, in which difference is *overcome*, awareness fostered and understanding achieved, with the aim to 'guarantee' a harmonious diversity. Instead, Giroux and Guilherme (2006) encourage modes of critical engagement *with* students' complex and contested experiences. Here, cultural difference does not just become a precondition for the existence of intercultural language education, or a problem that needs fixing through pedagogy. In other words, critical pedagogy sees difference not as a universal, abstract asset or obstacle, but as a fully embodied phenomenon; one that cannot be regarded in separation from particular living and breathing bodies and the contested social realities these bodies find themselves in. In her critical discussion of Byram's (1997) intercultural competence model, Hoff (2014) explains how the five *savoirs*-model's underlying notion of human universality could in this respect run the risk of working towards undisturbed educational spaces in a mode of passivity, rather than result in an active stance of critical inquiry:

> [T]he wish to highlight universal aspects of the human condition is made at the expense of actively and inquisitively investigating cultural difference. (Hoff, 2014: 512)

Rather than promoting an active engagement with different perspectives and (multi-sensory) manifestations of migratory experience, Hoff (2014) argues, Byram's model might inadvertently support uncritical processes of socialisation – in a mode of 'adopting' the other's cultural and behavioural values. Although Byram's (1997) intercultural competence model encompasses forms of knowledge (of self and other) and skills (relate, interpret, discover, value) which encourage critical engagement, these are always employed with a view towards the more conceptually closed aims of awareness-raising and intercultural understanding.

On the one hand, the *savoir être*-dimension of the model, for example, explicitly encourages curiosity, openness and a mode of de-centring from (universalising) cultural beliefs (Byram *et al.*, 2002: 12). On the other hand, the model cannot fully disengage itself from its tendency towards a cultural relativist framework, in which the 'intercultural narrative is realised through the process of mediation' (Dasli, 2011).

> While these forms of knowledge stem from an increased understanding of one's sense of Self and that of the Other, they are constantly put into question during the process of mediation. This process, which initially swings from one reason-modelled conviction to the other, provisionally settles in a relativised context where the intercultural narrative is realised. (Dasli, 2011: 26)

In the same vein as Dasli (2011), MacDonald and O'Regan (2009, 2013) caution against a conceptual reliance on relativist or universalist frameworks. Unlike Alred *et al.* (2006: 125) who commend the Universal Declaration of Human Rights as a useful starting point in the everyday intercultural negotiation of value positions, MacDonald and O'Regan (2013) caution against such reliance. The Universal Declaration of Human Rights, they argue, might work well as a wider moral framework but could lead to ethical inertia when faced with concrete 'exorbitant acts of the other' (MacDonald & O'Regan, 2013: 6) in everyday life. Everyday intercultural improvisations often require 'on-the-spot' ethical judgement 'as part of a necessary and ongoing reflexive intercultural praxis' (MacDonald & O'Regan, 2013: 6). A reliance on moral universalisms might potentially lead to an *incapacity to act* and the closure of an open discursive terrain. In its extreme form, a desire for 'conceptual purity' can actively prevent communication:

> The Western alliance's 'War on Terror' and the Jihadism of Al-Qaeda are both examples of claims which are being used in this [universalising] way. They each represent a will to truth which colonises the discursive terrain according to its own perceptions, based as they are on the presupposed obviousness of their own moral privilege. (MacDonald & O'Regan, 2013: 8)

MacDonald and O'Regan (2009, 2013) thus rightly problematise wider, universalising tendencies inherent in intercultural communication concepts and pedagogies. These can run the danger of preempting the 'transformation' of the other – towards the 'higher ideals' of awareness-raising, openness or intercultural understanding – and erasing the difference between self and other.

> A politics of presence is stalking the corridors of intercultural communication. This is an Enlightenment desire for plenitude, for the satisfactory repletion of ideas and outcomes, and the resolution of difference. In other words, it is the desire we as interculturalists have for fulfilment and purity in the concepts that we employ in our work and in the consequences which they portend; and so there is a desire for justice, equality, understanding, openness, truth, etc., an organic ordering of the intercultural whole, in which these elements are all neatly ordered and arranged. (MacDonald & O'Regan, 2009: 6)

MacDonald and O'Regan (2009) caution that even well-intentioned educational ideals can result in pedagogic practices that can lead to discursive closure and ethical inertia which stall open dialogue and critical action. 'Progressive' intercultural concepts can prove vacuous, or even function to hold wider, inequitable structures in place, if they do not actively acknowledge people's concrete, lived realities. 'Difference' should not just be defined 'culturally' but as always in relation to people's wider life conditions (materially, politically, psychologically). Intercultural concepts and pedagogies can potentially do damage to students like Nam Ha and Yun, when they do not take their real-world experiences – often of injustice and inequality – into account for their formulations of justice, equality, understanding, etc. Phipps (2014) explains the negative effect that universal frameworks can have on students who are more vulnerable to structural inequality:

> Intercultural Dialogue may work and make sense in stable, secure jurisdictions where there is relative 'freedom from fear and want' (Nussbaum, 2011), but it is at best limited and at worst dangerous when used in situations of conflict, vulnerability, insecurity and aggression. (Phipps, 2014: 115)

Phipps explains this conceptual paradox in the context of UNESCO's (2013), the British Council's (2013) and the Council of Europe's (2008) definitions of 'Intercultural Dialogue' – as 'open and respectful exchange between individuals and groups of different cultural backgrounds' (Council of Europe, 2014: 116). Groups, such as asylum seekers and refugees, who do not enjoy equitable status, Phipps (2014: 115) writes, 'act as symbolic examples of a subaltern who are excluded from the lofty aims of Intercultural Dialogue as equal exchange in many of their encounters, thus troubling the ideal and exposing its vacuousness'. The 'desire for conceptual fulfilment' (MacDonald & O'Regan, 2013) in intercultural pedagogies can then entail a structural violence when it is unequivocally assumed that the equitable discursive structures for 'respectful dialogue' are already established. The other's (e.g. the asylum seeker's, the refugee's) 'transformation' towards the preconceived value of 'respectful exchange', which he/she doesn't have the agency to determine, can then become an obligatory moral act. It safeguards the purity of the intercultural concept but holds existing, inequitable structures in place.

## An Ethical Praxis of Responsibility

> Without responsibility, the hope which is carried in the possibility of the other that, for example, things might be different one day, as well as the praxis which such hope implies, would be denied. (MacDonald & O'Regan, 2009: 13)

With reference to Ricoeur (1992), Lévinas (1997) and Derrida (1981), MacDonald and O'Regan (2009, 2013: 11) call for an ethical praxis in intercultural education which avoids universalising truth claims but takes as its guiding principle an 'ethics of responsibility for the other'. Ethical considerations are linked to people's concrete hopes and life experiences and aim 'at the good life with and for others, in just institutions' (Ricoeur, 1992: 170, quoted in MacDonald & O'Regan, 2009: 9). Here, the otherness of the other is not transformed and difference erased. It is brought out for active, critical inquiry and a formulation of educational practices that can resist 'deficit orientations' (Grainger, 2013; Grainger & Jones, 2013) towards students. In such ethical praxis of responsibility, students' hopes for 'at-homeness' (Lederach & Lederach, 2010) can then find expression from within the process of working towards more equitable relationships in 'just institutions'. In her critical review of cosmopolitan education, educational philosopher Todd (2007, 2008) affirms the importance of not basing educational conceptualisations on the premises of preconceived appeals to human universality and dignity, as found, for example, in liberal arts education models (e.g. Nussbaum, 1997). 'Humanity', so Todd writes, should not be considered as an abstract, given fact or a legitimisation for education. Instead, 'humanity' should act as a 'provocation' and lead to praxis-based reflections on the validity of those concepts and educational practices, which we evoke in the name of a humanity-oriented education.

> The respect, dignity and freedom, which have become signs of humanity, are not bred from within, but in relation to the disturbing and provocative event of being confronted by another person [radically different to oneself]. It is here, in this provocation, where I see the promise of education itself. For it allows into education the difficult prospect of responding to others as an actual practice of justice (however incomplete such practices might be) without deferring it to some future that will one day arrive. (Todd, 2008: 9)

Not unlike MacDonald and O'Regan (2009, 2013), Todd locates the promise of an education that faces humanity 'head-on', within the imperfect, but responsibility-oriented pedagogies which emerge out of responding to students' concrete, present needs (psychologically, materially, politically) and hopes for their future lives (Figure 2.4). Educational practices, when located within this responsibility-oriented pedagogy–social justice link, do not claim an alleged neutrality. They act as moral and political practices. They involve resistance against discriminatory tendencies in wider educational structures and pay close attention to practices that allow students' experiences and concrete hopes for their future to be present in classroom learning. Students' 'humanity' – as for example manifested in Nam Ha and Yun's story of hope – then becomes a cause for praxis-based educational reflection on the possibilities for 'just' educational practices, rather than a foundational principle for universally applicable 'best' practices. An ethical praxis of responsibility in intercultural language education then asserts one of critical pedagogy's radical statements: 'every educational act is political and every political act should be pedagogical'

**Figure 2.4** What happens to people's hopes for a better future?

(Guilherme, 2006: 170). With reference to Freire (1973, 1995), Trueba and Bartolomé (2000) call into question notions of 'teacher neutrality' and 'best practice' prevalent in most teacher education programmes:

> According to Paolo Freire, beyond technical skills, teachers should also be equipped with a full understanding of what it means to have courage – to denounce the present inequities that directly cripple certain populations of students – and effectively create psychologically harmless educational contexts. (Trueba & Bartolomé, 2000: 289)

Teachers' critical engagement with how an ethical praxis might take shape in their specific educational contexts should thus be a key element of teacher education. This could, for example, involve reflection on how pedagogical activities can connect to students' complex lives, migratory experiences and hopes for a 'good life'. In other words, a sole focus on methodological questions, best teaching practices and notions of teacher neutrality might inadvertently hold hegemonic discursive structures in place, if these are not shaped and changed by students' presence and their lived realities. Students like Nam Ha and Yun might not benefit from an intercultural language education, which defines Intercultural Dialogue's 'respectful exchange' only methodologically. They can be educationally disadvantaged because the wider educational and societal structures that disable this important goal for them remain invisible and thus go unquestioned.

Educational practices and concepts that work *towards* humanity rather than conceptually presupposing it thus need to connect notions of competence and agency to the collective work of establishing the wider conditions in which the student's full 'narratorial self' (Kramsch & Gerhards, 2012: 76) can be present (Figure 2.5).

This also includes pedagogical attention to the damage that the loss of 'at-homeness' (Lederach & Lederach, 2010) might have exerted on students' minds (Bronstein & Montgomery, 2011; Halvorsen, 2002). Although a detailed discussion of this psychological dimension is beyond the scope of this chapter, language education should be mindful of the role that pedagogic activities might play in producing 'psychologically harmless educational contexts' (Trueba & Bartolomé, 2000: 289).

> These are practices which pay attention to the damage created by exposure to the multiple pervasive varieties of conflict, trauma and mistrust which are part of the present global condition or to the loss of identities caused by present circumstances [...]. (Phipps, 2014: 119)

In other words, 'restorative practices' (Phipps, 2013) recognise that notions of hope and resiliency, especially significant for students who have experienced trauma in their lives, are often associated with creative

**Figure 2.5** How can we encourage students' full narratorial selves?

processes (e.g. Harris, 2007; Rappaport, 2014; Tantia, 2014; Yohani, 2008). In addition to these restorative dimensions, the inclusion of performative approaches in intercultural language education also asserts language and intercultural learning itself as a visceral, physical and subjective process. It always involves students with their whole bodies (Kramsch, 2009; Kramsch & Gerhards, 2012; Phipps & Gonzalez, 2004; Schewe, 2013).

> [L]anguage teachers should be much more aware that the bodies they have in front of them in the classroom are, in fact, acquiring the language with all their senses; not just their brains, but their eyes, their ears, their touching, their smell, their taste, and that they should appeal to the senses in a much greater way than they usually do. (Kramsch & Gerhards, 2012: 75)

Language and intercultural learning is a multisensory process. This should be reflected in intercultural language pedagogies which place students' subjectivity and sensory experiences at the centre. In a turn away from skills/competence-oriented intercultural models, Phipps and Gonzalez (2004: 115) propose in this respect the terms 'languaging' and 'intercultural being'. These are terms which capture the performative dimension of language and intercultural learning. 'Languaging' pedagogies thus promote collaboration and creative processes. They cultivate a notion of narration in intercultural language education which is linked to subjective and affective dimensions. Can drama pedagogy serve as an example of a 'languaging pedagogy' that facilitates a critical and multisensory engagement with difference in intercultural language education?

## Drama Pedagogy: A Languaging Practice?

> Over the last two decades, drama pedagogy has helped to lay the foundations for a new teaching and learning culture which accentuates physicality and centres on 'performative experience'. (Schewe, 2011)

Drama pedagogy has long acted as an important reference discipline for foreign language didactics (see Schewe, 2011, 2013). This brought forth various drama-based approaches which emphasise to varying degrees the methodological, psychological and political dimensions in intercultural language learning. What unites the various approaches that emerged in the wake of the performative turn in language and intercultural education is their kinaesthetic orientation and stance as dynamic learning tools. They are employed for the purpose of 'intercultural training' (Feldhendler, 1994, 2007), 'expanding students' multi-lingual and multi-modal self-expression' (Rothwell, 2011), 'reducing learners' language anxiety' (Piazzoli, 2011) or providing opportunities for 'reflective and transformative explorations of self and other' (Donelan, 2002) (Figure 2.6).

Concerning intercultural education in particular, we find a methodological focus on the potential of drama pedagogy to realise intercultural competence objectives. Kessler and Küppers (2008) as well as Boehm (2011), Choi (2004) and Cunico (2005), for instance make the case for drama pedagogy as a holistic way to put into practice intercultural (communicative) competence (Byram, 1997). Drama pedagogy is thought to foster awareness of the interpersonal dimension, including the moods, emotions and attitudes that are embedded in the languages

**Figure 2.6** Learning cultures that accentuate performative experiences

we use (Cunico, 2005). Corporeality and sense experience are described as the constitutive elements of an intercultural language learning that combines linguistic, ethical, action-oriented, affective and cognitive learning objectives (Kessler & Küppers, 2008). The drama-based language classroom thus becomes a space of experimentation and kinaesthetic learning, in which cultures, and both one's own and others' identities, can be explored, questioned, developed and invented, all within the 'safe space' of the drama (e.g. Donelan, 2002; Fleming, 2003, 2004) – and to transformative effect.

Does drama pedagogy, when used in service of these intercultural competence objectives, conceptually rely on a universalist orientation? Does drama pedagogy implicitly promote discursive closure when it is in service of the 'higher ideals' of intercultural understanding and awareness-raising? Asked in reverse, does drama pedagogy's focus on students' bodies and lived experiences not (implicitly) assert a critical pedagogical orientation? Does drama pedagogy not 'automatically' promote an active stance of inquiry in intercultural language education; one that opposes a consumer-oriented 'banking education' (Freire, 1973) and the creation of 'docile' student bodies? In other words, does the use of drama pedagogy in intercultural language education not guarantee a mode of 'languaging', which cultivates forms of engagement that are aesthetically unencumbered by a desire for conceptual purity?

I would argue that the caution and reflection concerning universalising intercultural conceptualisations (MacDonald & O'Regan, 2009, 2013; Phipps, 2013, 2014; Todd, 2007, 2008) equally applies to drama pedagogy when used in the work with learners who are more vulnerable to structural inequality. Dunn *et al.* (2012) give an example from their drama work with newly arrived refugee children:

> In choosing to base the drama upon a playful, fantasy-based narrative, we were hoping to avoid the kind of responses to resettlement and resilience that apply a deficit model or focus on the challenges this experience brings. (Dunn *et al.*, 2012: 496)

Dunn *et al.* (2012) carefully connect their methodological objectives – the development of English language skills as a key aspect of supporting refugee children's resilience – to the wider psychological and political dimensions at play in their students' lives. Through the use of a fictional narrative that is centred around Rollo, a young robot who has travelled to Earth from a distant planet with her robot dog Sparky, the educator-researchers invite their students to inhabit positions of expertise (e.g. as interpreters for Sparky who cannot speak English). They build on students' strengths, real-world interests (in animals, robots) and their sense of play. Narrative practices which put students in a position of lack or deficit (e.g. of English language skills) or forces them to relive traumatic events are avoided.

In addition to Dunn *et al.*'s (2012) example, Arizpe *et al.* (2015) reveal the benefits of using fictional, fantasy-based narratives. Arizpe *et al.* work with the wordless picture book *The Arrival* (Tan, 2006) to develop a form of 'intercultural literacy' which takes newly arrived refugee children's life experiences and hopes for their own futures as the starting point for multimodal activities and conversations. Drawing on school-based ethnographic work in a multilingual classroom, Ntelioglou *et al.* (2014) also show that performative approaches, especially within a multi-literacies (The New London Group, 1996) approach, can build on students' personal, cultural and multiple language experiences and put them in a position of expertise rather than deficit. Educational psychologist Yohani (2008) emphasises how using photographs and an image-based 'hope quilt' can foster discussions based on hope and strength that are led by the children. Dennis (2007, 2008) reminds us, however, to consider that the telling of stories is no neutral affair.

> The personal story in the refugee context represents a complex, cultural, political and social currency. [...] It is thus necessary to question how theatre [and other performative approaches] translates to the refugee context where people are required to tell their stories – over and over and over again. Who is listening? [...]. The refugee context is structured around the repeated requirement to tell within a culture of institutional disbelief [...]; a story is represented as currency to earn the next stage of entry. (Dennis, 2007: 357)

The act of storytelling in performative pedagogies, far from being universally empowering for every participant, is caught up in a complex net of psychological, social and political effects. These can resonate beyond the specific pedagogical situation. In a context like our ESOL classroom, for example, where students like Nam Ha and Yun have experienced the pressure and potential trauma of having to tell and retell their personal story in an institutional setting (the UK's Home Office), careful ethical reflection on how the performative method constitutes and reconstitutes its tellers and listeners is imperative.

## Conclusion

Performative approaches in intercultural language education hold the potential to be powerful languaging practices which stand in the tradition of critical pedagogy and defy the modernist templates of adoption models. Drama pedagogy, for example, can work from students' embodiment and from within the complex overlap of aesthetic, affective and political dimensions *towards* 'just' educational practices. I suggest, therefore, that we have to be careful not to put performative approaches too quickly in service of universalising moral aims and methodological objectives. Instead, I propose that performative pedagogies in intercultural language education should not be regarded as a dynamic intercultural learning tool only but as complex, aesthetic translation practice. Such aesthetic translation practice embraces fiction, multi-modality and a narrative practice full of metaphoric gaps. The performance-based 'identity texts' (Cummins, 2001) that emerge from such aesthetic translation practice, as Nam Ha and Yun's story demonstrates, do not necessarily produce 'authentic stories'. They cannot be easily 'consumed' as just another intercultural narrative flowing smoothly within our existing concepts. The students' relentless story of hope, love and home place, in the face of the very complex and often (socially, politically, psychologically) contested lives they live in the real world, upsets our social relations and educational status quo. It confronts and challenges us educators and researchers to position ourselves in the face of such hope and examine how our pedagogies hold up to the pressure. Theatre scholar Ridout (2009: 12) says that 'it is in the situation of doubt, in the moment of choice, when you ask yourself, "How shall I act?"' that you are opening up the space of ethics. Performative approaches might be regarded as ethical praxis in intercultural language education not when they offer anything of the ethical in and of itself, but when their aesthetic processes lead us (teachers, researchers, students) into critical reflection on the kind of educational and societal spaces we build in the name of 'humanity'.

## Acknowledgements

I would like to thank artist Simon Bishopp for the aesthetic translation of Nam Ha and Yun's text into the images which illustrate this chapter. Thank you also to Alison Phipps for her feedback on the manuscript.

## References

Arizpe, E., Colomer, T. and Martínez-Roldán, C. (2015) *Visual Journeys Through Wordless Narratives: An International Inquiry with Immigrant Children and the Arrival.* London/New York: Bloomsbury.

Blommaert, J., Collins, J. and Slembrouck, S. (2005) Spaces of multilingualism. *Language & Communication* 25, 197–216.

Boehm, S. (2011) Affektiv ist effektiv: Dramatische Aktivitäten als Hilfsmittel zur Erlangung einer interkulturallen Sensibilität im Fremdsprachenunterricht. *Scenario* V (2), 59–72.

The British Council (2013) Intercultural dialogue. See http://activecitizens.britishcouncil.org/content/intercultural-dialogue-icd (accessed 15 January 2016).

Bronstein, I. and Montgomery, P. (2011) Psychological distress in refugee children: A systematic review. *Clinical Child and Family Psychology Review* 14, 44–56.

Byram, M. (1997) *Teaching and Assessing Intercultural Communicative Competence*. Clevedon: Multilingual Matters.

Byram, M., Gribkova, B. and Starkey, H. (2002) *Developing the Intercultural Dimension in Language Teaching: A Practical Introduction for Teachers*. Language Policy Division, Directorate of School, Council of Europe, Strasbourg. See http://www.coe.int/t/dg4/linguistic/Source/Guide_dimintercult_EN.pdf (accessed 15 January 2016).

Byram, M., Fleming, M. and Alred, G. (eds) (2006) *Education for Intercultural Citizenship – Concepts and Comparisons*. Clevedon: Multilingual Matters.

Choi, Y.J. (2004) Being outside and inside: Dialogic identity and intercultural communication through drama in teaching English as an international language. *Research in Drama Education: The Journal of Applied Theatre and Performance* 9 (1), 101–102.

Council of Europe (2008) *White Paper on Intercultural Dialogue: 'Living Together as Equals with Dignity'*. See http://www.coe.int/t/dg4/intercultural/source/white%20paper_final_re-vised_en.pdf (accessed 15 January 2016).

Cummins, J. (2001) *Negotiating Identities: Education for Empowerment in a Diverse Society*. Los Angeles, CA: California Association for Bilingual Education.

Cunico, S. (2005) Teaching language and intercultural competence through drama: Some suggestions for a neglected resource. *The Language Learning Journal* 31 (1), 21–29.

Dasli, M. (2011) Reviving the 'moments': From cultural awareness and cross-cultural mediation to critical intercultural language pedagogy. *Pedagogy, Culture & Society* 19 (1), 21–39.

Dennis, R. (2007) Inclusive democracy: A consideration of playback theatre with refugee and asylum seekers in Australia. *Research in Drama Education: The Journal of Applied Theatre and Performance* 12 (3), 355–370.

Dennis, R. (2008) Refugee performance: aesthetic representation and accountability in playback theatre. *Research in Drama Education: The Journal of Applied Theatre and Performance* 13 (2), 211–215.

Derrida, J. (1981) *Positions*. London: The Athlone Press.

Donelan, K. (2002) Engaging with the Other: Drama, and intercultural education. *Melbourne Studies in Education* 43 (2), 26–38.

Dunn, J., Bundy, P. and Woodrow, N. (2012) Combining drama pedagogy with digital technologies to support the language learning needs of newly arrived refugee children: A classroom case study. *Research in Drama Education: The Journal of Applied Theatre and Performance* 17 (4), 477–499.

Feldhendler, D. (1994) Augusto Boal and Jacob L. Moreno: Theatre and therapy. In M. Schutzman and J. Cohen-Cruz (eds) *Playing Boal* (pp. 87–109). London: Routledge.

Feldhendler, D. (2007) Playback theatre. A method for intercultural dialogue. *Scenario* I (2), 48–59.

Fleming, M. (2003) Intercultural experience and drama. In G. Alred, M. Byram and M. Fleming (eds) *Intercultural Experience and Education* (pp. 87–100). Clevedon: Multilingual Matters.

Fleming, M. (2004) Drama and intercultural education. *German as a Foreign Language* 1 (4), 110–123.

Frank Tantia, J. (2014) Mindfulness and dance/movement therapy for treating trauma. In L. Rappaport (ed.) *Mindfulness and the Arts Therapies: Theory and Practice* (pp. 95–107). London/Philadelphia, PA: Jessica Kingsley.

Freire, P. (1973) *Pedagogy of the Oppressed*. New York: Seabury.

Freire, P. (1995) *Pedagogy of Hope: Reliving Pedagogy of the Oppressed*. Trans. Robert R. Barr. New York: Continuum.

Grainger, K. (2013) The daily grunt: Middle-class bias and vested interests in the 'Getting in Early' and 'Why Can't They Read?' reports. *Language and Education* 27 (2), 99–109.

Grainger, K. and Jones, P.E. (2013) The 'language deficit' argument and beyond. *Language and Education* 27 (2), 95–98.

Guilherme, M. (2006) Is there a role for critical pedagogy in language/culture studies. An interview with Henry Giroux. *Language and Intercultural Communication* 6 (2), 163–175.

Halvorsen, K. (2002) Separated children seeking asylum: The most vulnerable of all. *Forced Migration Review* 12, 34–36.

Harris, D.A. (2007) Dance/movement therapy approaches to fostering resilience and recovery among African adolescent torture survivors. *Torture* 17 (2), 134–152.

Hoff, H.E. (2014) A critical discussion of Byram's model of intercultural communicative competence in the light of bildung theories. *Intercultural Education* 25 (6), 508–517.

hooks, b. (1994) *Teaching to Transgress: Education as the Practice of Freedom.* New York/London: Routledge.

Kessler, B. and Küppers, A. (2008) A shared mission. Dramapädagogik, interkulturelle Kompetenz und holistisches Fremdsprachenlernen. *Scenario* II (2), 3–24.

Kramsch, C. (2009) *The Multilingual Subject.* Oxford: Oxford University Press.

Kramsch, C. and Gerhards, S. (2012) Im Gespräch. An interview with Claire Kramsch on the 'multilingual subject'. *Die Unterrichtspraxis/Teaching German* 45 (1), 74–82.

Lederach, J.P. and Lederach, A.J. (2010) *When Blood and Bones Cry Out: Journeys through the Soundscape of Healing and Reconciliation.* New York/Auckland/Capetown: Oxford University Press.

Lévinas, E. (1997) *Entre nous: On Thinking-of-the-Other.* London: Athlone Press.

Levine, G.S. and Phipps, A. (2012) *Critical and Intercultural Theory and Language Pedagogy.* Boston, MA: Heinle.

MacDonald, M.N. and O'Regan, J.P. (2009) The Ethics of Intercultural Dialogue. Working paper presented at the 38th Annual Meeting of the Philosophy of Education Society of Australasia, Imin International Conference Center, Honolulu, Hawaii, 3–6 December.

MacDonald, M.N. and O'Regan, J.P. (2013) The ethics of intercultural communication. *Education Philosophy and Theory* 45 (10), 1005–1017.

Malkki, L. (1995) Refugees and exile: From 'refugee studies' to the national order of things. *Annual Review of Anthropology* 24, 495–523.

The New London Group (1996) A pedagogy of multiliteracies: Designing social futures. *Harvard Educational Review* 66 (1), 60–93.

Ntelioglou, B.Y. (2011) But why do I have to take this class? The mandatory drama-ESL class and multiliteracies pedagogy. *Research in Drama Education: The Journal of Applied Theatre and Performance* 16 (4), 595–615.

Ntelioglou, B.Y., Fannin, J., Montanera, M. and Cummins, J. (2014) A multilingual and multimodal approach to literacy teaching and learning in urban education: A collaborative inquiry project in an inner city elementary school. *Frontiers in Psychology* 15 (5), 533. See http://www.coe.int/t/dg4/intercultural/source/white%20 paper_final_re-vised_en.pdf (accessed 15 January 2016).

Nussbaum, M. (1997) *Cultivating Humanity: A Classical Defense of Reform in Liberal Education*. Cambridge, MA: Harvard University Press.

Piazzoli, E. (2011) Process drama: The use of affective space to reduce language anxiety in the additional language learning classroom. *Research in Drama Education: The Journal of Applied Theatre and Performance* 16 (4), 557–573.

Phipps, A. (2013) Intercultural ethics: Questions of methods in language and intercultural communication. *Language and Intercultural Communication* 13 (1), 10–26.

Phipps, A. (2014) They are bombing now: Intercultural dialogue in times of conflict. *Language and Intercultural Communication* 14 (1), 108–124.

Phipps, A. and Gonzalez, M. (2004) *Modern Languages: Learning and Teaching in an Intercultural Field.* London/Thousand Oaks, CA/New Delhi: Sage Publications.

Phipps, A. and Guilherme, M. (eds) (2004) *Critical Pedagogy: Political Approaches to Language and Intercultural Communication.* Clevedon: Multilingual Matters.

Prato, G.B. (2009) *Beyond Multiculturalism – Views from Anthropology.* Farnham/Burlington, VT: Ashgate Publishing.

Rappaport, L. (2014) *Mindfulness and the Arts Therapies.* London/Philadelphia, PA: Jessica Kingsley Publishers.

Ricoeur, P. (1992) *Oneself as Another.* Chicago, IL/London: University of Chicago Press.

Ridout, N. (2009) *Theatre & Ethics.* Basingstoke/New York: Palgrave Macmillan.

Rothwell, J. (2011) Bodies and language: Process drama and intercultural language learning in a beginner language classroom. *Research in Drama Education: The Journal of Applied Theatre and Performance* 16 (4), 575–594.

Schewe, M. (2011) Die Welt auch im fremdsprachlichen Unterricht immer wieder neu verzaubern. Plädoyer für eine performative Lehr- und Lernkultur! In A. Küppers, T. Schmidt and M. Walter (eds) *Inszenierungen im Fremdsprachenunterricht. Grundlagen, Formen, Perspektiven* (pp. 20–31). Braunschweig: Diesterweg.

Schewe, M. (2013) Taking stock and looking ahead: Drama pedagogy as a gateway to a performative teaching and learning culture. *Scenario* VII (1), 5–28.

Tan, S. (2006) *The Arrival.* London/Sydney: Hodder Children's Books.

Todd, S. (2007) Promoting a just education: Dilemmas of rights, freedom and justice. *Educational Philosophy and Theory* 39 (6), 592–603.

Todd, S. (2008) Facing Humanity: The Difficult Task of Cosmopolitan Education. Paper presented at the Philosophy of Education Society of Great Britain annual conference. See http://www.philosophy-of-education.org/conferences/pdfs/Sharon_Todd.pdf (accessed 15 January 2016).

Trueba, E.T. and Bartolomé, L.I. (2000) *Immigrant Voices: In Search of Educational Equity.* Oxford/Lanham, MD: Rowman and Littlefield.

Turner, T. (1994) Anthropology and multiculturalism: What is anthropology that multiculturalists should be mindful if it? In D.T. Goldberg (ed.) *Multiculturalism. A Critical Reader* (pp. 406–425). Oxford/Cambridge, MA: Blackwell.

UNESCO (2013) Intercultural dialogue. See http://www.unesco.org/new/en/culture/themes/dialogue/intercultural-dialogue/ (accessed 15 January 2016).

Yohani, S.C. (2008) Creating an ecology of hope: Arts-based interventions with refugee children. *Child & Adolescent Social Work Journal* 25 (4), 309–323.

# 3 Diadrasis: An Interactive Project on Language Teaching to Immigrant Families in a Greek School

Evi Kompiadou, Antonis Lenakakis and Roula Tsokalidou

## Introduction

The research and methodological principles upon which this chapter is based relate to (a) theater-pedagogic techniques, (b) multimodal texts and (c) identity texts (discussed in the section: Multimodality and Identity Texts) as educational tools in contexts of language and culture contact, such as the Greek multicultural school. It is a case study and a pilot application within a research program called 'Diadrasis' (=Interaction), promoting social and digital literacy in mixed groups of parents and children.[1] Its main aim was to create a bridge of communication between vulnerable social groups[2] and the dominant society. Although this is an important educational aspiration at all times in Greece, the existence of earmarked funding during the academic year 2013–2014 allowed for the realization of a specific project. The school selected for the implementation of the program was the Intercultural Primary School of Neoi Epivates in the prefecture of Thessaloniki.

According to Statute 2413/96, which regulates matters regarding, on the one hand, the provision of Greek language education to the Greek diaspora and, on the other, the provision of 'intercultural education' (the ministry's term) in Greece, the purpose of the latter was the foundation and operation of primary and secondary schools that would 'provide education to young people with a specific educational, social or cultural identity' (the ministry's translation). Following the implementation of the law, a total of 26 'intercultural' schools were established throughout Greece. Although they were supposed to cater to the needs of a 'special' student population through the use of specially designed curricula and materials, in reality this has not been achieved. Students of non-Greek-background do not find themselves in a cognitively challenging and stimulating environment that would enhance their potential (Gkaintartzi *et al.*, 2014; Mitakidou *et al.*, 2007).

Through the Diadrasis program, immigrant and Greek-background families (parents and children) met at the school premises on weekends and shared their knowledge and experiences. Thus, a twofold goal was achieved: the sensitization of Greek families to issues of migration and the support of immigrant families in the process of becoming full members of the dominant Greek community. Our particular study was aimed at the negotiation of theater-pedagogic theory and praxis, using identity texts as a method of activating the linguistic and cultural capital of students and their families and of establishing a context of communication, cooperation and trust among the groups involved. In this way, immigrant children and parents would also further develop their Greek language skills.

## Issues of Students' Language and Culture in the School Context

The school is a place of meeting and social exchange for children from different social backgrounds as well as for their families. As a space for social interaction, the school becomes the place where information sharing, mutuality, social development and integration take place. It is our view that the establishment of a context of promoting heterogeneity – as an element of enrichment, encouragement and the strengthening of immigrant-background students and their families – provides a fertile educational and linguistic context for both immigrant and Greek-background students and families.

The negative effects of ignoring students' linguistic and cultural backgrounds within the school context, as well as the school's role in rejecting students' bilingualism, have been well documented in the scientific literature (Cummins, 1995; Wong-Fillmore, 1991). As a result, students' bilingualism remains 'invisible' (Tsokalidou, 2005). The maintenance of the language of origin is considered a responsibility of the family, although research findings show that the efforts of individual families and communities do not suffice for the reduction of language loss, much less for the development of bilingualism (Valdés & Wiley, 2000). Children and their families are, directly or indirectly, forced to assimilate to the dominant school language and culture. Wong-Fillmore (1991: 343) stresses the negative consequences of family language loss for the communication between family members: 'What is lost is no less than the means by which parents socialize their children: When parents are unable to talk to their children, they cannot easily convey to them their values, beliefs, understandings, or wisdom about how to cope with their experiences'.

We believe that, in language and culture contact environments, the implementation of innovative practices that acknowledge the linguistic and cultural background of all children is necessary to address the challenge of multicultural education (Tsokalidou, 2012: 117). The familiarization of Greek-background children with the existing and diverse linguistic and cultural wealth in their classes can take place in a productive and natural manner through the use of the arts. More specifically, through theater-pedagogic practices, we can visualize and gain awareness of the various 'voices' in a safe context, where every participant can freely offer his/her own suggestions and solutions for every problem/issue and test out their effects.[3]

## Aspects of Theater-Pedagogic Theory and Praxis

*Theater pedagogy* combines the practice of play and theater with the science of pedagogy, and it finds application at all levels of education. The two core terms, *theater* and *pedagogy*, meet in a new synthesis, without, however, losing their autonomy. The result is not the sum total of the two but a dynamic and complex interrelationship, in which new areas of research are laid open (Lenakakis, 2008).

Theater pedagogy and its techniques cannot of course be considered a universal tool for the educational management of all social and pedagogical matters. On the contrary, its use as a tool goes against its very nature. Theater pedagogy survives and affects its recipients as long as it maintains its playful, experimental and interactive character, at the very point where the play with aesthetic forms, focus, exaggeration, the unexpected and the haphazard find time and space to flourish (Lenakakis, 2012: 121). The power of theater pedagogy lies in the potential it generates for activating sensory impulses through scenery, symbolism, metaphor, hypothetical 'if' and intonation (Lenakakis, 2004). Activating sensory impulses, however, makes players aware of their expressive means, which are subsequently developed to generate potentially multisensory expressions and representations. Becoming aware of, visualizing and symbolically presenting contradictions within a safe setting enables players to freely put forward and try out their own solutions. Art is a rare and valuable area of freedom, but at the same time it is also a special area of real and effective learning as children are taught to listen, watch and observe themselves, others and life itself. Theater as a form of play provides areas of negotiation, exploration, partnership, communication and interaction through enjoying what is a shared outcome (Kondoyianni *et al.*, 2013).

Just as knowledge, emotion and the cultivation of the soul are all in a dynamic interaction, so too our meeting with art needs to be promoted through multifaceted activities within and outside the school context. In this light, music, theater, audiovisual material and video art are intertwined and coexist within a 'Pedagogy for all the Arts' (Grammatas, 2011). The role of art is to create, for its recipients, relations with objects and to lead to the activation of their sensory impulses in order for them to comprehend the self and the other, while surpassing the constraints of subjectivity, within the safe space of play (Lenakakis, 2013). Through theater and other art forms, we can best understand human behavior and the surrounding world and deal with problematic situations on both a personal and a social level (Kondoyianni *et al.*, 2013).

## Multimodality and Identity Texts

Contemporary multicultural societies face the challenge of diversity, a reality that enriches pedagogical thinking with new points of view regarding the study of the text, connecting it with a variety of genres and technology and transforming it into a 'multimodal text': a text that combines a variety of forms, such as pictures, writing, sounds, etc. Multimodality is an important text quality for children because of their everyday contact with multimodal texts within and outside the school environment (Chatzisavvidis, 2011). It directly relates to 'cultural diversity' through the significant issues which arise from the multicultural nature of the classroom and has little to do with a superficial engagement with customs, music and other folkloric products (Duncker, 2009). The concept of multimodality has a direct relation to diversity as an asset in the educational process. It allows for new meanings to be given to the texts that are under negotiation. We can thus move away from power and class relationships in order to build relations of cooperation and autonomy (Chatzisavvidis, 2014). Moreover, different language resources contribute to the expansion of the meaning of texts and encourage multiple expressions of identity, which are brought to the surface and placed under negotiation (Cummins, 2003; Kalantzis & Cope, 1999).

In the teaching scenario presented in this chapter, we use multimodal texts as the vehicle for the expression of the participants' identities. They are utilized therefore as 'identity texts' which help broaden the children's perspectives and encourage critical thinking. Through the involvement of parents, we attempt to create an environment that enables and supports the development and the expression of the multilingual and multicultural identities of children and parents alike.

Identity texts can act as mirrors of children's identities and observable behaviors, while multimodal texts in a school environment foster and encourage language development (Cummins & Early, 2011; Kourtis-Kazoullis, 2011; Skourtou, 2011). Additionally, the scenario presented below suggests that the same texts can become 'identification texts' for their readers, who can identify with the experiences of the texts' writers/creators (Kompiadou, 2013). Through such texts, the language(s), knowledge and experiences that children and parents bring from home become visible and a source of wealth for the whole class to share (Tsokalidou, 2012).

## A Case Study: An Example of Interaction and Multisensory Expression

The case study we present in what follows is part of a series of training sessions in the context of the Diadrasis program, which was implemented in the Intercultural Primary School of Neoi Epivates in the prefecture of Thessaloniki and lasted for a total of 16 weeks.

The program had an intergenerational nature: 4 immigrant and 11 Greek-background families participated, i.e. children who studied at the aforementioned school during the academic year 2013–2014 and their parents. The ages in the group ranged from 5 to 54 years old. In the following case study, a teaching scenario was implemented with a group of students who attended the meetings on May 30 and 31, 2014. These meetings took place on Saturday afternoons for five hours each time. The researchers and the group of parents and students met and got involved in the interactive activities that are described below.

### The research sample

The research sample consisted of 10 individuals who formed the group of participants: 5 were children, 8–12 years old (4 boys and 1 girl) and 5 were mothers, 32–43 years old (average children's age: 9.8, average mothers' age: 36). Three of the children were of Greek origin and the other two were of Albanian origin, while two mothers were of Greek origin, one was a Russian speaker and another two were of Albanian origin.

### Methodological issues: Stages of the research

The research included two levels/stages. At the first stage, the participants were involved in live training sessions which preceded an intensive multisensory theatrical introduction; the second stage included "the teaching scenario 'Five meetings on stage'." We describe the two research stages below.

The first research stage, with the live training sessions preceding an intensive multisensory theatrical introduction, included communication and self-expression games and exercises (Figure 3.1).[4] At the end of every session, the members of the group recorded or wrote down their experience in an open questionnaire (Figure 3.2), in any language or manner they could, stating their opinion on the specific session. They were invited to write short comments and expressions regarding the feelings and thoughts

**Figure 3.1** The intensive multisensory theatrical session

during the session they had participated in. This furnished the researchers with collected data for an evaluation of the session.

The second research stage, the teaching scenario 'Five meetings on stage' that we present below, was designed as an intercultural, interactional *meeting* which was titled: 'Five meetings on stage'. The overall communicative context included the technique of *stage improvisation of realistic situations.*[5] Improvisation meant that the participants had the freedom to choose the 'theatrical material' which they would transform into a 'theatrical scene'.

## Planning of the teaching scenario

The following four methodological steps outline the necessary stages which carried the individuals all the way to stage action and presentation. The instructions and the necessary explanations were given by the researchers to the group. The group was given paper and color markers.

- First step: Finding the character
  'Think of a person, either real or imaginary. This person will be your character. You could also be that person yourself and you do not need to tell us. Decorate your T-shirt with a message which expresses the identity of your own character. Draw, write words or

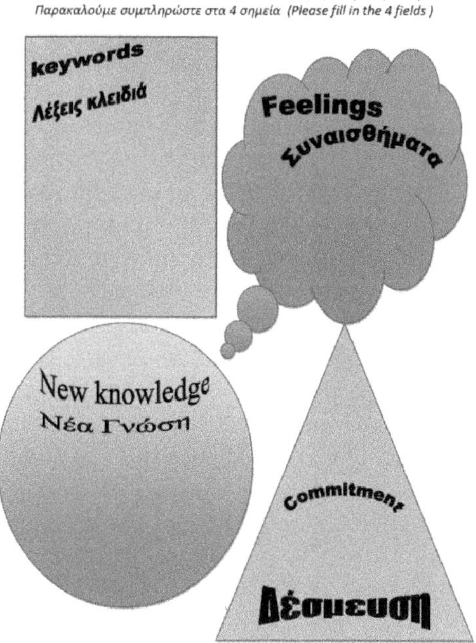


**Figure 3.2** Questionnaire

phrases, artistically express yourself and exhibit the T-shirts you have made'.

- Second step: Presenting the character
  'Present your character to the group in any way you like'.
- Third step: The theatrical convention/the meeting of the *characters*
  'Draw a picture from the box and form couples based on the picture's color'.
- Fourth step: Stage action
  'Every couple will create their own story, answering the questions provided. The story can be presented either through narration or through acting. Do not forget to include the picture-symbol of your group in the story. Finally, give your story a title'.

These four steps gradually led the group from individual to group exercises, engaging all participants in the presentation of the stories and eventually leading to a meeting in pairs. We will now analyze these steps and how they relate to the theoretical context we presented.

Below we present the research stages in detail and the findings from each stage.

## Research findings

The research data collected from the two stages, presented below, were analyzed based on the grounded theory of Strauss and Corbin (1996) through open, axial and selective coding in addition to *in vivo* coding for creating codes based on the participants' language to identify prominent themes and patterns rooted in the participants' own language. Conclusions were arrived at by taking participants' *snapshots* during the program. This data analysis approach proved to be the most suitable and, to a great extent, the most relevant one because of the qualitative nature of our research. Based on seeking repetitive patterns and evidence that can lead to reliable results, grounded theory includes open, axial and selective coding to decipher human behaviors attitudes and thoughts. In addition, elements were borrowed from van Dijk's (2001) theoretical model focusing on specific linguistic features, mostly lexical forms, word meaning and word choices, all of which 'index' the world views of the participants. Although the participants had the freedom to choose any language on stage, they mostly used Greek, a choice which allowed for the Greek language to be reinforced and taught during the program.

## Stage one

The research data from the first stage are presented/analyzed in four main axes, following the principles of grounded theory and van Dijk's (2001) model according to which the material analyzed is the naturally occurring text and talk in the participants' original contexts. These axes resulted from the analysis of the data on the evaluation forms, and they demonstrate the positive atmosphere that was created in the live sessions. The four axes are the following:

(1) The *keywords* which the participants used to describe the atmosphere of the sessions.
(2) The *feelings* recorded by the participants during the sessions.
(3) The *new knowledge* the participants felt they had acquired.
(4) The *commitments* they felt that they were ready to make after each session.

Through the rethinking of these sessions and the workshops, two main categories arose: diversity as a challenge with a focus on effective communication and solidarity among individuals. The level of contact and familiarization through the intensive multisensory program created the necessary framework for the implementation of the teaching scenario presented below (Table 3.1).

**Table 3.1** The four axes are presented in the languages of origin (Greek, Albanian, Russian) and are translated in the parenthesis

| *Λέξεις κλειδιά/key words* | *Συναισθήματα/ feelings* | *Νέα γνώση/new knowledge* | *Δεσμεύσεις/commitments* |
|---|---|---|---|
| Спасибо (Thank you) | Gëzim (Joy) | Русский (Russian) | *«Να μάθω νέες λέξεις»* *('To learn new words')* |
| Ενότητα (Unity) | Eqeshur (Laughter) | Συνύπαρξη (Coexistence) | *«Να τους μάθω αλβανικά να γράφουν και να διαβάζουν»* *('To teach them how to write and speak in Albanian')* |
| Διαφορετικότητα (Diversity) | Ngrohtësi (Warmth) | *«Πόσο σημαντική είναι η μητρική γλώσσα για έναν μετανάστη»* *('How important is the mother language for an immigrant')* | *«Θα μάθω και θα ενδιαφέρομαι για τις γλώσσες» ('I will learn and be more interested in languages')* |
| Ιδαιτερότητες (Specificities) | Ικανοποίηση (Satisfaction) | *«Είναι κέρδος να μαθαίνεις γλώσσες»* *('It is a benefit to learn languages')* | *«Θα ζητώ από τις φίλες μου που μιλούν άλλες γλώσσες να μου λένε λέξεις»* *('I'll ask my friends to teach me some words in their language')* |
| Më afër (Closer) | Ελευθερία (Freedom) | Спасибо (Thank you) | *«Θα συμμετέχω στα κοινά περισσότερο»* *('I will participate in public affairs more often')* |
| Μετανάστευση (Immigration) | Ζωντάνια (Liveliness) | да (Yes) | *«Μεγαλύτερη επαφή με ελληνίδες»* *('I will keep in contact with Greek women more')* |
| Μητρική γλώσσα (Mother tongue) | Έκπληξη (Surprise) | | |
| Διγλωσσία (Bilingualism) | Ενθουσιασμός (Enthusiasm) | | |
| Επικοινωνία (Communication) | Αισιοδοξία (Optimism) | | |
| Ελευθερία (Freedom) | | | |
| Dashuri (Love) | | | |
| Grup (Group) | | | |
| Μάθηση (Education) | | | |
| Κοινωνικός γραμματισμός (Social literacy) | | | |
| Γλώσσες (Languages) | | | |
| Συναισθήματα (Emotions) | | | |
| Biseda (Conversation) | | | |

## Stage two

### *Analysis of the steps included in the research stage 'Five meetings on stage'*

(1) First step: The workshop started at the level of individual involvement. Each participant had to search for and collect his/her own data (either real or imaginary), i.e. the characteristics of the characters he/she chose to enact on stage. Then they would record these characteristics in a multimodal text and draft their own identity text. Their research was based on memories, biographical or fictional incidents which would render each character 'real'. The participants were invited to illustrate the identity of their characters on a T-shirt (Figure 3.3a), creating multimodal texts and identity texts by combining languages, cultural elements, pictures and symbols which they would illustrate artistically (Figure 3.3b–k). The texts were considered identity texts, as participants in a drama play combine elements from the real world with imaginary situations in a manner that expresses the materials of their own lives (Lenakakis, 2012).

**Figure 3.3** The identity of each character on a paper T-shirt

(2) Second step: Every participant was invited to exhibit the profile and the identity she/he had attributed to her/his characters and to present them to the other participants.
(3) Third step: Pairs were randomly created so that gender, age and origin would differ, after having chosen parts of pictures (Figure 3.3) with different colors. Then the participants were paired up according to the color of the pictures they chose, regardless of whether the parts made up the same picture or not. The pictures chosen would provide the starting point for the pairs to develop the stage action and would also help create a common basis for the theatrical choices of the group.
(4) Fourth step: Finally, the meetings of the characters were presented, calling for the engagement of the entire group of participants in the presentation of the stage action. The questions provided to the group members (also referred to as *action questions*) formed the core of the action and were the following: *Who? Where? When? What? Why? With whom? Against whom?* The questions aimed at offering the initial context of the stage improvisation and providing a direction for the process of group creation. The answer to the question of *When?* was decided by the researchers before the workshop, so that the improvisations would have a common meeting point: that of time. The stage meeting had been set for a *Saturday at 3 pm!*
(5) In the presentations that followed, which we present below, we realized that *When?* was not the only common element shared by the group (Figure 3.4).

### *Presenting the stage meeting*

We will now focus on the pairs that were formed (see fourth step) and on the stories behind these *stage meetings.*

- The chosen couples are:
  (1) Lionel Messi and Mrs Helen
  (2) Chrysa and Savio
  (3) Evelina and Giorgos
  (4) Rena's and Elli's moms
  (5) Grandma Kyriaki and Gioni
- The stories of the five *stage meetings* were the following:
  (1) Messi and Mrs Helen met at the sea, which they both liked. The weather was beautiful. Mrs Helen has a daughter who is a fan of Messi and she wanted to get her an autograph. Messi was visiting Greece with his son in order to help children with cancer and children who are addicted to drugs. One of these children was Mrs Helen's daughter! (Figure 3.5a)
  (2) Chrysa and Savio met at a birthday party which took place at a park with a slide, many trees, swings and various other playsets.

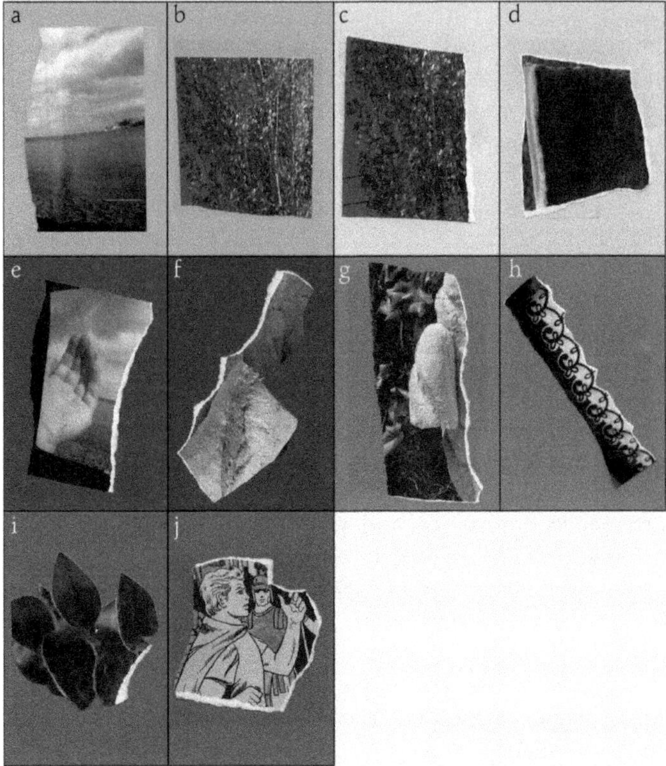


**Figure 3.4** The chosen colored pictures

They played games, some of which were group games. They played football with some other children, but the rival team got upset because they were losing, and they ended up quarreling. This way, the two of them got closer! (Figure 3.5b)

(3) Evelina and Giorgos want peace and love to prevail throughout the world. Many areas of the world suffer from hunger, drought and most importantly illnesses. They told us during the performance: 'We met in Sierra Leone in order to provide help, because we sympathize with our fellow human beings. We will talk to locals about the help we wish to provide. A nice local person helped us communicate with the poor, interpreting for us'. They also took a stand against the government which has brought the country to this state (Figures 3.5c and d).

(4) Rena's and Elli's moms met at Elli's place in order to get to know each other. Their daughters are friends. Elli had invited them over for dinner. Elli's mom talked about her daughter whom she missed, and Rena's mom talked about her daughter who lives here,

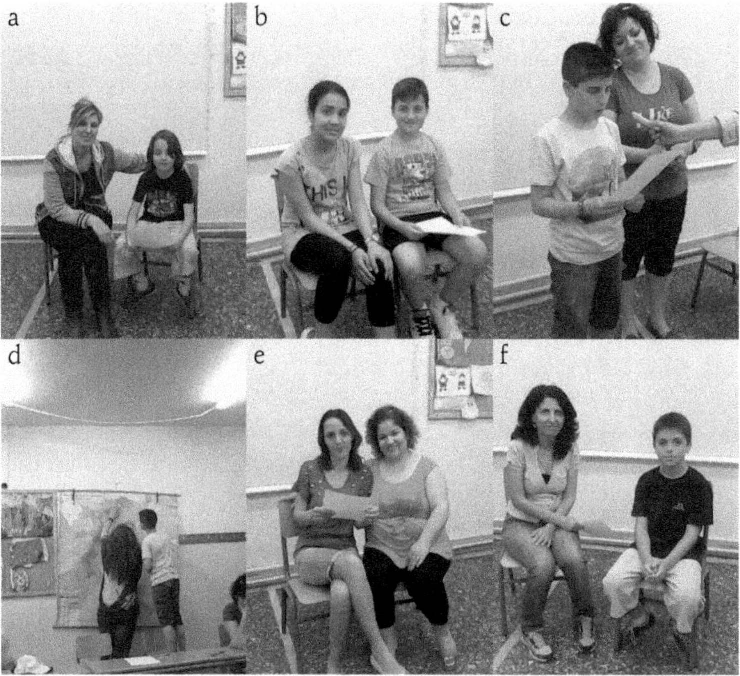

**Figure 3.5** The chosen couples

in Greece, and knows full well how hard it is to be unemployed (Figure 3.5e).

(5) Grandma Kyriaki and Gioni, who is 10 years old, met by chance at the village square. They introduced themselves and started a conversation. Grandma Kyriaki is a refugee, while Gioni comes from a family of migrant workers. His parents came to Greece seeking a better life, while Kyriaki fled her country due to war. In their conversation, they both expressed bitterness, both for the poor financial circumstances which force people to migrate and for the evil people who rule the world and cause wars in countries (Figure 3.5f).

### *The analysis of stage action*

In the stage meetings discussed above, theatrical convention turned into the creation and the expression of a personal story, of a stage discourse with many autobiographical elements and lived experiences. Real characters met as in the case of Pair 1, namely the well-known football player Lionel Messi, as embodied by the young player who is a great fan of his, and Mrs Eleni, troubled with serious issues, a story with many autobiographical elements (Figure 3.5a). Likewise, in Pair 5, grandmother Kyriaki was a role with many references to the grandmother of the player who was very dear to her. Gioni, in the same pair, was in fact the cousin of the young player of Albanian-background who lived in Albania and was missed. The common experiences of two families of immigrants and refugees met on stage and created a shared story (Figure 3.5f). Pair 4, the mothers of Rena and Elli, engaged in a stage dialogue and shared the agony and difficulty of being immigrant mothers (Figure 3.5e). World problems and the diachronic values of humanity came to the surface in the story of Pair 3 (Figure 3.5c and d) and simple everyday issues like football, play and the love of life were expressed through the stage action of Pair 2 (Figure 3.5b).

The interplay between role, embodied character and actor leads to the creation of a subjective normality which has a unique pedagogic value (Kondoyianni *et al.*, 2013; Lenakakis, 2004). The safety provided by the role taken on in play becomes the means for lifting the existing emotional load. At the same time, the normality of real life is transformed into the normality of play, and the two relate in a dynamic and subversive manner. The player as a subject, an object and a means of the artistic process is involved holistically (body, mind, emotion), plays and constructs forms and discovers himself/herself utilizing all the materials that make up the self. To play means to experiment freely and to construct, for as long as the performance lasts, one's own world with one's own conventions and terms. The player discovers, realizes and gives meaning to the normality of the world, of which she/he is a subject. While play through illusion and hypotheses happens in a special place and time of action away from the real world, the materials of which the dream and the illusion are made, in fact, are the materials of one's own life (Lenakakis, 2012).

Through the meetings described in this chapter, the members of the group came closer and were involved in a dialogue utilizing the materials of their own biographies and desires. Both the adults and the children, through their multimodal identity texts (drawings, photos, colors, sounds) expressed their love, memories and dreams for a better life. Through these simple everyday communicative experiences, people create their own narrative worlds which include not only facts but, more importantly, memories and feelings (Archakis & Tsakona, 2011).

## Discussion

A context of constructing and consolidating relations of communication, interaction, cooperation and trust was created among all the groups and individuals involved. The cultural, linguistic and social obstacles were surpassed and a new form of interactive and multisensory communication was achieved, as the researchers adhered to the need for unraveling (van Dijk, 2001) the dominant mechanisms in discourse and strengthening the participants in their effort to propose alternative meanings. Through multimodal texts, identity texts and an overall multilingual context of action, we created the basis for the acknowledgement of linguistic and cultural heterogeneity and the consolidation of cohesion within the group. The texts that were documented, presented on stage and discussed with reference to personal experiences were in the purest sense 'identity texts', in which children and parents integrated parts of their own histories, families, homes and countries. The parents' stories were expressed in their own languages, often with the help of the Greek-speaking parents and their children as translators in a trans-generational and mutually enriching communication. The choice of languages involved much more than the dominant Greek language, as the process was multisensory. The native speakers had the opportunity to deconstruct their sense of linguistic uniqueness, as the activities realized in other languages were equally interesting and convincing. The whole group and its members recognized and acknowledged the familiar and the unfamiliar alike, the latter living next to us, among us and even within us. The realization and the verbalization of any possible resistance to the unfamiliar led the way to the inclusion of the experiences of all participants and to a fertile dialogue between the school and home contexts. The project gave parents the opportunity to participate in their children's classes and share a school activity that allowed them to connect their personal life stories, their languages and cultures with the school context.

All in all, on the level of dramatic expression, our intention had not been to create a final scenic product which could be presented to a wider audience. The group composition, its dynamics and the limited time available led us to a conscious decision to put forward the emotional and social aspects for the empowerment of the specific group of participants as learners of Greek as a second language. However, the dramatic actions that took place during the project were such that a powerful and extremely emotional atmosphere was created which kept all participants constantly involved. Our main future aim for the continuation of the project is to focus on and further cultivate the dramatic forms that appeared in the group with the intention of sharing a more complete theatrical product to a wider audience.

## Conclusion

A theater pedagogy-based educational program that raises cultural awareness and aims at the construction and consolidation of relations of authentic communication, interaction, cooperation and trust can function as an ally to parents and children in their effort to be critical toward the dominant language and culture and to form a new identity and new social relations. On the other hand, it offers participants the possibility of acknowledging the variety of languages and cultures, and thus of surpassing cultural and other barriers. In such a context of mutuality and theatrical play, the teaching of the dominant school language, Greek in our case, took on completely new and exciting dimensions for all participants. More importantly, bridges connecting the school language with the parents' home languages were built, and the strengthening of Greek as the target language was achieved through a multisensory theater-pedagogy that strengthened researchers and participants alike.

## Notes

(1) Diadrasis, Educational Programme of Lifelong Learning, funded by the General Secretariat of Lifelong Learning of the Greek Ministry of Education. See http://diadrasis.web.auth.gr/diadrasis/el (accessed 15 June 2016).
(2) 'Vulnerable social groups', according to the Programme 'Diadrasis', are immigrant and return migrant populations (http://diadrasis.web.auth.gr/diadrasis/el), a definition followed by the European Community Fund (http://www.eye-ekt.gr/) and the Ministry of Labour and Social Solidarity (http://www.opengov.gr/minlab/?p=1764); all links accessed 15 June 2016.
(3) On the development of intercultural dialogue through theater pedagogy, see e.g. Lenakakis (2004, 2012).
(4) See Lenakakis (2010).
(5) This technique is based on theatrical exercises developed by Stanislavsky and Strasberg. For more information see Strasberg (2001) and Wermelskirch (2003).

## References


Archakis, A. and Tsakona, V. (2011) *Taftotites, Afigiseis kai Glossiki Ekpaidefsi* [*Identities, Narrations and Language Education*]. Athens: Patakis (in Greek).

Chatzisavvidis, S. (2011) I polytropikotita sti sychroni egrammati koinonia os proion metaforas tou biomatos: pros mia nea morfi logou [Multimodality in contemporary literate society as a product of the transfer of experience: A new form of discourse]. In M. Pourkos and E. Katsarou (eds) *Vioma, metafora kai polytropikotita: efarmoges stin epikoinonia, tin ekpaidefsi, ti mathisi kai ti gnosi* [*Experience, Transfer and Multimodality: Applications in Communication, Education, Learning and Knowledge*] (pp. 103–13). Thessaloniki: Nisides (in Greek).

Chatzisavvidis, S. (2014) Apo ton grammatismo ston polygrammatismo [From literacy to multiliteracies]. In A. Kyridis (ed.) *Efpatheis koinonikes omades kai dia viou mathisi* [*Vulnerable Social Groups and Lifelong Learning*] (pp. 325–337). Athens: Gutenberg (in Greek).

Cummins, J. (1995) Canadian French immersion programs: A comparison with Swedish immersion programs in Finland. In M. Buss and C. Lauren (eds) *Language Immersion: Teaching and Second Language Acquisition* (pp. 7–20). Vaasa: University of Vaasa Research Papers.

Cummins, J. (2003) *Taftotites ypo Diapragmatefsi. Ekpaidefsi me skopo tin Endynamosi se mia Koinonia tis Eterotitas* [*Negotiating Identities: Education for Empowerment in a Diverse Society*] (E. Skourtou, ed.; S. Argyri, trans.). Athens: Gutenberg (in Greek).

Cummins, J. and Early, M. (2011) *Identity Texts, the Collaborative Creation of Power in Multilingual Schools*. Stoke-on-Trent: Trentham Books.

Dijk van, T.A. (2001) Critical discourse analysis. In D. Schiffrin, D. Tannen and H.E. Hamilton (eds) *The Handbook of Discourse Analysis* (pp. 352–371). Malden, MA: Blackwell.

Duncker, L. (2009) Polytropikotita kai diapolitismiki mathisi. Mia theoritiki prosegisi [Multimodality and intercultural learning. A theoretical approach]. In Chr. Govaris (ed.) *Keimena gia ti didaskalia kai ti mathisi sto polypolitismiko scholeio* [*Texts for Teaching and Learning in Multicultural School*] (pp. 37–49). Athens: Atrapos (in Greek).

Gkaintartzi, A., Chatzidaki, A. and Tsokalidou, R. (2014) Albanian parents and the Greek educational context: Who is willing to fight for the home language? *International Multilingual Research Journal* 8 (4), 291–308.

Grammatas, Th. (2011) To Theatro os Pammousos Paidagogia – Prokliseis kai zitoumena tis ekpaidefsis stin epochi tis ysteris neoterikotitas [Theatre in Education – Educational challenges in the era of late modernity]. In M. Argyriou and P. Kambylis (eds) *Technes kai Ekpaidefsi: Dimiourgikoi tropoi ekmathisis ton glosson. Praktika Diethnous Synedriou, t. A'* [*Art and Education*] (pp. 71–76). Athens: EEMAPE (e-book) (in Greek).

Kalantzis, M. and Cope, B. (1999) Polygramatismoi [Multiliteracies]. In A.F. Christidis (ed.) *Ischyres kai astheneis glosses stin Evropaiki Enosi: opseis tou glossikou igemonismou* [*Strong and Weak Languages in the European Union: Facets of Linguistic Hegemonism*] (pp. 680–695). Thessaloniki: KEG (in Greek).

Kompiadou, E. (2013) Paidagogiki axiopoiisi tis glossikis kai politismikis eterotitas sto nipiagogio [Educational exploitation of linguistic and cultural diversity in kindergarten]. Unpublished postgraduate thesis, Aristotle University of Thessaloniki (in Greek).

Kondoyianni, A., Lenakakis, A. and Tsiotsos, N. (2013) Intercultural and lifelong learning based on educational drama. Propositions for multidimensional research projects. *Scenario* 7 (2), 27–46.

Kourtis-Kazoullis, V. (2011) Identity journals in multicultural/multilingual schools in Greece. In J. Cummins and M. Early (eds) *Identity Texts: the Collaborative Creation of Power in Multilingual Schools* (pp. 88–96). Stoke-on-Trent: Trentham Books.

Lenakakis, A. (2004) *Paedagogus ludens. Erweiterte Handlungskompetenz von Lehrer(inne)n durch Spiel- und Theaterpädagogik* [*Paedagogus Ludens. Broadened Action Competence of the Teachers through Drama and Theatre Pedagogy*]. Berlin/Milow: Schibri (in German).

Lenakakis, A. (2008) I Theatropaidagogiki os neo mondelo paremvasis stin Agogi atomon me embodia sti zoi kai sti mathisi [Theatre pedagogy and special education]. In H. Kourkoutas and J.P. Chartier (eds) *Paidia kai efivoi me psychokoinonikes kai mathisiakes diataraches* [*Children and Adolescents with Psychosocial and Learning Disabilities*] (pp. 455–470). Athens: Topio (in Greek).

Lenakakis, A. (2010) To paichnidi kai to theatro sti didaskalia tis (ellinikis os) xenis glossas. Mia didaktiki protasi [Play and theatre in the teaching of (Greek as) a foreign language. A teaching proposal]. *Paidagogikos Logos* 3, 81–105 (in Greek).

Lenakakis, A. (2012) Oi andistaseis mas sto anoikeio os proklisi: Efkairies diapolitismikis synandisis kai epikoinonias meso Theatropaidagogikis [Theatre pedagogy and interculturalism]. In G. Androulakis, S. Mitakidou and R. Tsokalidou (eds) *Stavrodromi Glosson & Politismon: Mathainondas ektos scholeiou* [*Crossroads of Languages and Cultures: Learning Outside the School*] (pp. 114–128). Thessaloniki: Polydromo and Faculty of Education A.U.Th. (in Greek).

Lenakakis, A. (2013) I Theatropaidagogiki stin ekpaidefsi: Taseis kai staseis [Theatre pedagogy in education: Trends and positions]. *Paidagogika Revmata sto Aigaio* 6–7, 1–12 (in Greek).

Mitakidou, S., Tressou, E. and Daniilidou, E. (2007). Cross-cultural education. A challenge or a problem? *International Journal of Educational Policy, Research & Practice: Reconceptualizing Childhood Studies* 8 (1), 67–81.

Skourtou, E. (2011) *I Diglossia sto Scholeio* [*Bilingualism in the School*]. Athens: Gutenberg (in Greek).

Strasberg, L. (2001) *Schauspielen & Das Training des Schauspielers* [*Acting and the Actor's Training*] (W. Wermelskirch, ed.). Berlin: Alexander Verlag (in German).

Strauss, A.L. and Corbin, J. (1996) *Grundlagen qualitativer Sozialforschung* [*Basic of Qualitative Research. Grounded Theory. Procedures and Techniques*]. Weinheim: Beltz.

Tsokalidou, R. (2005) Raising bilingual awareness in Greek primary schools. *International Journal of Bilingual Education and Bilingualism* 8 (1), 48–61 (in German).

Tsokalidou, R. (2012) *Choros gia dyo. Themata diglossias kai ekpaidefsis* [*Space for Two: Issues of Bilingualism and Education*]. Thessaloniki: Zygos (in Greek).

Valdés, G. and Wiley, T.G. (2000) Editors' introduction. Heritage language instruction in the United States: A time for renewal. *Bilingual Research Journal* 24 (4), i–v.

Wermelskirch, W. (ed.) (2003) *Texte für Vorsprechen und Acting-Training. 110 Solo- und Duo-Szenen des 20. Jahrhunderts* [*Texts for Auditions and Acting Training. 110 Solo and Duo Scenes of the 20th century*]. Berlin: Alexander Verlag (in German).

Wong-Fillmore, L. (1991) When learning a second language means losing the first. *Early Childhood Research Quarterly* 6, 323–346.

# 4 Developing Empathy Through Theatre: A Transcultural Perspective in Second Language Education

Joelle Aden

*To my mind, acting and experiencing communication in a foreign language are the same thing. In both cases, one remains oneself while using words that aren't one's own or at least aren't those that one would use spontaneously. More importantly, both activities are a profound experience of freedom.*

Jeanne Balibar, French actress (2014)

## Introduction: What is the Connection Between Theatre and Languages?

According to Jeanne Balibar (2014), acting and experiencing communication in a foreign language allow us to feel free. But from what confines do they release us? And via what mechanisms? In an interview, the actress reveals what it is that, for her, makes the connection between foreign languages and theatre: both are an intimate encounter with the unknown, an experience within oneself of somebody else's words, rhythm and unique way of perceiving the world. Erving Goffman (1959) developed a theory of this language-theatre connection based on his observation of everyday conversations, in which he compared ritualised speech acts with 'cultural performances'; but his theory remains on the surface of language with its standards and conventions, and only gives us limited insight into the nature of how we co-construct meaning. As for the actress, she evokes her intimate world of theatre: to speak another language or do theatre is to live through the eyes of others and feel inhabited by their gestures, sounds and postures; it's for an actor to invent a fictional character and at the same time be invented by the thoughts and feelings of the character. It is to create a reciprocal resonance between self and other.

In essence, Balibar is speaking of empathy, *Einfühlung*. Used for the first time by the German philosopher Robert Vischer (1873), this term was taken up by the phenomenological movement in philosophy and psychology. Neurology is now uncovering the neural systems that enable us to have this experience of 'other in self' or of 'self in other',[1] and showing that theatrical performance, like ordinary conversation, relies largely on invisible mechanisms such as kinaesthetic and emotional empathy. Empathy, as the basis of interaction, places language at the heart of human relationships without separating the linguistic aspects from all the neurophysiological and psychological sub-mechanisms that constitute the act of 'languaging'.[2] It is also important that this relationship be imbued with an empathetic concern for the Other. However, as Varela *et al.* (1993: 333) remind us, while empathy is something people do, it cannot be caused by 'simple rationalist standards or injunctions'. An attitude of empathy must be rooted in the body (as a form of sensory experience) and enacted (brought forth through action into the social world). Hence, we might ask, what role and what forms must be given to this construct in language teaching and learning?

We will see, on the one hand, that the ability to perceive a situation from another person's perspective without losing one's own sense of self is the biological and psychological foundation of our linguistic intersubjectivity, and forms the backdrop for the teaching and learning of language. On the other hand, pro-social attitudes develop from mechanisms of empathy that foster cooperation and tolerance of difference. In this regard, empathy is also the bedrock of intercultural competencies. In this chapter, I will show, through several plurilingual and cross-cultural artistic projects, the ways in which artists draw on these two levels of empathy. Then I will discuss different types of partnerships between artists and teachers that offer students the opportunity to 'enact' attitudes of empathy as part of a performative approach to language learning.

## The Need for a Paradigm Shift in Foreign Language Teaching

At the crossroads of academic knowledge, social demands and the power struggles surrounding language policy, the field of language teaching has already experienced many methodological turns: communicative, cultural, task based, intercultural, plurilingual. But today the field is at the dawn of a larger paradigm shift that is taking shape as a result of two key observations.

(1) Unprecedented levels of mobility and migration at a global level and the thinning of physical and symbolic boundaries have disrupted generally accepted ideas and practices in connection with languages.

Languages are complex systems tightly woven into the cultures of which they are an intrinsic part. They reflect different ways of perceiving our relationship to reality. All linguists agree on the richness of each human language and on the importance of their preservation. Contemporary views are radically calling into question the post-colonial hierarchy that at one time granted superior status to some languages over others. As living organisms, languages are changing and hybridising more and more rapidly through inter-cultural and cross-cultural encounters. The model of the mass teaching of a few dominant languages at the expense of those languages spoken by plurilingual people 'on the move' is beginning to crack on all sides. The question is, what languages do we teach to 'inter-understand' one another and function together in mutual respect and within a plurilingual and pluricultural framework, and '[w]hat does it mean concretely to have languages "interrelate and interact?" To have "values circulate across borders?" To have speakers "operate between languages?" Whether in one language or many, or in a mix of languages, intercultural communicative competence is in search of a pedagogy that transcends the duality L1-L2/C1-C2 and operates at the interface between multiple languages, subjectivities and identities' (Kramsch & Aden, 2012: 56).

(2) Our second observation is based on advances in cognitive science. The Cartesian idea that designates the neocortex (the cognitive brain) as the ontological seat of rational thought formed by the accumulation of abstract knowledge no longer holds. We adapt and learn constantly; in the words of H. Trocmé-Fabre (2006), we are 'born to learn' via our perceptions in social interactions. The discovery of the neural basis of empathy ('mirror neurons') led to the emergence of social neuroscience[3] which posits that 'our neurons absolutely require the physical presence of others and an empathetic connection to them' (Van Eersel, 2012: 68). We also know that in children's language development, the act of mimicking is the biological starting point for relationships to others (Jeannerod, 2002). It turns out that the theatre is based on these same kinaesthetic and emotional resonance mechanisms, which suggests a strong connection between theatre and language learning. Experiencing a story as a spectator is to feel a fictional situation as if it were real, i.e. what theatre theorists call the 'suspension of disbelief' and which corresponds exactly to the definition of empathy: to truly feel the emotions of the Other while remaining aware of not being that Other.[4] Whether we play or see others playing in other languages, we simulate the action of the 'other in self' or of 'self in the other'. It is not just unconscious imitation, but a form of resonance, for to mimic is to *bodily be one with* and therefore, to understand better (Lecoq, 1997). According to Edward Bond, the simulation within the (observing) self of what the characters experience on stage forces the spectator to change perspectives and thus to question himself/herself and engage morally.

> Drama puts us on the stage and gives us responsibility for the dilemmas that the characters we meet face. This makes the audience and participants creative, and the decisions they take are an act of self-creation. Each of us must dramatise our own life but also the lives of our communities. We are the dramatic species and we need drama in order to create the human self. The 'shared self' is social and therefore cultural and at the heart of a culture's story. (Cooper, 2015: 35)

## A Transcultural Experience Through Theatre

> Building a planetary civilisation requires a manifest interest in the Other with whom we bring forth a world. (Varela *et al.*, 1993: 328)

Artists have long engaged socially and politically for the emancipation and personal development of young people. The first project I have chosen to present is a poignant illustration of this engagement. Initiated by Palestinian artists, this project, titled *Gaza Monologues*, diffused the symbolic boundaries surrounding the occupied Palestinian territories so that the young people, victims of a conflict that engulfed their lives, could escape their imprisonment. By inviting youngsters from other cultures to put themselves in the shoes of the inhabitants of Gaza, they drew significantly on the phenomenon of emotional resonance, one of the mechanisms related to empathy.

In 2008, 22 days of intense aerial bombardment of the Gaza Strip resulted in a great number of civilian casualties. The state of terror and a feeling of helplessness had extinguished the hope of young Gazans. The artists from the Ashtar Theatre in Ramallah decided to run workshops enabling adolescents between the ages of 14 and 18 to put into words what they were experiencing. A writing process ensued and everyone recounted intimate moments: 'The house was full of smoke but my father lit a cigarette and smoked... as if we needed more smoke!'; 'I feel like running, running, running in the street till my headscarf flies in the sky and I fly after it...'. The experience could have limited itself to a form of art therapy, a kind of catharsis, but the artists decided to go further, turning it into a political act, establishing relationships, prohibited by the war, with other young people throughout the world (Figure 4.1).

The monologues of the young Palestinians were translated into 18 languages and distributed in 33 countries to more than 50 theatre companies around the world who, in turn, organised theatre workshops based on the Gaza monologues with a view to performing them. The aim was to put oneself in the shoes of young Gazans and to incorporate their voices in order to understand their plight in a way other than that used by the media. On a single day, 17 October 2010, the play was performed in all 18

**Figure 4.1** A writing workshop: Ashtar Theatre, Palestine, 2008

languages in Gaza City, Ramallah, Abu Dhabi, Cairo, Stockholm, Ghent, Vancouver, Harare, Beijing, Sydney and many other cities around the world. The choice to perform the play simultaneously in many different places was meant to reduce the distance between self and others, so much so that it would produce a sense of fusion between all the actors and spectators (Pacherie, in Berthoz, 2004: 176). In this process of mass contagion, well known to crowd psychologists, emotions spread among individuals, temporarily ridding them of their egos. Unlike empathy, individual selves merge into a collective self (sympathy) (Pacherie, in Berthoz, 2004: 176). This mechanism has to do with 'spindle neurons' that in mere milliseconds trigger archaic processes outside awareness that make it possible to detect and feel the emotions of others (Van Eersel, 2012: 72). This collective resonance produces very powerful emotional effects that can be negative (blind submission) or positive (compassion). Obviously, further work is required to become aware of and learn how to react to one's own emotions (Goleman, 1996) (Figure 4.2).

This is how more than 1700 young people around the world performed this play, affecting thousands of spectators, as borne witness to by the testimonies collected by the company: 'I just wanted to [say] how deeply moved I was on reading the monologues. They are one of the most important things I have ever read' (USA); '[I]t was an emotional experience that moved and humbled my friend and me. Your young writers eloquently conveyed the reality of their daily lives in Gaza ...' (UK). Educators who participated in this global project could work on

**Figure 4.2** Young Gazans performing the Gaza Monologues, Palestine, 2010

the texts and translations, i.e. on languages but as embodied in a very authentic, yet foreign experience.

This project transcends the scope of language and culture and provides an answer to the major challenge identified by Jeremy Rifkin (2010: 613): 'Human beings are forever searching for "universal intimacy", a sense of total belonging [...] The quest for universal intimacy is the very essence of what we mean by transcendence'. In his 'Seven complex lessons in education for the future', Edgar Morin (1999: 49) shares this point of view, suggesting that in order to develop understanding among peoples, 'we touch on the truly spiritual mission of education: teaching understanding between people as a condition and the protection of humanity's moral and intellectual solidarity'.

It seems that education systems throughout the world, although caught up in the game of rival nationalisms, are becoming increasingly aware that we need to build and live in a global community. Many are activists for a sustainable society, but such a society will not come about without first being a caring, empathetic society. Either that or it will be sustainable for only a minority of humanity. As we see it, building a truly sustainable society involves giving clear priority to transcendence, intercultural relationships and empathy over linguistic knowledge.

## Why Should We Address Intercultural Competencies Through Theatre?

### Reason 1: Our perceptions of cultural differences are partially below the threshold of awareness

Educational and language policies are putting more and more emphasis on the need to develop positive intercultural attitudes as part of young peoples' foreign language learning. Since the pioneering work of Hawkins (1984) on language awareness, many studies and pluralistic approaches have been developed to promote attitudes of tolerance and acceptance of other cultures and languages. Geneviève Zarate (2003: 15) puts forward the notion of cultural mediation within the framework of a political project for building a plurilingual Europe 'that raises the question of social values, be they negatively-charged (conflict, xenophobia, racism) or positively-charged (empathy, openness to others, xenophilia)', which must be addressed as a goal of intercultural education. Such a form of education cannot be based on reasoning alone.

The notion of embodied cognition is particularly interesting because it is based on the finding that cognitive processes are deeply rooted in the interaction between living organisms and their environment, a relationship that Varela calls 'structural coupling'. When an individual comes into contact with distant cultures and attitudes, foreign languages and unfamiliar behaviours, it is the non-conscious, neurophysiological and phenomenological mechanisms that determine the perception of and reaction to such difference or otherness. Our limbic brain triggers protective reflexes that can spawn racist attitudes. Pierre Bustany describes an epiphenomenon:

> After our birth, we develop the ability to analyze the faces of those ethnicities whose features become so familiar to us that we are able to recognize thousands of facial details in a matter of a few tenths of a second. But if we suddenly find ourselves in a foreign country, where the features are different, we become extremely imprecise in our analysis, unable to distinguish between individuals who are different but appear similar to us, thus rendering us less capable of empathy towards them. It is a neural basis of racism. (Bustany, 2012: 92–93)

Theatrical techniques are an indispensable, complementary resource for intercultural education because they develop the capacity to read faces and attitudes. They allow learners to embrace feelings of often negative strangeness by experiencing them first-hand rather than by fleeing them or feeling guilty about them. It is necessary to learn to recognise the emotions that emerge within the self and then to seek understanding of the kinds of behaviour they can push us to. Exercises such as 'hot-seating', used by actors to build foreign characters, or the 'Forum Theatre', for example, are extremely effective for becoming aware first-hand of our greater or lesser ability to feel empathy.

## Reason 2: Coping with the unknown engages emotions

The work of A. Damasio (2005) demonstrated that our choices and decisions are emotionally grounded and that our neocortex rationalises them after the fact. We are beyond Krashen's (1982) 'affective filter' which stresses the importance of developing a climate of trust and security in the classroom. This is of course essential; but recent studies on the links between the limbic system and the neocortex show that the emotional mechanisms are built into the cognitive system and that they codetermine our understanding of reality. For the neurologists Immordino-Yang and Damasio (2007: 5), '[h]idden emotional processes underlie our apparently rational real-world decision making and learning':

> In fact, one could argue that the chief purpose of education is to cultivate children's building of repertoires of cognitive and

> behavioural strategies and options, helping them to recognize the complexity of situations and respond in increasingly flexible, sophisticated, and creative ways. In our view, out of these processes of recognizing and responding, the very processes that form the interface between cognition and emotion, emerge the origins of creativity - the artistic, scientific, and technological innovations that are unique to our species. Further, out of these same kinds of processing emerges a special kind of human innovations: the social creativity that we call morality and ethical thought. (Immordino-Yang & Damasio 2007: 7)

In a similar vein, the French psychiatrist Christophe André stresses that 'it is essential to rediscover that we are thoroughly made up of basic emotions that are as natural to our functioning as breathing [...] Equally important, both empirically and practically, is the discovery that we have the possibility to modulate these flows of energy within' (André, in Van Eersel, 2012: 147).

Once again, theatrical practices offer a unique way to work on our awareness of and ability to regulate this system, since they allow us to live, feel and react to emotions and to work on a pre-verbal level of meaning *before* putting our sensory perceptions into words and reflecting on the shift from one language to another based on that experience.

When we think we are developing tolerance in young people by appealing to their conscious and rational understanding of a given social injustice, we are reaching merely the visible tip of the iceberg, based on what differentiates us. In such circumstances, our teaching has but a relatively weak and superficial impact in terms of bringing about change in negative intercultural attitudes. On the other hand, if we engage students in an aesthetic, in-the-flesh theatrical experience of this injustice, we reach a sensitive interface below the threshold of awareness that connects us to others as humans. Addressing contentious issues through the theatre opens new pathways for understanding the world and questioning the ready-to-think beliefs and attitudes often conveyed by the media. Because learning does not appeal to reason alone but to the dynamic network of sensory experience and non-conscious beliefs that bring knowledge into awareness, the knowledge transmission model as we know it must be revamped. In its stead, Varela has suggested speaking of the 'path of transformation' (in Trocmé-Fabre, 1994: video no. 4[5]). This non-conscious and emotional reality within the self that constitutes us and directs our actions should be widely present across the curriculum, and not only in the offices of school psychologists.

## Reason 3: Our ability to understand others relies on empathy mechanisms

In 1992, E. Rizzolatti and Sinigaglia (2008) showed the existence of a class of neurons they called 'mirror neurons' and which, from birth, become active both when an individual executes an act and when he/she observes it being executed by others. This ability to imitate or mimic by putting oneself literally 'in the body' of another person while remaining aware of one's own perspective clearly has much in common with the everyday work of actors. Not surprisingly, Rizzolatti and Sinigaglia (2008) open the preface to their book *Mirrors in the Brain: How Our Minds Share Actions and Emotions* by making an explicit connection between their discovery and the theatre:

> In an interview some time ago, the great theatrical director, Peter Brook commented that with the discovery of mirror neurons, neuroscience had finally started to understand what has long been common knowledge in the theatre: the actor's efforts would be in vain if he were not able to surmount all cultural and linguistic barriers and share his bodily sounds and movements with the spectators, who thus actively contribute to the event and become one with the players on the stage. This sharing is the basis on which the theatre evolves and revolves, and mirror neurons [...] now provide this sharing with a biological explanation. (Rizzolatti & Snigaglia, 2008: 7)

Soon afterward, it was discovered that this 'mirror system' unconsciously codifies not only the other person's actions but also their intentions and emotions. The direct connection established between perceiving and doing was described as a motor resonance (Rizzolatti & Craighero, 2004). A person uses his/her own motor repertoire to understand the meaning of movement 'while bypassing any process of analysis, representation or inferential reasoning' (Berthoz & Petit, 2006: 59).

We use this mechanism in our theatre workshops in the foreign language classroom: actors lead activities exclusively in the foreign language, even for beginners who, despite full immersion, manage to participate in all the activities using their other repertoires, i.e. gestural, emotional and aesthetic. They thus rely on low-level empathy phenomena (such as imitation and resonance) and associate the second language (L2) (or other languages) to a speech-related semantic network already in place in their first language (L1) (Aden, 2013). We have noted that it is essential to facilitate action, especially for beginners, by offering them situations and prototypical narrative contexts (stories) related to their own sensory and emotional experiences.

But whereas we use our own perspective, including spatial perspective, to understand the actions, feelings and emotions of others (Berthoz, 2004), further research has revealed that more complex psychological mechanisms are needed to understand the intentions and beliefs of others. We must remember that empathy is a particularly complex notion. Thirioux *et al.* (2014) describe a multifaceted socio-cognitive construct that combines 'emotional/automatic and cognitive/regulatory processes':

> [T]he automatic and emotional components of empathy correspond to the internal reproduction of another person's subjective experience and associated mental state, as if individuals were experiencing this given mental state themselves. On the other hand, the cognitive and regulatory components refer to a controlled process whereby people understand the mental states of others while adopting their psychological point of view based upon perspective-taking and self-other distinction. These are very akin to the second-person-like process involved in the Theory of Mind.[6] (Thiroux *et al.*, 2014: 287)

In drama workshops in second language evaluation (SLE), we use the low-level mechanisms as clues to understand the situations and as bridges to other languages. We consistently observe that students grasp the meaning of things without using analytic processes or inferential reasoning (Aden, 2014).

## A Study of the Use of Empathy Mechanisms in Theatre Workshops

In 2009, I conducted a study to better understand how actors used low-level empathy mechanisms in a plurilingual and pluricultural context. I wanted to know (a) if it was possible to rely on kinaesthetic and emotional empathy to conduct an educational project even when learners do not share a common language; (b) if the use of these low-level mechanisms could potentially help young people to learn, perceive and react in intercultural settings; and (c) if these mechanisms could foster positive attitudes, such as tolerance, willingness to help or the desire to meet others despite linguistic barriers.

The European research project entitled 'An Intercultural Meeting Through Applied Theatre'[7] (Aden, 2010) involved 54 young Europeans, aged between 12 and 18, for 10 days in France. Sixty percent of them had recently immigrated with their families to one of the six partner countries (Germany, UK, France, Greece, Italy and the Netherlands). These adolescents spoke a total of 25 languages and originated from 29 different countries spanning four continents (Table 4.1). Eight theatre practitioners from different

**Table 4.1** Languages spoken by the artists and the adolescents in each group (Aden, 2010: 90)

| | *Artists 1st Languages* | *Artists 2nd Languages* | *Languages of partner countries* | *Languages sopken in the groups* |
|---|---|---|---|---|
| Group 1 | English<br>Dutch | French/<br>German<br>English | German<br>English<br>French<br>Dutch<br>Italian<br>Greek | Albanian, German, English, Arabic, Armenian, French, Greek, Dutch, Italian, Lithuanian, Pashtu, Russian, Turkish, Ukrainian. |
| Group 2 | French<br>Spanish | English<br>Greek | | Albanian, German, English, Arabic, Armenian, French, Greek, Dutch, Italian, Kabyle, Lithuanian, Persian, Russian. |
| Group 3 | German<br>French | English | | Albanian, German, English, Arabic, Armenian, Spanish, French, Greek, Dutch, Ibamo (Nigeria), Italian, Macedonian, Neapolitan. |
| Group 4 | German<br>Italian | English/<br>French<br>French | | German, English, Bulgarian, Spanish, Greek, Dutch, Italian, Latvian, Portuguese, Romanian, Russian. |

theatrical backgrounds (clowning, mask work, drama, contact dance) were paired randomly just before starting the experimental workshops. They had never met before and did not share a common language.

A detailed analysis of the videos allowed us to identify cognitive threads woven of verbal and non-verbal languages. The artists organised activities in a continuum between awareness of one's own body in space (self-location experience) and awareness of others in space by progressively putting the students physically, emotionally and mentally 'in other people's shoes', thus operating a progressive change in perspective. We identified recurring patterns in the choice and sequence of activities in the four workshops. Starting with silence,[8] the artists initially relied on motor imitation (movements, rhythms, imagination, exchanges) and emotional resonance (looks, gestures, touch, 'mimo dynamism'), gradually introducing an element of psychological distance towards the self and other as part of an increasingly subtle game. (See a description of the progression of activities in Aden [2010: 101–110]). Our observations showed activities predominantly related to spatial perception, starting with the self, the self in relation to the other and then in relation to the group. The artists used activities that covered a full range of physical distances alternating between egocentric and allocentric[9] perspectives. According to Berthoz's (2004) spatial theory of empathy these mechanisms, which allow for the manipulation of spatial perspectives, are also used to manipulate cognitive perspectives, including representations and beliefs:

> It may seem bold to spatialize the problem of empathy. Yet there are several reasons for this. First, the fact that to change perspective is to change one's 'reading' of reality, i.e. how one solves a spatial problem. Putting oneself in the place of another is to see things his or her way. Changing points of view is changing perspectives. Furthermore, empathy is the way I look out at the world from the viewpoint of others. That said, the physiology of sight is a physiology of the manipulation of space through action, emotion, attention and intention. (Berthoz, 2004: 255)

We hypothesise that these spatial exercises can help develop mental plasticity in perspective-taking and foster cognitive empathy. But more than the use of space, it is the ability to navigate between egocentric and allocentric frames of reference that leads to the development of mechanisms of empathy. This gives rise to a mental agility and can help young people break away from various forms of conditioning, as will be discussed below. More studies looking into these issues are needed (Figure 4.3).

In this intercultural meeting, all the participants were constantly changing not only their spatial referents (through the theatre) but also their linguistic referents (all spoke or understood at least two languages, often more) as well as their cultural referents (differences in the perception of the body, ideas and emotions). Participants were thus 'pushed' rather intensively to adopt different perspectives of various kinds. The experiment provided the ecological conditions for what I called 'a space of potentialisation' (Aden, 2009), allowing for the emergence of an effective and altruistic transcultural dialogue. In 2007, I had suggested that empathy should be introduced in language education as a key component of communication and, further to this study, I suggested that empathy could be seen as the basis for transcultural competence. I make a distinction between 'intercultural', which suggests links between existing cultural

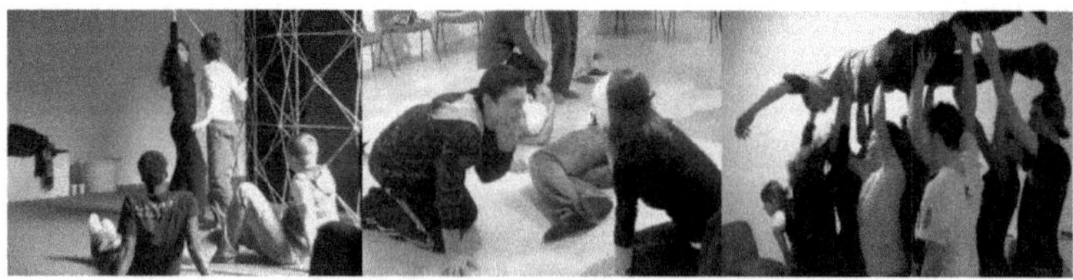

**Figure 4.3** Spatial exercises. Forbach, France, 2009

entities, and 'transcultural', which implies more complex and dynamic relationships across, through and beyond various cultures.

## Transcultural Competence and Empathy-Inhibiting Factors

Research in psychology and the neurosciences suggests that we are wired not for aggression, violence and utilitarianism, but for sociability, attachment and affection, and that our first drive is to belong (Rifkin, 2010). Thanks to the popularisation of the aforementioned research in the neurosciences, empathy has been identified as a key factor in the regulation of social relationships and has become increasingly popular among educators, but it is sometimes promoted in education as an over-simplified response, a magic cure in the form of ready-to-use tool kits of which we should be rather wary.

Although acting in several languages is not enough to develop pro-social attitudes, theatre does contribute significantly to the creation of conditions that foster such attitudes. I will envisage theatre and the aesthetics of theatre as the point of departure for teaching meaningful language that can help pupils build a global, transcultural identity. To do so, I will refer to the work of Simon Baron-Cohen (2011), the British psycho-pathologist specialising in the study of autistic disorders. According to his model, empathy comes by degrees on a spectrum, which spans from high to low levels of empathy. He differentiates the cognitive component, which enables us to imagine other people's thoughts and feelings, from the affective component, which is the drive to respond with a socially appropriate emotion to what someone else is thinking or feeling (Figure 4.4). According to him, both forms of empathy must be taken into account in order to understand the 'empathy circuit' in people's social

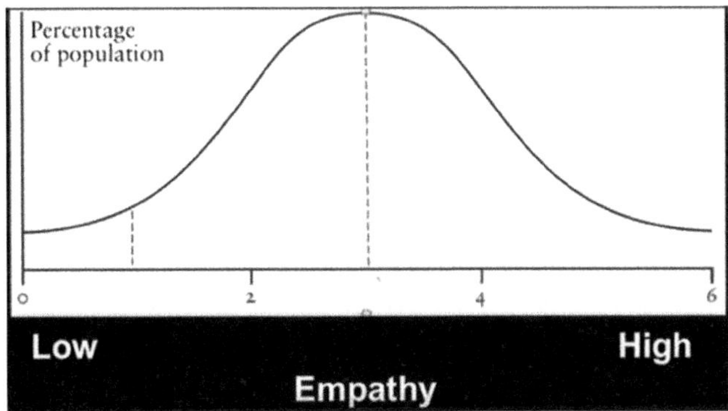


**Figure 4.4** The empathy bell curve (Baron-Cohen, 2011: 14)

behaviour. For instance, low affective empathy explains human cruelty as individuals can hurt and torture without any appropriate emotional response. But a low affective empathy combined with a high degree of cognitive empathy characterises cruel people who can at the same time manipulate, deceive, read people's minds and abuse them without feeling emotional distress. In this case, the 'other' is seen as an object and is dehumanised.

For an education of empathy, students can be helped to become aware of their own differences and those of others with respect to this 'bell curve' and learn to regulate them. In his work, Baron-Cohen (2011: 117) identifies 12 factors[10] that influence the 'empathy circuit' and suggests that 'Forms of role-play that involve taking the victim's perspective may be worth trying' in order to prevent low empathy (Baron-Cohen, 2011: 105). Teachers can thus rely on some of these factors for developing empathetic attitudes. The project described in the following section focuses on three sociological factors with a view to fostering awareness of self and other:

(1) **Obedience to authority and blind conformity** can erode empathy. It was first demonstrated in 1961 with Milgram's experiment: ordinary people can become torturers. When asked by an authority figure to inflict suffering against all standards of morality, relatively few people have the resources needed to disobey orders, even when the destructive effects of their action become very clear. We believe that an empathetic education should support students in developing a questioning attitude, a capacity to make informed ethical choices and the strength to resist arbitrary authority.
(2) **Ideological confinement** is another factor. It has also been shown that some people score very low on empathy when they are convinced that what they are doing is more important than the victims' suffering. Exploiting the human need to belong, religious or political groups can entrap young people and progressively erode their ability to empathise with people who are portrayed as enemies. As educators, it is our job to empower students so that they have the resources to become aware of ideologies and to question them.[11]
(3) Finally, another well identified factor is what Baron Cohen calls **ingroup/outgroup relations**. In creating a distance between one group and another, he states that the 'out group' becomes dehumanised. The dissociation can be created through repeated propaganda, through virtual reality (shooting at dehumanised targets in video games) or imposed violence as in the case of child-soldiers. The in-group loses their grip on reality and the out-group becomes sub-human. When we dehumanise a group as an enemy or even as a distant victim, we pave the way for low empathy.

## Replaying the 11th of September to Question the World

> Our era is characterized by '[t]wo extreme and regressive tendencies – the resurgence of religious extremism and outmoded belief systems, and the entrenchment of scientific materialism and reductionism'. (Thompson & Batchelor, 2015)

To an unprecedented extent in the history of mankind, young people nowadays are subjected to the influence of media and social networks, which not only virtualise relationships, making others somehow seem less 'real', but also foster blind adherence to information, thereby eroding the individual's ability to empathise with others. The French philosopher Pierre Le Coz (2014) points to what he calls 'emotional harnessing', whereby emotional and sensory stimulation invades our mental world without leaving enough room for rational intelligence. Schools that neglect the development of emotional and social intelligence cannot meet this anthropological challenge. In this regard, the theatre is ahead of the educational world: it has long cultivated its subversive role by combining thought and aesthetics. It is therefore hardly surprising that totalitarian regimes seek to silence theatre artists.

In the project described below, we will see how artists worked with teachers to help bring young teenagers to an understanding of the events of September 11 and its ideological implications. In 2010, an entrepreneur from outside the field of education discovered the text of a play published in two languages, entitled *September 11, 2001*. He convinced the French author, Michel Vinaver, to produce it for the commemoration of the 10th anniversary of September 11. So far, it represents a standard artistic production project. But the director, Arnaud Meunier, decided to turn it into a transcultural educational experience and to stage the play with adolescent students from a multicultural suburb outside Paris and the professional actors from his company.

He wanted them to experience this event of which they had only a vague and limited understanding based mainly on the media's constant rehashing of it. He wished they could revisit the past (they were barely seven years old at the time) and question their present in a new light. Throughout the school year, three groups of 11th grade students, aged 15–17 with no background in the theatre, became involved in the study and staging of a work through readings, meetings with the author and theatre workshops.[12] Among them, 45 volunteer students committed to working with the company on weekends and during school holidays in order to rehearse the play which was scheduled on September 11, 2011. They performed to a full house in one of the most prestigious national theatres in Paris. The educational challenge for the adults working with the teenagers was to accompany them as young people, many of whom were growing up in immigrant families, and to encourage them to think outside the framework of their daily lives, often steeped in negative values (conflict, xenophobia, Islamophobia, racism), i.e. environments that schools on the whole cannot manage to transform (Figure 4.5).

> I wanted an intermingling of words and situations, of the extraordinary and the banal, like a primitive chaos prior to any form of interpretation; it was a way to reproduce the event itself, things that shatter into a million pieces before ascribing any meaning. (Vinaver, 2015: 55)

As in the *Gaza Monologues* project, the play *September 11, 2001* consists of verbatim transcripts. Vinaver incorporates the words of the victims, the politicians and the terrorists, without any hierarchy, and the French students, like the young people from Gaza, do the same kind of work involving shifts in perspective. Here, they are not rooted in the biographical narrative of their own stories, but rather they navigate between cultures, ideologies and beliefs; they find themselves between a personal search for meaning and geopolitical issues of great importance. A documentary produced and based on this project showed its impact on the young people's ability to feel empathy for others. As students revealed in follow-up interviews, the theatre-based experiences and work they were involved in helped them transcend a good-versus-evil vision of this event.

**Figure 4.5** Performance at the Théâtre de la Ville, Paris, Septembre 2011 (copyright Pierre-Etienne Vilbert)

But above all, they tell how this work changed their perception of their fellow high school students from other suburbs. As one student said, 'At first I had my doubts. On TV the kids from the other neighbourhoods come across as losers, people you wouldn't want to hang out with, but in fact, you really see people differently when you meet them and have the chance to talk with them'.

Another noteworthy aspect of the project is the way in which the artists and the teachers were able to emancipate the youngsters from the 'emotional magma' they were in. Teachers from various disciplines used the students' aesthetic experience to deepen their academic thinking and develop their creativity. We will cite the example of two teachers (of French and English), who ran joint writing workshops based on the model of the play by Michel Vinaver. In January 2011, the international press was focused on the Arab Spring. Students patiently began collecting data on this event. They consulted a variety of media outlets in several languages, assembled an eclectic mix of the 'serious' and the 'trivial' and worked together to produce a text they called 'January 14, 2011'. When, in March 2011, Michel Vinaver came to meet them in their school, the students read him their text. Moved, Michel Vinaver told the students how much he admired them and invited them to stage their own text. The students published it on the project's Facebook page[13] and, against all odds, a Tunisian blogger Slim Amamou, recognised himself in their text. He had been one of the revolutionary protagonists of the Arab Spring. At the time he discovered the students' play, he had been appointed Secretary of State for Youth and Sports of the transitional government. He wrote to the class and congratulated them. The writing and voices of the students in this class from the suburbs of Paris had crossed the Mediterranean.

## Conclusion: Is it Possible to Teach Empathy Through the Theatre in Formal Educational Contexts?

In the projects described above, I have sought to understand how artists transcend cultures and languages through the aesthetic dimension, which is an integral part of people's relationships to others, the world and themselves. We have seen that an aesthetic relationship is by definition an empathetic one because it provides access to a sensory and in-the-flesh understanding of the world and can give rise to intellectual questions. To conclude this chapter, I would like to mention an experiment that took place in a middle school and that builds on the main lines of these projects, suggesting ways to rethink the connections between the arts and languages.

Over a period of four years, from 2011 to 2015, we integrated theatre into our teaching of English and German in a plurilingual school near Paris. Known as AiLES (Arts in Language Education for an Empathic Society), this project was organised around a multilingual community of practice made up of artists, teachers, researchers and cultural mediators. Over the months and as questions surfaced, this community developed artistic activities related to various academic disciplines. Two hours per week were devoted to theatre workshops conducted in several languages in which teachers also took part. Here are five key ideas that have enabled students to develop their linguistic and intellectual autonomy and encouraged attitudes of empathy and curiosity about cultural difference:

(1) To start with 'meaningful questions' related to the emotional and cognitive development of the students. In AiLES, young people chose the topics of their projects: either based on their experiences during the second year, where they were asked about the limits placed on their freedom of thought in school, or inspired by professional shows that we went to see with them. During the third year, they asked themselves the following question: 'Should one comply or rebel?' At the same time, they expressed the desire to put on a play in which they could act, dance and sing. In order to meet this request while supporting them in this philosophical exploration, we chose a play by the German author Lutz Hübner entitled *Creeps*. Hübner, intrigued by our project, wanted to meet the students in their middle school and he subsequently decided to write a play with them in German and English entitled *Simply the Best*. Tailored for the class, the play highlighted their concerns as teenagers living in a multicultural neighbourhood. After performing the play in the theatre of their town, the students gave a moving performance at the 'Lingue in scena' festival in Torino in April 2015 (Figures 4.6 and 4.7).

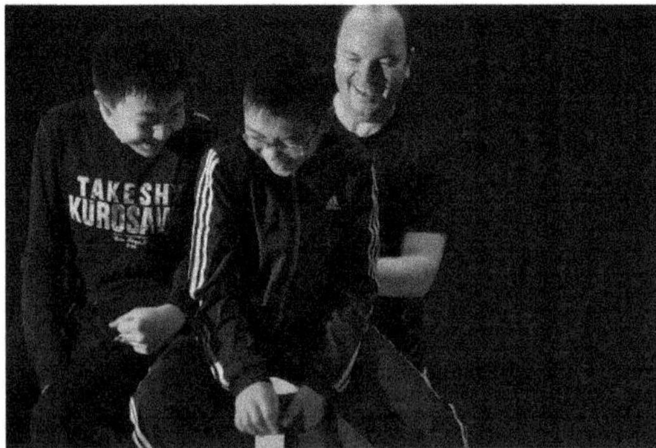


**Figure 4.6** Lutz Hübner and the students at J-P Timbaud, Bobigny. France. October 2014

**Figure 4.7** Performance of Simply the Best in April 2015. Festival Lingue in Scena, Torino

(2) To bring together the languages taught in school and those of all the project participants (students and their families, teachers, facilitators, artist, etc.). From the very first hours of the workshops, adults from the community used their L1s and invited the students to improvise, write and act not only in German and English, but in all their other languages. Numerous studies on bi- and plurilingualism denounce the psychological violence done to students who are asked to ignore the languages and cultures of their families and the cognitive inhibitions that it causes (Dehn *et al.*, 2011; Krumm, 2013; Moro, 2011). That is why we put at the heart of our project the rehabilitation of the languages that made up the multicultural identity of our group. Thus, students gradually became interested in the languages of their friends, their teachers, the artists and all the adults around them. We found much evidence of connections re-established between children and their families, as illustrated in the case of one student who expressed regret at not being able to speak her mother's language at home. Following one of the activities, she asked her mother to translate the text she had improvised into Portuguese Creole, which she then learned and acted out, sparking a strong emotional response among spectators on the day of the public performance.

(3) To develop a physical, corporal awareness among students and teachers. The students experienced the embodied dimension of language both as actors when they participated in the theatre workshops and as spectators when they attended professional performances in class outings. These theatrical activities were transferred to the language classes. To take just one example, with the help of Ursula Hirschfeld from the University of Halle-Wittenberg, we designed translingual body-based activities in order to work on phonetics, rhythm and intonation: warming up the voice was often conducted in several

languages at the same time, and many exercises involved the embodied passage from one language to another, as, for example, in the game where students passed an imaginary object, represented by a ball, which they associated with a word and an emotion. Two balls were being passed simultaneously around the circle, a red ball for German and a yellow ball for English (Figure 4.8).

(4) To elicit various forms of empathy in order to develop language skills, starting with the low-level mechanisms and taking into account the factors that inhibit empathy. Over the four years, the team implemented activities specifically designed to develop these mechanisms: for example, asking a student to improvise a story mimed while a classmate speaks his thoughts 'for him', interpreting his friend's attitudes, actions and facial expressions. These practices, described in a doctoral dissertation[14] and in a research report, required a number of adjustments. Such work could not be done over the course of a single year, and it seemed essential that the artists' residencies as well as the teacher–artist partnerships should develop over time.

(5) To learn to translanguage, i.e. to teach students to use, without inhibition, all the language repertoires they have at their disposal: kinaesthetic, sensory, emotional and linguistic. For that, the adult community must foster a climate of respect and trust, and demonstrate benevolent concern for others. The community brought about deep transformations for the students as well as for the researchers, teachers and artists.

To come full circle, let's return to our original question: what do theatre and languages release us from? They can help us 'escape' from our own identities and free ourselves from the familiar that conditions our choices. Because theatre and languages allow us to move back and forth between ourselves and others, they are antidotes to the closing of the mind, to self-centredness and to the fear of difference. Artistic and academic subjects play an equally important role in young people's education as there are no walls that separate our emotional and rational lives or that

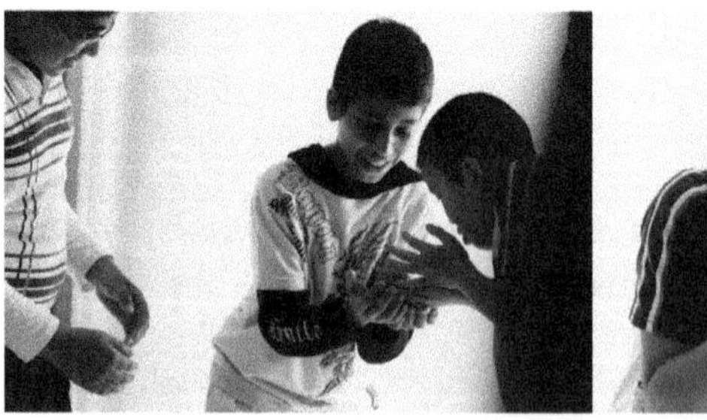

**Figure 4.8** AiLES Workshop in 2011 (copyright Fred Furgol)

compartmentalise our ideas, imaginings, motor commands, feelings and fears (Trocmé-Fabre, 1999). That is why 'we have no choice but to learn by way of the body' (Aden, 2013: xx). F. Varela, who introduced the concept of 'enaction' on which my work is based, defines the intelligence we need to cultivate in schools in the 21st century not as the ability to solve problems but as the ability to enter and be part of a shared world.[15] Learning to translanguage is a means towards achieving this goal, and the theatre associated with language learning is a promising way forward.

## Notes

(1) Most notably mirror and spindle neurons.

(2) 'It is by languaging that the act of knowing, in the behavioral coordination which is language, brings forth a world. We work out our lives in a mutual linguistic coupling, not because language permits us to reveal ourselves but because we are constituted in a continuous becoming that we bring forth with others' (Maturana & Varela, 1987: 234–235).

(3) A movement which began with the publication of an article by Cacioppo and Berntson (1992).

(4) Cinema studies make similar claims (see Coëgnarts & Kravanja, 2015).

(5) See http://www.canal-u.tv/video/cerimes/ne_pour_creer_du_sens_avec_francisco_varela.12824 (accessed 22 September 2015).

(6) The theory of mind is the ability to attribute mental states (beliefs, intentions, desires) to oneself and others and to understand that others' beliefs or intentions are different from one's own.

(7) Zeitschrift für interkulturellen Fremdsprachenunterricht (ZiF), 19, Jahrgang Nummer 1 (April 2014). See http://tujournals.ulb.tu-darmstadt.de/index.php/zif/issue/view/8 (accessed 3 April 2017); http://tujournals.ulb.tu-darmstadt.de/index.php/zif/article/view/28/25 (accessed 3 April 2017).

(8) '[S]ilence is the common element from which it is possible to draw out the "common poetic source", thus establishing a new code of communication through a physical and emotional intelligence' (Aden, 2010: 90).

(9) An egocentric perspective takes the self as a point of reference whereas an allocentric perspective takes external objects as points of reference.

(10) The factors fall into three categories: genetic, hormonal and environmental.

(11) The French neurophysiologist Alain Berthoz (2004: 254) also supports this idea.

(12) Cf. pedagogical file: See http://crdp.ac-paris.fr/piece-demontee/pdf/11-sept_total.pdf (accessed 22 September 2015).

(13) See https://www.facebook.com/11septembre2001?fref=ts (accessed 22 September 2015).

(14) Sandrine Eschenauer (in preparation): Médiations: langages et empathie: Une pédagogie énactive pour un apprentissage sensible, esthétique et encorporé des langues-cultures (translangageance), au travers de la pratique théâtrale au collège. Université Paris-Est Créteil.

(15) 'L'idée fondamentale est donc que les facultés cognitives sont inextricablement liées à l'historique de ce qui est vécu, de la même manière qu'un sentier au préalable inexistant apparaît en marchant. L'image de la cognition qui s'ensuit n'est pas la résolution de problèmes au moyen de représentations, mais plutôt le faire-émerger créateur d'un monde, avec la seule condition d'être opérationnel: elle doit assurer la pérennité du système en jeu' (Varela, 1996: 111–112).

## References

Aden, J. (2009) Improvisation dans le jeu théâtral et acquisition de stratégies d'interaction. In J. Aden (ed.) *Didactique des langues- cultures: univers de croyance et contextes* (pp. 77–99). Paris: Manuscrit Recherche – Université.

Aden, J. (2010) *An Intercultural Meeting Through Applied Theatre*. Berlin: Schibri-Verlag.

Aden, J. (2013) Apprendre les langues par corps. In Y. Abdelkader, S. Bazile and O. Fertat (eds) *Pour un Théâtre-Monde. Plurilinguisme, interculturalité et transmission* (pp. 109–123). Bordeaux: Presses Universitaires de Bordeaux.

Aden, J. (2014) Theatre Education for an Empathic Society. In C. Nofri and M. Stracci (eds) *Performing Arts in Language Learning* (pp. 52–71). Rome: Edizioni Novacultur Rome.

Balibar, J. (2014) Interview in Libération online. See http://next.liberation.fr/cinema/2014/08/03/jeanne-balibar-langue-vivante_1074993 (accessed 30 January 2016).

Baron-Cohen, S. (2011) *Zero Degrees of Empathy: A New Theory of Human Cruelty and Kindness*. London, Penguin.

Berthoz, A. (2004) Physiologie du changement de point de vue. In A. Berthoz and G. Jorland. *L'Empathie* (pp. 251–275). Paris: Éditions Odile Jacob.

Berthoz, A. and Petit, J-L. (2006) *Phénoménologie et physiologie de l'action*. Paris: Odile Jacob.

Bustany, P. (2012) Entretien avec Pierre Bustany. In P. van Eersel (ed.) *Votre cerveau n'a pas fini de vous étonner* (pp. 79–99). Paris: Albin Michel.

Cacioppo, J.T. and Berntson, G.G. (1992) Social psychological contributions to the decade of the brain: Doctrine of multilevel analysis. *American Psychologist* 47, 1019–1028.

Coëgnarts, M. and Kravanja, P. (eds) (2015) *Embodied Cognition and Cinema*. Leuven: University Press.

Cooper, C. (2015) Edward Bond: Imagination et démocratie. In J. Aden (ed.) *Théâtre et Éducation dans le monde. De nouveaux territoires d'utopies* (pp. 33–40). Bruxelles: Lansman Editeur.

Damasio, A. (2005) *Descartes' Error: Emotion, Reason and the Human Brain* (revised Penguin edition). New York: Putnam.

Dehn, M., Oomen-Welke, I. and Osburg, C. (2011) *Kinder und Sprache(n): Was Erwachsene wissen sollten*. Leipzig: Klett.

Goffman, E. (1959) *The Presentation of Self in Everyday Life*. New York: Anchor Books.

Goleman, D. (1996) *Emotional Intelligence. Why It Can Matter More than IQ*. London: Bloomsbury.

Hawkins, E. (1984) *Awareness of Language: An Introduction*. Cambridge: University Press.

Immordino-Yang, M.-H. and Damasio, A. (2007) We feel, therefore we learn: The relevance of affective and social neuroscience to education. *Mind, Brain and Education* 1 (1), 3–10.

Jeannerod, M. (2002) *Le cerveau intime*. Paris: Editions Odile Jacob.

Kramsch, C. and Aden, J. (2012) ELT and intercultural/transcultural learning. In J. Aden, F. Haramboure, C. Hoybel and A-M. Voise (eds) *Approche culturelle en didactique des langues* (pp. 39–60). Paris: Éditions Le Manuscrit-université.

Krashen, S.D. (1982) *The Natural Approach: Language Acquisition in the Classroom*. Oxford: Pergamon Press.

Krumm, H-J. (2013) Multilingualism and identity: What linguistic biographies of immigrants can tell us. In P. Siemund, I. Gogolin, M.E. Schulz and J. Davydova (eds) *Multilingualism and Language Diversity in Urban Areas: Acquisition, Identities, Space, Education* (pp. 165–176). Hamburg: John Benjamins Publishing Company.

Lecoq, J. (1997) *Le Corps poétique: un enseignement de la création théâtrale*. Paris: Actes Sud-Papiers.

Le Coz, P. (2014) *Le Gouvernement des émotions … et l'Art des déjouer les manipulations*. Paris: Albin Michel.

Maturana, H. and Varela, F. (1987) *The Tree of Knowledge. Biological Basis of Human Understanding* (revised edition). Boston, MA: Random House.

Morin, E. (1999) *Seven Complex Lessons in Education for the Future*. Paris: UNESCO Publishing. See http://unesdoc.unesco.org/images/0011/001177/117740eo.pdf (accessed 22 September 2015).

Moro, M-R. (2011) *Enfants d'ici venus d'ailleurs*. Paris: Ed. Pluriel.

Rifkin, J. (2010) *The Empathic Civilization: The Race to Global Consciousness in a World in Crisis*. New York: Jeremy P. Tarcher.

Rizzolatti, G. and Craighero, L. (2004) The mirror neuron system. *Annual Review of Neuroscience* 27, 169–192.

Rizzolatti, G. and Sinigaglia, C. (2008) *Mirrors in the Brain: How Our Minds Share Actions, Emotions and Experience*. Oxford: University Press.

Thirioux, B., Mercier, M.R., Blanke, O. and Berthoz, A. (2014) The cognitive and neural time course of empathy and sympathy: An electrical neuroimaging study on self-other interaction. *Neuroscience* 16 (267), 286–306.

Thompson, E. and Batchelor, S. (2015) *Waking, Dreaming, Being: Self and Consciousness in Neuroscience, Meditation and Philosophy*. New York: Columbia University Press.

Trocmé-Fabre, H. (1994) «Né pour apprendre», 7 vidéos, ENS Éditions ENS Fontenay/ St Cloud , Université de La Rochelle. See https://www.canal-u.tv/video/cerimes/ne_pour_organiser_avec_francisco_varela.12133 (accessed 3 April 2017).

Trocmé-Fabre, H. (1999) *Réinventer le métier d'apprendre*. Paris: Editions d'Organisation.

Trocmé-Fabre, H. (2006) *Né pour apprendre*. La Rochelle: Éditions Être et Connaître.

Van Eersel, P. (2012) *Votre cerveau n'a pas fini de vous étonner*. Paris: Albin Michel.

Varela, F. (1996) *Invitation aux sciences cognitives*. Paris: Seuil.

Varela, F., Thompson, E. and Rosch, E. (1993) *The Embodied Mind: Cognitive Science and Human Experience*. Cambridge/London: The MIT Press.

Vinaver, M. (2015) D'un 11 Septembre à l'autre: le théâtre comme expérience de la démocratie. In J. Aden (ed.) *Théâtre et Éducation dans le monde. De nouveaux territoires d'utopies* (pp. 53–60). Bruxelles: Lansman Editeur.

Vischer, R. (1873) *Über das optische Formgefühl – ein Beitrag zur Aesthetik* [*On the Optical Sense of Form: A Contribution to Aesthetics*]. Leipzig: Hermann Credner Verlag (in German).

Zarate, G. (2003) *Médiation culturelle et didactique des langues*. Centre Européen pour les Langues Vivantes, Editions du Conseil de l'Europe. See http://archive.ecml.at/documents/pub122F2003_zarate.pdf (accessed 22 September 2015).

# Part 3

# Focus on Teacher Training

# 5 Interculturality in Foreign Language Teacher Training: Performing Arts Projects Across National, Language and Cultural Borders

Micha Fleiner

## Interculturality: Questions of Definition

This contribution explores the role of interculturality in the specific area of foreign language teacher training. Taking into account the growing interest in performative approaches to foreign language education, the question will be raised of how the performing arts (drama, theatre, music, dance, etc.) can lend support to an authentic and playful understanding of interculturality. Underlying theoretical principles on which an interculturally accentuated 'performative foreign language didactics' (Schewe, 2013: 16) might be based will be discussed, as well as the particular importance of arts-based cross-border projects for prospective language teachers. For this reason, the present contribution is rounded off by a concrete insight into a bicultural performing arts project, which was developed by the University of Education Freiburg (Germany) and the Université Lumière Lyon 2 (France) for pre-service teachers of German and French as a foreign language.

In view of the fact that '[t]he importance of world exchanges has led to an economic, professional, cultural and student hypermobility, showing a rapid rate of growth' (Szende, 2014: 33), it is no exaggeration to say that '[n]o one can escape the challenges posed by the encounter of cultures that our current world favors' (Szende, 2014: 33). But what is meant by 'cultural encounter' in a deeper sense? This seems to be a legitimate question, especially when one considers that '[t]he term "culture" has come to cover a host of phenomena that mean different things to different people' (Kramsch, 2006: 328). The broad spectrum of content-related dimensions such as 'literate tradition or high culture, level of civilization, way of life, ethnic membership, country of origin, nationality, ideology, religious affiliation, or moral values' makes it increasingly 'difficult to find a common objective denominator' (Kramsch, 2006: 328). Such a blurring of boundaries is not without consequences for the definitional approach of '*inter*cultural communication', as can be seen in the following:

> The term 'intercultural' literally means 'between cultures', and so, at one level, 'intercultural communication' could refer to all communication between members of two (or more) different social/cultural groups. This, in fact, is how the term has traditionally been used. Difference in nationality or mother tongue has typically been taken as the criterion for membership of different social/cultural groups, and communication between people of different nationalities or different mother tongues has then automatically been classified as intercultural. However, there are several problems with this. If culture is associated with social groups, then nationality and mother tongue are not the only social groups we each belong to. We are all simultaneously members of numerous other groups, such as regional, professional and religious, and so, if communication between members of different social groups is classified as intercultural, virtually all communication would thereby be defined as intercultural. Such a broad definition is clearly unsatisfactory [...]. (Işik-Güler *et al.,* 2012: 572)

These kinds of conceptual challenges become even more significant in the specific area of teaching and learning foreign and second languages since '[l]anguage learning is a personal, communal, and political act that involves border-crossings' (Fels & McGivern, 2002: 20) and social group dynamics at all times and in every way. In recent years, different approaches have been proposed to make the idea of 'interculturality' more tangible in language teaching (e.g. Bazin, 2012; Blanchet & Coste, 2010; Byram & Hu, 2009; Fetscher, 2013; Godley, 2012; Heringer, 2014; Işik-Güler *et al.*, 2012; Szende, 2014; Thiem, 2014). Building on the idea that '[c]ulture has always been an integral component of language teaching' (Kramsch, 2006: 322) which 'has retained a sense of the irreducible, the sacred, that touches the core of who we are – our history and our subjectivity', we might say that '[c]ulture is embodied history' (Kramsch, 2006: 328). Such a close connection between culture, history and embodiment proves helpful because, firstly, the process of teaching and learning languages, literatures and cultures cannot be imagined without an active implication of the learners' temporally and spatially anchored biographies and self-concepts, such as 'past actions, goals, intentions, interests, future sel[ves]' (Dermitzaki, 2011: 731) and lived experiences. From this point of view, it is possible to understand culture as 'that precarious third place where our historical and subjective self gets constructed across utterances and turns-at-talk between the self we have just been and the self we might still become' (Kramsch, 2006: 328). Secondly, the idea of embodiment in foreign and second language education sharpens students' awareness for a richer and more intuitive understanding of interculturality:

> [I]t is the entire body that creates meaning. The relationship between verbal communication (so often stereotypical) and non-verbal communication (not any less ritualized) varies from one language to another. Every culture has its ways of carrying itself and of adopting body postures, while every gesture bears a particular significance within its culture. Expressing oneself means entering into a rapport with others' words. [...] Much misunderstanding can arise from mismanagement of the corporeal co-presence. Expressing oneself in another language means being conscious of the capacity of the words to play a role in discourse organization – and also to go from one 'talking body' to another 'talking body'. Showing lack of respect of conventions that regulate non-verbal behaviour in a communication situation could produce disruption, indeed even rupture, in communication. (Szende, 2014: 232–234)

Taking into account the different aspects that have been developed so far, it almost seems as if interculturally fruitful experiences in the field of teaching and learning foreign and second languages could be linked to a dynamic interplay between subjectivity, lived history and embodied communication. Alternatively, as Schewe states with regard to Gardner's (1993) model of multiple intelligences, one could call it a creative connection of 'bodily-kinesthetic and linguistic intelligences, but also [...] spatial, interpersonal, and intrapersonal intelligences' (Schewe, 2002: 89). Following this approach, it can be seen that '[f]oreign- and second-language education, after all, consists of more than learning how to speak, listen, read, and write' (Schewe, 2002: 89). Instead, a major emphasis in modern language classrooms should rather be put on a symbiotic relationship 'between body and language [...] that leads to doubts, questions, and insights for learners interacting with themselves and others and their linguistic and cultural identity' (Bräuer, 2002b: x). One promising way to create such a 'meaningful dialogue between one's own culture and the one yet to be discovered' (Bräuer, 2002b: x), and, consequently, to translate an interculturally sensitive approach into practice for language students and their teachers, may lie in the recently developed concept of a 'performative foreign language didactics' (Schewe, 2013: 16). This idea, including its theoretical background, its methodological principles as well as its didactical benefits, will be described in more detail in the following section.

## Towards a Culturally Sensitive Conception of Performative Teaching and Learning

The basic intention behind a performative foreign language didactics is to 'avail of the wealth of forms found in the arts for teaching and learning purposes' (Schewe, 2013: 16).[1] This is achieved by a playful neglect of 'clear-cut lines between science and art, theory and practice' (Schewe, 2013: 16). From this perspective, foreign languages, literatures and cultures are taught, learnt and practised by entering into an inspiring 'dialogue and exchange with the arts, in particular with theatre arts and also school/university subjects related to the aesthetic field (including music, visual art, dance, literature, film)' (Schewe, 2013: 16). The implementation of such body- and performance-centred teaching and learning methods in the German-speaking area was initially established by the pioneering work of Schewe (1993). A follow-up publication (Schewe & Shaw, 1993) took up selected core ideas from an international perspective. Since then, additional research accentuations have been set (e.g. Dufeu, 2003; Huber, 2003; Lutzker, 2007; Sambanis, 2013; Tselikas, 1999), each of them contributing to the development of a performative teaching and learning culture.[2] Nevertheless, the reciprocal relationship between performativity and interculturality has been the subject of language-centred publication projects only on a relatively sporadic basis (e.g. Bräuer, 2002a; Byram & Fleming, 1998a; Kessler, 2008). This is surprising, as a creative and well-considered use of performing arts in language studies and foreign language teacher training would offer interesting potential – both practically and theoretically – for a vivid and corporeal understanding of interculturality. These considerations will be further explained by taking the art form of theatre as an archetypical example of cultural mediator:

> [I]f culture is the arena of a continuous struggle over meanings between various social groups, then theatre is an ideal site to enact and dramatise these conflicts and present them, as it were, in actu. Theatre is a major constituent in the politics of culture and thus also in the negotiation of intercultural relations. And since cultural identity is established performatively, what better space to study this struggle over the meaning of culture than through the signifying practices of the stage itself, where a natural and inevitable dialogue takes place between processes of production and activities of consumption. (Huber *et al.*, 2010: 9–10)

If one considers 'culture' as a form of 'embodied history' (Kramsch, 2006: 328) that can be incorporated and experienced intra-individually as well as inter-individually, at once the idea of performativity becomes pedagogically tangible. Culture, from this point of view, becomes physically visible, mentally perceptible and, perhaps most important, emotionally available. This, in turn, creates a particular level of awareness, solidarity and energy – and herein lies a primary pedagogical importance of performativity:

> It is action that enables us to make differences among and between us, [...] [P]erformativity [...] engages an audience that does not necessarily share common grounds [...]. Yet the process is again one of gifting, giving the audience member that gift of self-gifting, the choice of making a difference and changing their self with respect to the presence performed. [...] As a performer, I interact with the audience, engaging with their responses, their energy. (Hunter, 2014: 106–107)

Taking this line of thought further, one could argue that such an energetic and culturally responsive 'teaching and learning with head, heart, hands and feet' (Schewe, 1993: 8, translation Micha Fleiner) is particularly suitable for use in the context of language studies and foreign language teacher training because, in the future foreign language classroom, 'the goal is not merely the intellectual mastery of a certain body of knowledge, but the embodied, impassioned and intuitive grasp of a new way of communicating' (Crutchfield, 2015: 2). Performative teaching and learning elements should, therefore, form an integral part of initial and ongoing teacher training programmes.[3] This is not just because the process of teaching has always been a body-centred profession (Schewe, 2008: 127), but also, essentially, because the act of performing offers prospective language teachers the possibility to reflect and question intercultural communication and encounter situations from an intuitive and emotive perspective – even if these situations turn out to be burdened by cultural tensions or conflicts: They 'are explored more searchingly and vividly, it seems, in theatre than they are in political discourses or journalistic articles' (Huber *et al.*, 2010: 11). One potential reason might be that 'art has the power to individualise problems of globalisation, cultural conflict and social change, thus making them emotionally accessible' (Huber *et al.*, 2010: 11). Of course, these communication processes 'may take the form of tragedy or parody, of satire or documentary drama' (Huber *et al.*, 2010: 11). The potential feelings and moods of any performer or spectator involved should not be underestimated: 'Plays dealing with interculturality may [...] shock them, it may make them laugh or rouse them to furious protest – but they rarely leave them emotionally detached' (Huber *et al.*, 2010: 11). This latter point is all the more significant in light of an increasing degree of standardisation and economisation in the area of higher and tertiary education, where learning outcomes and competence measurement occupy a comparatively dominant position (Schewe, 2011: 20–21).[4] The training of future foreign language teachers is not an exception to this overall scenario, and yet it is exactly in these contexts of pedagogical education where a vibrant interplay between 'body, intellect, emotions, and imagination in the crucible of an audience's attention' (Crutchfield, 2015: 30) would be desirable and necessary, because teachers – be it in the primary, secondary or tertiary education sector – are not solely communicators of encyclopaedic knowledge and testable competences; they are, to the same extent, critical communicators of cultural and social interaction:

> [T]eachers [...] themselves continue to learn and develop their capacities as intercultural speakers. This is an advantage. Teachers who take seriously the cultural dimension of language learning [...] will not expect to know and teach everything about a specific society and its culture(s). They will place more emphasis on developing their learners' and their own awareness of the nature of intercultural interaction, and the skills and competences which allow them to relate to cultural difference. In the final analysis, even teachers who have never personally experienced a particular society and the people of many different social identities within it, can help their learners to engage with texts and documents where those identities are expressed. Their task, and expertise, as teachers is to enable learners to enquire into the beliefs, values and cultural practices they embody [...]. (Byram & Fleming, 1998b: 9)

Needless to say, the development of such an 'intercultural speaker' (Byram & Fleming, 1998b: 9) will not arise of itself; it is much rather the result of an ongoing and dynamic learning process which needs to be encouraged and empowered during the teacher training phase at university level. A culturally sensitive conception of performative teaching and learning, tailored to the specific professional needs of prospective teachers of languages, literatures and cultures, can play a key role here in several ways.

Firstly, on a personal level, '[i]t promotes the learning process in which verbal and nonverbal expression are integrated in a comprehensive working method' (Feldhendler, 1993: 172). This means that 'body, pose, gesture, movement, feelings, emotions and voice' (Feldhendler, 1993: 174) are of substantial relevance for the development of a 'personal authenticity and hence personal authority' (Crutchfield, 2015: 30).

Secondly, on a social level, the combination of performativity and interculturality offers the potential to generate 'a creative interactive space within which participants negotiate multiple possibilities of action and, through shared participation and reflection, learn from each other both within and outside the drama' (Fels & McGivern, 2002: 21). With regard to the students' future workplace – educational institutions including multiple interaction processes with pupils, colleagues or parents – the necessity of a distinctive social competence in the form of appreciative 'relationships with others both within and outside the classroom' (Fels & McGivern, 2002: 21) cannot be emphasised often enough.

Thirdly, on a subject-specific level, the targeted use of performative teaching and learning practices helps learners reduce linguistic inhibitions (Gilardi *et al.*, 2005: 218) and develop linguistic sensitivity and diversity in the areas of 'pronunciation, idiomatic expressions, grammar, spelling, [and] accent' (Axtmann, 2002: 48). Developing a sensitivity to the expressive richness of the target language in the context of pre-service education is all the more justified, since prospective teachers 'must have a level of awareness of language that enables them to assess, analyse and present it to learners in ways that will enhance acquisition' (Jourdenais, 2009: 652). In addition, a more distinct feel for language gained through performative approaches forms a plausible basis for the creation and further development of literary competences and aesthetic awareness. The use of dramatic poetry, for instance, enables learners 'to become familiar with a particular text extract but also encourages them to think about meaning and the way meaning is determined by context' (Fleming, 2011: 103). These contexts can differ greatly, and they open up the possibility to 'transform [...] the four walls of a classroom into a variety of situations, environments and relationships' (Fels & McGivern, 2002: 20). Transformations of this kind, in which performative, aesthetic and improvisational dimensions are intimately connected, possess the capacity to stimulate so-called 'in-between-worlds' (Schewe, 1998: 220), meaning 'productive interplay[s] between inner and outer activities' (Schewe, 1998: 220). From that perspective, the confrontation with literature 'offers a particular corpus for entry into the culture of the Other and, through a mirror effect, his own culture as well' (Szende, 2014: 194). One of the main reasons for this may lie in the fact that '[a]rt often challenges us to see things in new ways and to question assumptions' (Fleming, 2011: 8).

Finally, the implementation of a culturally sensitive conception of performative foreign language didactics in teacher education programmes also provides benefits on a methodological level. Organisational and planning skills, for example, can be fostered by '[a]nticipating the final performance in front of an audience' (Fonio & Genicot, 2011: 81) or 'by translating and adapting dramatic texts for performance in a specific location and cultural setting' (Schewe, 2013: 15). Furthermore, '[i]n order to stage a foreign language play, students have to decode its cultural component first, thus passing through a dramaturgic analysis process' (Fonio & Genicot, 2011: 83). This can be seen as a characteristic example for the development of analytical and strategic competences.

As shown in the examples above, the idea of a stronger nexus between performativity and interculturality in higher education programmes would be a rewarding experience for future teachers of languages, literatures and cultures – on a personal and social level as well as from a subject-specific and methodological point of view. One possible way of putting such an interculturally sensitive performative foreign language didactics into practice in the higher education sector would be to arrange arts-based cross-border projects for prospective language teachers. Over the last few years, the considerable educational potential arising from performing arts projects across national, language and cultural borders has been the subject of various teaching and learning initiatives (e.g. Boyd & Schewe, 2012; Fleiner, 2014; Holl, 2011; Kulovics & Terler, 2014; Oelschläger, 2011; Riedmüller, 2014). Why not systematically translate this idea into the area of foreign language teacher education? Why not enrich traditional university curricula with elements of artistic live performances in the light of an international teaching and learning environment? Why not, finally, seize the opportunity to give future language teachers an authentic insight into embodied interculturality?

To enrich a further understanding of the practical implementation of this approach, the following section offers a concrete insight into a bicultural performing arts project which is currently being developed by the University of Education Freiburg and the Université Lumière Lyon 2 for students of German and French as a foreign language. However, to avoid a misunderstanding in this context, it is worth mentioning that the dynamic nature of a performative foreign language didactics, which fully embraces 'the aesthetic field, or rather the various arts (theatre, music, visual art, dance, film, performance art)' (Schewe, 2013: 15), cannot and should not be restricted to ready-made models of teaching and learning – be it in teacher training, in continuing education, in language lessons at school or elsewhere. Such a narrow approach would appear incompatible with the 'elusive character of art forms' (Barone & Eisner, 2012: 5) and the idea of an open-ended and aesthetically transformative 'border[land] between fact and fiction' (Zipsane, 2009: 176). In other words, '[t]he arts are examples of activities in which ends are held flexibly' (Eisner, 2002: 206). It is with this in mind that the subject of the next section, the description of a culture-oriented performing arts project between German and French student teachers, shall be presented. The project description is based on a strategic plan developed by the University of Education Freiburg (Germany) and the Université Lumière Lyon 2 (France) beginning in 2014. It should be noted that the actual implementation of the project in 2016 had to be modified in certain respects for financial, staffing-related and organisational reasons.

## Practical Approach: Setting up a Bicultural Performing Arts Project in Foreign Language Teacher Training

The idea of setting up a performing arts project across national, language and cultural borders within the specific context of foreign language teacher training initially arose from an educational strategy meeting between the University of Education Freiburg and the Université Lumière Lyon 2 which took place in 2014. The aim was twofold: The first step was to forge tighter links between teacher training institutions in Germany (state of Baden-Württemberg) and France (region of Auvergne-Rhône-Alpes). The second step was to develop these binational links within the horizon of an interactive and aesthetic understanding of interculturality. Inspired by the first international SCENARIO forum conference on performative teaching, learning and research, which was held early in the summer of 2014 at University College Cork, Ireland,[5] the project leaders decided to pursue this double aim by way of body-centred teaching and learning practices, with a particular focus on cross-national performing arts projects. The realisation of this project, which received financial support from the Franco-German Youth Organisation,[6] was expected to take place during the summer term of 2016. The target group consisted of students of German and French as a foreign language, most of whom were ongoing language teachers with an emphasis on primary or secondary education. As this performative teaching and learning project was to be open to all students of German and French as a foreign language, it was expected that the target group would exhibit various levels of linguistic competences and intercultural communication skills. Furthermore, it was assumed that the students' previous experiences with performing arts might vary considerably: The spectrum could range from complete novices to students with basic experiences in different art forms and on to experts with several years of practice in the fields of drama, theatre, dance or music. However, in this context, diverging levels of skills and knowledge – either linguistically, interculturally or performatively – were not considered an obstacle but rather an additional advantage for the students' learning process. The reason for this was that they allowed for internal differentiation and mutual assistance within the same learning group – a promising way to create a supportive Franco-German performance ensemble.

Regarding the project leadership, a binational team of four members covered different areas of activity: Two of them (a French stage director and a DAAD[7]-lecturer with specialised training in drama pedagogy) were primarily responsible for the artistic part of the project, the other two (lecturers in the area of French didactics and teacher training) devoted particular attention to the development and application of linguistic, literary and intercultural objectives. From an organisational point of view, the division of the project process into two sub-processes – an artistic-performative one and a theory-based one – proved useful as it allowed an allocation of preparatory tasks, individual responsibilities and pedagogic competences. This seemed all the more pertinent in view of the fact that the implementation of cross-national performance formats in the vast majority of cases 'is very time consuming [...] demands high motivation and enormous dedication from the participants and can only be realised as an extra-curricular activity' (Schewe, 2013: 12).

With regard to pedagogical objectives, this Franco-German performing arts project was based on three overarching target dimensions: performativity, aesthetics and interculturality. In concrete terms, this meant the following: Firstly, future language teachers would be introduced to performative teaching and learning practices. They would experience an embodied understanding of the French and the German language, including a deeper awareness of voice, movement, gestures and facial expression within the scope of holistic communication processes. Secondly, students would be personally confronted with the concept of aesthetic education and different forms of art. In this respect, the project members were expected to develop a heightened awareness of aesthetic experiences and artistic imagination. Thirdly, active participation and creative involvement in performative teaching and learning processes across language, national and cultural borders would provide the French and German student teachers with the possibility to discover variations and peculiarities in culture-specific meanings, values and practices between two neighbouring European countries. Thus, the participants would be enabled to gain a change in perspective and, as explained above, to 'develop their capacities as intercultural speakers' (Byram & Fleming, 1998b: 9) in a binational field of artistic experimentation.

In order to appropriately communicate these three pedagogic target dimensions, the project plan is based on a three-phase model including the following activities: during an introductory phase (Phase 1), students are given initial insights into the interplay between foreign languages, aesthetics and performing arts. This opening phase, which is realised separately and in the form of compact seminar sessions, includes acting warm-ups as well as performative hands-on exercises. The students are introduced to selected drama techniques such as tableaux, spotlighting, questioning in role or teacher in role. These learning elements are complemented by further-reaching activities with a special focus on literary, visual and musical dimensions: Every project participant is asked to pre-select pieces of prose or poetry, personal photographs, paintings or film clips, favourite songs or short dance sequences, and to present them to their fellow students. The importance here is that the chosen elements stand in direct relation to the respective target country, both linguistically and culturally. They form the basis for non-, mono- or bilingual short-term performances, imaginary journeys, creative writing exercises and text-based improvisations, to name but a few. Moreover, both the Freiburg-based and the Lyon-based learning groups are engaged in the task of preparing a drama pedagogical teaching unit in the corresponding target language. The underlying idea of this first project phase is to arouse the students' curiosity and to performatively prepare them for the next step of the project: the face-to-face encounter with the ensemble members from their partner country.

For this contact phase (Phase 2), the starting point is a three-day meeting between the French and the German student teachers on the campus of Université Lumière Lyon 2, France. Directly afterwards, the entire learning group travels back to Germany, where it spends another three days together – this time on the campus of the University of Education Freiburg, Germany. During this one-week exchange phase, the Franco-German tandem partners become involved in a varied programme of linguistic, cultural and arts-based activities. First of all, this includes the realisation of joint performance processes: The students are invited to present and share their prepared activities; to experience binational improvisation processes; to co-develop drama pedagogical teaching units; and to explore, exchange and put into action selected drama techniques and performative practices for the future foreign language classroom. Binational roundtable discussions and a cultural discovery tour of the partner city, including visits to professional theatre performances in Lyon and Freiburg, round off the programme on site. In the course of this week, the participants have an opportunity not only to put their newly acquired knowledge and skills into performative practice but also to make professional contacts and develop personal friendships with future foreign language teachers from a different cultural and linguistic environment.

A third phase of final reflection and documentation (Phase 3) marks the official end of the Franco-German exchange project. Approximately three weeks after the encounters in Lyon and Freiburg, the students participate in a closing session at their respective home university. The major objective of this final meeting is to encourage the project participants to reflect on their experiences during this performative teaching and learning project from an individual and social perspective as well as from an educational and professional point of view. In this connection, a closing feedback round, as well as a personal reflection paper provide further support and guidance. In this last step, the future language teachers are invited to critically discuss and document their learning experiences (such as personal motivation and relation to the project, linguistic progress, intercultural and performative key moments, impact on future teaching roles, etc.). The project leaders envisage that, upon successful completion of this binational performative teaching and learning project, the French and German student teachers will have gained valuable insights into their own personality and their future field of work: culturally, professionally and, not least, artistic-corporally. This would represent a further step in the ongoing development of 'a new approach to teaching and learning, whereby emphasis is placed on forms of aesthetic expression' (Schewe, 2013: 16) – and on the idea to regard the process of foreign language 'teaching as a performing art' (Crutchfield, 2015: 29).[8]

## Conclusion

Bearing in mind the fact that 'the deeper aspects of interculturalism are closely related to drama as an art form and to art more generally' (Fleming, 2011: 8), the present chapter represents an attempt to reflect on the role of interculturality within the scope of an aesthetically accentuated foreign language teacher education. As a first step, different definitional aspects of interculturality were explored. Following the idea to locate the notion of interculturality in a field of creative tension between subjectivity, history and embodiment, the concept of performative teaching and learning was brought into play in a second step. It was demonstrated that the performing arts possess an interesting potential to lend support to an authentic and interactive understanding of interculturality. Since teachers of foreign and second languages play a substantial role in communicating, representing and performing social and cultural meanings, values and practices, the idea of a culturally sensitive conception of a performative foreign language didactics was then translated into the specific area of teacher training. In order to illustrate theoretical backgrounds, methodological principles and didactical benefits of this approach, the present contribution was rounded off by a description of a bicultural performing arts project developed by the University of Education Freiburg and the Université Lumière Lyon 2 for future language teachers.

When the project was implemented in the spring and summer of 2016, the expectation was that it would become clearer during the different phases of the project to what extent the declared intentions of this performative teaching and learning project had been achieved. It should, however, be recalled that pedagogical aspiration and practical reality may diverge considerably. This is particularly true for the dynamic interplay between languages, cultures and performing arts – and it should be regarded as a key potential of arts-based foreign language education. The image of an improvising jazz musician might be helpful here.

'The capacity to improvise, to exploit unanticipated possibilities' and to appreciate the fragile and fleeting moment of surprise 'is a substantial cognitive achievement fundamentally different from the lockstep movement of prescribed steps toward a predefined goal' (Eisner, 2002: 206). Teachers, students and practitioners who are committed to the idea of a culturally sensitive conception of performative teaching and learning should pay careful attention to that latter point on every occasion. Against this backdrop, and with a special eye to the future, three necessary and desirable further steps towards an interculturally accentuated performative foreign language didactics should be mentioned: Firstly – and this cannot be stressed enough – the dissemination of such an idea requires international communication channels, otherwise it will remain unheard and gradually disappear. A promising platform in this regard is the bilingual online journal *SCENARIO*, which its editors envision as 'the driving force in the building of bridges between the arts and the field of foreign language teaching and learning' (Schewe, 2013: 11). It is hoped that this development will continue to expand in the years to come.

Secondly, concrete ways have to be found to implement intercultural performing arts projects in higher education programmes. This includes especially the fields of foreign language teacher education and curriculum development. A worthwhile goal – which seems, however, fairly unrealistic at the present time – would be to transform future foreign language teachers into 'well-trained and professionally experienced performing artists' (Crutchfield, 2015: 29) with a core competence in intercultural reflexivity.

Thirdly, it may be beneficial to involve the individual art forms more systematically and at all levels in the development of a culture-oriented performative language education. Drama and theatre offer tremendous potential for linguistic, literary and cultural teaching and learning processes. Sometimes, however, the leading role of drama and theatre goes hand in hand with a slight marginalisation of neighbouring art forms such as music, dance, visual arts or performative hybrid genres. Performing arts projects across national, language and cultural borders in higher education programmes would present an ideal opportunity to fully embrace the rich – virtually infinite – range of artistic expression. Such a performatively comprehensive approach could make us even more sensitive to a playful, and – as shown in the concluding thought below – colourful understanding of interculturality:

> Isn't the understanding of culture similar to an understanding of a piece of art? Doesn't each new stroke that we see in a painting alter the pattern and each new nuance in colour we discover affect our perception of the whole? Don't we have to go back to a painting and look at it again

and again to be able to create new meaning for ourselves? If (foreign) culture was like a painting with many different surfaces, shapes and deep layers, wouldn't we have to become more aware of its resonances? (Schewe, 1998: 221)

## Notes

(1) 'The term "performative" [...] is derived [...] from "perform", the usual verb with the noun "action"' (Austin, 1962: 6). In the context of drama and theatre studies, performativity is closely related to the notions of corporeality and aesthetic experience (e.g. Fischer-Lichte, 2014: 474–475; Lehmann, 2014: 58–61).

(2) For a comprehensive overview on past and current developments in the area of performative language education, see Schewe (2013).

(3) Admittedly, an ultimate model of teacher training programmes does not and cannot exist (Schroeter, 2014: 46–53). However, if one considers that '[t]he bodily elements of interaction and the semiotics of visible behavior are part and parcel of language use around the world' (Dingemanse & Floyd, 2014: 467), it is no exaggeration to call for a general and systematic implementation of 'nonverbal core competences' in higher education programmes (Simmons, 2015: 91–99).

(4) The orientation towards harmonised competences has far-reaching impacts 'on educational standards, [...] new curricula, [...] and relevant further education programmes' (Weidinger, 2014: 34). For a recent discussion of the methodological limitations of empirical education research, see Wimmer (2014: 391–429).

(5) For further information on the 'Scenario Forum International Conference: Performative Teaching, Learning, and Research', see http://www.ucc.ie/en/scenario/scenarioarchive/ (accessed 8 September 2015). Also note Even and Schewe (2016).

(6) Deutsch-Französisches Jugendwerk (DFJW)/Office franco-allemand pour la jeunesse (OFAJ).

(7) DAAD=Deutscher Akademischer Austauschdienst (German Academic Exchange Service).

(8) See especially Lutzker (2007: 222–240) and Schewe (1993: 195–223).

## References

Austin, J.L. (1962) *How to Do Things with Words: The William James Lectures Delivered at Harvard University in 1955*. Cambridge, MA: Harvard University Press.

Axtmann, A. (2002) Transcultural performance in classroom learning. In G. Bräuer (ed.) *Body and Language: Intercultural Learning Through Drama* (pp. 37–49). Westport, CT: Ablex Publishing.

Barone, T. and Eisner, E.W. (2012) *Arts Based Research*. Thousand Oaks, CA: Sage.

Bazin, L. (2012) Anthropologie et interculturalité en didactique du FLE. Du mal-entendu au mieux-disant. In F. Dervin and B. Fracchiolla (eds) *Anthropologies, interculturalité et enseignement-apprentissage des langues* (pp. 35–48). Bern: Lang.

Blanchet, P. and Coste, D. (2010) Sur quelques parcours de la notion d'interculturalité. Analyses et propositions dans le cadre d'une didactique de la pluralité linguistique et culturelle. In P. Blanchet and D. Coste (eds) *Regards critiques sur la notion d'«interculturalité». Pour une didactique de la pluralité linguistique et culturelle* (pp. 7–27). Paris: L'Harmattan.

Boyd, S. and Schewe, M. (2012) *Welttheater. Übersetzen, adaptieren, inszenieren*. Berlin: Schibri.

Bräuer, G. (ed.) (2002a) *Body and Language: Intercultural Learning through Drama.* Westport, CT: Ablex Publishing.

Bräuer, G. (2002b) Introduction. In G. Bräuer (ed.) *Body and Language: Intercultural Learning Through Drama* (pp. ix–xvi). Westport, CT: Ablex Publishing.

Byram, M. and Fleming, M. (eds) (1998a) *Language Learning in Intercultural Perspective: Approaches Through Drama and Ethnography.* Cambridge: Cambridge University Press.

Byram, M. and Fleming, M. (1998b) Introduction. In M. Byram and M. Fleming (eds) *Language Learning in Intercultural Perspective: Approaches Through Drama and Ethnography* (pp. 1–10). Cambridge, MA: Cambridge University Press.

Byram, M. and Hu, A. (eds) (2009) *Intercultural Competence and Foreign Language Learning. Models, Empiricism, Assessment.* Tübingen: Narr.

Crutchfield, J. (2015) Creative writing and performance in EFL teacher training. A preliminary case study. *Scenario: Journal for Drama and Theatre in Foreign and Second Language Education* 1 (IX), 1–34.

Dermitzaki, I. (2011) Self-concept. In P.C. Hogan (ed.) *The Cambridge Encyclopedia of the Language Sciences* (pp. 731–732). Cambridge, MA: Cambridge University Press.

Dingemanse, M. and Floyd, S. (2014) Conversation across cultures. In N.J. Enfield, P. Kockelman and J. Sidnell (eds) *The Cambridge Handbook of Linguistic Anthropology* (pp. 447–480). Cambridge: Cambridge University Press.

Dufeu, B. (2003) *Wege zu einer Pädagogik des Seins. Ein psychodramaturgischer Ansatz zum Fremdsprachenerwerb.* Mainz: Éditions Psychodramaturgie.

Eisner, E.W. (2002) *The Arts and the Creation of Mind.* New Haven, CT: Yale University Press.

Even, S. and Schewe, M. (eds) (2016) *Performative Teaching, Learning, Research – Performatives Lehren, Lernen, Forschen.* Berlin: Schibri.

Feldhendler, D. (1993) Enacting life! Proposals for a relational dramaturgy for teaching and learning a foreign language. In M. Schewe and P. Shaw (eds) *Towards Drama as a Method in the Foreign Language Classroom* (pp. 171–191). Frankfurt am Main: Lang.

Fels, L. and McGivern, L. (2002) Intercultural recognitions through performative inquiry. In G. Bräuer (ed.) *Body and Language: Intercultural Learning Through Drama* (pp. 19–35). Westport, CT: Ablex Publishing.

Fetscher, D. (2013) Les incidents critiques dans l'enseignement de la communication interculturelle. Un exercice de heuristique interculturelle. In A.-C. Gonnot, N. Rentel and S. Schwerter (eds) *Dialogues entre langues et cultures* (pp. 177–190). Frankfurt am Main: Lang.

Fischer-Lichte, E. (2014) Performativität der Dinge. In S. Aue, H. Parzinger and G. Stock (eds) *ArteFakte. Wissen ist Kunst. Kunst ist Wissen. Reflexionen und Praktiken wissenschaftlich-künstlerischer Begegnungen* (pp. 469–478). Bielefeld: Transcript.

Fleiner, M. (2014) *Zur Notwendigkeit einer performativ-ästhetischen Fremd sprachenlehrerausbildung im deutschsprachigen Hochschulraum. Zusammenfassende Einblicke in Theorie und Praxis.* In N. Bernstein and C. Lerchner (eds) Ästhetisches Lernen im DaF-/DaZ-Unterricht. Literatur, Theater, Bildende Kunst, Musik, Film (pp. 179–190). Göttingen: Universitätsverlag.

Fleming, M. (2011) *Starting Drama Teaching.* London: Routledge.

Fonio, F. and Genicot, G. (2011) The compatibility of drama language teaching and CEFR objectives: Observations on a rationale for an artistic approach to foreign language teaching at an academic level. *Scenario: Journal for Drama and Theatre in Foreign and Second Language Education* 2 (V), 75–89.

Gardner, H. (1993) *Frames of Mind. The Theory of Multiple Intelligences.* London: Fontana Press.

Gilardi, P., Rohrbach, R. and Sauter, P. (2005) Parola, corpo, movimento, spazio. Apprendre une langue avec des activités théâtrales. Ein mehrsprachiges Experiment.

In A. Gohard-Radenkovic (ed.) *Plurilinguisme, interculturalité et didactique des langues étrangères dans un contexte bilingue* (pp. 207–225). Bern: Lang.

Godley, A.J. (2012) Intercultural discourse and communication in education. In C.B. Paulston, S.F. Kiesling and E.S. Rangel (eds) *The Handbook of Intercultural Discourse and Communication* (pp. 449–481). Malden, MA: Blackwell.

Heringer, H.J. (2014) *Interkulturelle Kommunikation*. Tübingen: Francke.

Holl, E. (2011) Sprach-Fluss. Theaterworkshops mit Jugendlichen aus 16 afrikanischen Ländern. Theaterpädagogik zwischen kultureller Bildung und Fremdsprachendidaktik. *Scenario: Journal for Drama and Theatre in Foreign and Second Language Education* 2 (V), 13–31.

Huber, R. (2003) *Im Haus der Sprache wohnen. Wahrnehmung und Theater im Fremdsprachenunterricht*. Tübingen: Niemeyer.

Huber, W., Novak, J. and Rubik, M. (2010) Introduction. In W. Huber, J. Novak and M. Rubik (eds) *Staging Interculturality. Contemporary Drama in English 17* (pp. 9–17). Trier: Wissenschaftlicher Verlag Trier.

Hunter, L. (2014) *Disunified Aesthetics: Situated Textuality, Performativity, Collaboration*. Montreal: McGill-Queen's University Press.

Işik-Güler, H., Spencer-Oatey, H. and Stadler, S. (2012) Intercultural communication. In J.P. Gee and M. Handford (eds) *The Routledge Handbook of Discourse Analysis* (pp. 572–586). London: Routledge.

Jourdenais, R. (2009) Language teacher education. In M.H. Long and C. Doughty (eds) *The Handbook of Language Teaching* (pp. 647–658). Malden, MA: Blackwell.

Kessler, B. (2008) *Interkulturelle Dramapädagogik. Dramatische Arbeit als Vehikel des interkulturellen Lernens im Fremdsprachenunterricht*. Frankfurt am Main: Lang.

Kramsch, C. (2006) Culture in language teaching. In K. Brown (ed.) *Encyclopedia of Language & Linguistics* (Vol. 3; pp. 322–329). Oxford: Elsevier.

Kulovics, N. and Terler, K. (2014) Herzstück. Performatives Lehren und Lernen am Beispiel eines Gemeinschaftsprojekts im universitären DaF-Bereich oder frei nach Schiller: Von der performativen Erziehung des Menschen. *Scenario: Journal for Drama and Theatre in Foreign and Second Language Education* 2 (VIII), 89–96.

Lehmann, S. (2014) *Die Dramaturgie der Globalisierung. Tendenzen im deutschsprachigen Theater der Gegenwart*. Marburg: Schüren.

Lutzker, P. (2007) *The Art of Foreign Language Teaching: Improvisation and Drama in Teacher Development and Language Learning*. Tübingen: Francke.

Oelschläger, B. (2011) Wenn man sieht, dass die Jugendlichen wirklich dabei sind. Das Schülertheaterprojekt der Partnerschulinitiative in Mittelosteuropa. *Scenario: Journal for Drama and Theatre in Foreign and Second Language Education* 1 (V), 54–65.

Riedmüller, A. (2014) K.B.M. – Mit einem interaktiven DaF-Theaterstück für Kinder auf Tournee durch Lateinamerika. *Scenario: Journal for Drama and Theatre in Foreign and Second Language Education* 1 (VIII), 70–73.

Sambanis, M. (2013) *Fremdsprachenunterricht und Neurowissenschaften*. Tübingen: Narr.

Scenario. Language, Culture, Literature. *Journal for Drama and Theatre in Foreign and Second Language Education*. See http://scenario.ucc.ie (accessed 8 September 2015).

Schewe, M. (1993) *Fremdsprache inszenieren. Zur Fundierung einer dramapädagogischen Lehr- und Lernpraxis*. Oldenburg: Zentrum für pädagogische Berufspraxis, Universität Oldenburg.

Schewe, M. (1998) Culture through literature through drama. In M. Byram and M. Fleming (eds) *Language Learning in Intercultural Perspective: Approaches Through Drama and Ethnography* (pp. 204–221). Cambridge: Cambridge University Press.

Schewe, M. (2002) Teaching foreign language literature: Tapping the students' bodily-kinesthetic intelligence. In G. Bräuer (ed.) *Body and Language: Intercultural Learning Through Drama* (pp. 73–93). Westport, CT: Ablex Publishing.

Schewe, M. (2008) Drama und Theater in der Fremd- und Zweitsprachenlehre. Blicke zurück nach vorn. In I. Hentschel, B. Wildt and J. Wildt (eds) *Theater in der Lehre. Verfahren, Konzepte, Vorschläge* (pp. 127–137). Münster: Lit.

Schewe, M. (2011) Die Welt auch im fremdsprachlichen Unterricht immer wieder neu verzaubern. Plädoyer für eine performative Lehr- und Lernkultur! In A. Küppers, T. Schmidt and M. Walter (eds) *Inszenierungen im Fremdsprachenunterricht. Grundlagen, Formen, Perspektiven* (pp. 20–31). Braunschweig: Diesterweg/Klinkhardt.

Schewe, M. (2013) Taking stock and looking ahead: Drama pedagogy as a gateway to a performative teaching and learning culture. *Scenario: Journal for Drama and Theatre in Foreign and Second Language Education* 1 (VII), 5–27.

Schewe, M. and Shaw, P. (eds) (1993) *Towards Drama as a Method in the Foreign Language Classroom.* Frankfurt am Main: Lang.

Schroeter, R. (2014) *Eine Bestandsaufnahme von Überzeugungen (beliefs) Lehramtsstudierender zu Lehrerbildung und Lehrerberuf.* Leipzig: Leipziger Universitätsverlag.

Simmons, K. (2015) Nonverbale Kompetenz. In D. Ufert (ed.) *Schlüsselkompetenzen im Hochschulstudium. Eine Orientierung für Lehrende* (pp. 91–102). Opladen: Budrich.

Szende, T. (2014) *Second Culture Teaching and Learning. An Introduction.* Bern: Lang.

Thiem, A. (2014) Interkulturelle Kompetenz als Herausforderung für das Lehramtsstudium. *Scenario: Journal for Drama and Theatre in Foreign and Second Language Education* 2 (VIII), 44–61.

Tselikas, E.I. (1999) *Dramapädagogik im Sprachunterricht.* Zürich: Orell Füssli.

Weidinger, W. (2014) Competence-oriented teaching in international projects. In G. Rabensteiner and P.-M. Rabensteiner (eds) *Interculturality* (pp. 34–49). Baltmannsweiler: Schneider.

Wimmer, M. (2014) *Pädagogik als Wissenschaft des Unmöglichen. Bildungsphilosophische Interventionen.* Paderborn: Schöningh.

Zipsane, H. (2009) Lifelong learning through heritage and art. In P. Jarvis (ed.) *The Routledge International Handbook of Lifelong Learning* (pp. 173–182). London: Routledge.

# 6 Exploring Diversity Through Drama Education: English–Turkish Perspectives on National German Stereotypes in Foreign Language Teacher Training

Almut Küppers

*This dancefloor is my temple. Here we don't care about things. We enjoy the randomness of life. And we love each other freely. And forget each other soon.*
(Istanbul, anonymous 2015)

## Introduction: We Can Only Change Our Own Behavior – Not That of Others[1]

To change their behavior is one of the hardest challenges for individuals. As human beings, we develop routines, habits and customs and often function best in fixed structures. Behavioral patterns smoothly guide the flow of our lives. Many features of our behavior can be extremely automated: morning routines, the way we organize our work space, how we prepare food. There is no need to think about actions we have performed hundreds and thousands of times, as we have internalized them. Automation while brushing teeth or making tea minimizes the cognitive effort, and thus makes space for other, more challenging tasks. But when it comes to behavior in communication, things get more complicated. Communication means dealing with complex human beings, not an inanimate toothbrush, teabag or kettle. However, not just in daily routines and work, but also in the way we speak, how we interact and in general how we look at the world and understand it, highly automated processes exist. Lippmann (1956) was the first to refer to the process of ordering the incoming data we receive from the ever more buzzing, dazzling and diverse world as 'stereotyping'. By generalizing and categorizing, this activity is, on the one hand, a necessity – if not an inescapable way to make sense of ourselves and the environment we live in. In everyday life, on the other hand, the term 'stereotype' almost always carries negative connotations. The familiar mantra – at least in the educational world – even aims at the exact opposite. 'Challenging stereotyping' has become one of the proclaimed objectives in many school curricula around the world. In times of rapidly growing diversity, avoiding conflicts and communicating openness and tolerance seem to have turned into a magic educational formula (e.g. KMK, 2004). Understanding others can be as enlightening as it is painful, and understanding *each other* can in fact be a tedious struggle, almost like hard work. As we finally arrive at the realization that we can only change our own behavior – never that of others – intercultural learning is often an aching process of readjusting positions or discarding old beliefs which we have held dear – a process of self-realization which can at the same time be intellectually challenging, emotionally disturbing and physically painful.

Lippmann's notion of stereotyping as an inevitable part of human nature and understanding, however, reminds us to not simply ignore, confront or condemn generalizing and stereotyping but rather to explore its manifestations, its accompanying intentions, motivations and consequences – which is possible in the safe context of the drama process and which will be the focus in this chapter.

## Foreign Language Teaching and Drama in Education: A Perfect Match?

It is one of the most overrated commonplaces that 'our world is evolving rapidly'. Change seems desirable, yet it brings about diversity. The real challenges in the wake of rapid change are the deep divides which are tangible almost everywhere in modern societies. Not only are the official outer worlds of politics, commerce, communication, entertainment or tourism rapidly evolving in modern societies, but also the inner worlds of their citizens who have access to the most distant spots on the globe through digital technology and who now spend considerable amounts of time online. For encounters in all those speedily evolving inner and outer spaces, intercultural communicative competencies have been hailed as an answer to overcoming conflicts, dealing with critical incidents and challenging communicative situations. However, the term 'intercultural' seems to put too much emphasis on the term 'cultural'.[2] For prospective foreign language teachers it seems of more practical value to understand the term 'cultural' in the broadest possible and most fluid sense and not to limit it to the outdated concept of fixed 'national cultures' (cf. Hu, 2007).

Conflicts among people emerge for all sorts of reasons, one of which can be their cultural predetermination. There are many more, however, such as differing character traits, conflicting values and beliefs but also differing ethnic, linguistic, social, religious, inter-generational standards or gender differences (cf. Sen, 2007). In huge urban areas where people of all colors and from all walks of life and professions are washed ashore, millions live next to each other in growing diversity and contribute to a diversification of lifestyles, sexual orientations and worldviews. Urban life has become the incubator of hybridity, and life's urban randomness is the dancefloor of unlimited possible encounters. It is here that expectations, values and ideologies clash – not necessarily cultures.[3]

Moreover, dealing successfully in international business encounters became an important requirement for the international workforce long ago. In the private sector in particular, intercultural training has developed into an established – and also very profitable – field of professional education as the new global economy not only requires mobile but also smart and flexible employees in order to boost profits (cf. Küppers & Bozdağ, 2015a: 5). Hence, the sensitivity to deal with diversity in personal encounters is a prerequisite not just for people who move on the urban dancefloors – but also for those who stay put and welcome newcomers. However, intercultural competencies cannot be seen as a set of skills which can be learned and applied like math formulae. Intercultural learning is at best identity negotiation and therefore not a fancy add-on subject to the school curriculum. It should much rather be seen as a new attitude toward learning which needs to be implemented across the curriculum (cf. Küppers & Bozdağ, 2015b: 41).

If we define intercultural communicative competencies as identity negotiation, it will be argued here that foreign language teaching complemented by a drama in education approach seems to be the perfect match. For quite some time, foreign language subjects have been regarded as the most apt curricular home for intercultural education. In the following, the notion of intercultural communicative competencies will firstly be defined along the lines of the most influential reference disciplines of foreign language education in the past, namely logocentric disciplines like linguistic and literary studies as well as, quite recently, cultural studies. However much elaborated theoretically, academic debates on intercultural competencies have been intense and often controversial, but without much added value with regard to the micro level of the classroom. After three decades of extensive academic discourse, there is still a substantial lack of approaches, materials and tools when it comes to teaching, and, what is more, learning intercultural competencies, let alone testing them. Relatively unnoticed alongside the more prominent topics like standardization and media integration, drama and theater education has evolved as a very lively and productive field in the realm of foreign language teaching in the past two decades and can now be regarded as firmly established (cf. Schewe, 2007, 2013). Hence, theater and the performing arts as new reference disciplines for foreign language teaching open up a new perspective on language. Language is no longer modeled as a text but celebrated as a multidimensional event. In contrast to the aforementioned classical text-based disciplines like linguistics or literature, where language is dealt with in written and spoken texts and a variety of different text genres, in the world of theater, communication takes place holistically and physically, and language is thus a manifestation of 'performative experience' (Schewe, 2013: 15).

In general, the 'drama in education' approach in foreign language teaching can be defined as a cooperative macro method (cf. Bonnet & Küppers, 2011), which due to its deliberate fictionalization of the learning context and the integration of movement and body language, also belongs to the much wider field of aesthetic learning. Hence, the drama teaching approach covers much common ground with foreign language teaching objectives, namely the aim to develop language learners holistically as intercultural speakers. However, the impact of drama in language teaching seems to be most powerful on the often neglected level of intercultural *interactions*. Employing activities taken from the world of drama and theater, it is possible to advance to the performative center of the language subjects. Schewe (2013) quite rightly calls for an overall performative foreign language didactics in order to avail ourselves of the wealth of forms found in the performing arts. In line with the distinction he makes between 'large-scale' and 'small-scale' forms of drama (Schewe, 2013: 8ff), in the teaching units which this chapter examines, the focus will be on the *drama process* in which students and teacher engage in a process of negotiating meaning by employing *small forms* of dramatic elements like improvisations, freeze frames, slow-motion, thought-tapping or hot seating.

## Intercultural Communicative Competence as Doing Diversity

Since the 'cultural turn', the formerly popular 'native speaker' no longer serves as a linguistic baseline in the foreign language subjects. The over-ambitious aim of near nativeness in pronunciation and language use of the 1970s has been substituted by the more prominent and more down-to-earth intercultural speaker who may speak with an accent but is more aware of potential pitfalls in intercultural encounters (cf. Schmenck, 2010). The new role model for language learners – at least according to academic discourse – is a person who can relate to other people and maintains this connection by communicating appropriately.

This person identifies possible difficulties in communication and deals with them in a sensitive way. Moreover, she or he is able to mediate between interlocutors from different cultures who speak different languages (Schmenk, 2010: 118 with reference to Byram, 1997). Hence, intercultural competencies – according to Schmenk and many others – can be understood as an important part of complex modern identities which are not static but always evolving in the spaces between places, cultures, languages and experiences. In a more interconnected world, the ways we communicate also evolve rapidly and have become more diverse, volatile, disembodied and digitized. The intercultural speaker is a person who is able to deal with those new demands in communication, with surprise situations and challenging people in a self-critical way, as she or he does not assume that everybody sees the world in the same way that she or he does. Critical self-appreciation of positions, ideas and long-held beliefs, based on the willingness to alter or even discard them when necessary, is an important feature of the successful intercultural speaker. Hence the moment of self-transformation and changeability is paramount to the modeling of the intercultural speaker, who not only accepts limits to understanding and can endure contradictions, but also knows that conflicts are not always solvable and that dilemmas are part of the human condition. Ideally, the worldview of an intercultural speaker is more colorful than black and white, and his or her awareness of the huge 'discomfort zone' when dealing with diversity and difference of any kind is well developed.

Michael Byram's (1997) influential model of Intercultural Communicative Competence (ICC) serves as an important reference point in foreign language teacher training. At the heart of his model of ICC, we find a category called 'self-critical cultural awareness' ('savoir s'engager'), which corresponds well with what Mall (2003) describes as 'normative self-transformation', and which translates into the ability to dismiss ethnocentric perceptions of absoluteness for the sake of living with and in differences and to struggle for understanding. Like other models, too, Byram's model conceives intercultural communication on three different levels that are all interconnected, namely the cognitive, the affective and the level of interaction. The cognitive dimension is called 'savoirs' and includes not only the knowledge of one's own as well as of other cultures but also knowledge of communication models and interaction processes (cf. Hu, 2010: 76). This area is factual in nature and close to what is also called 'socio-cultural background knowledge' or traditional cultural studies. The category 'savoir comprendre' relates to skills of interpretation and understanding. Going beyond text comprehension, this skill can be conceptualized as the ability also to comprehend interactions, and it takes into consideration influences from both the cognitive and the affective level. 'Savoir être' describes the affective dimension of Byram's model and refers to attitudes and values but also includes e.g. willingness to openness and tolerance. Moreover, the uneasiness, discomfort or irritation often accompanied by strong feelings as a by-product in distorted communication processes are rooted in this section, which is complemented by the readiness to distance oneself from ethnocentrism. 'Savoir apprendre' points to the level of interaction in communication and translates into the willingness to also learn from new situations in which we encounter differences and diversity. The English equivalent of 'skills of discovery and interaction' seems to encompass this dimension best, as it highlights the dimension of face-to-face interaction and includes the discovery of our own predetermination/s in such situations.

Byram's widely acknowledged model of ICCs is embedded in a linguistic dimension, since in communication all knowledge, attitudes and interactions find expression in language either verbally or through body language. The latter dimension, however, has not yet been reflected enough in Byram's model, and Benedikt Kessler has advanced it by adding the dimension of physicality, which he calls 'savoir percevoir' (Kessler, 2008; Kessler & Küppers, 2008). Changing perspectives, coordinating them and increasing understanding and knowledge are part and parcel of a learning process which acknowledges that not only our points of view but also our behavior in interactions is amendable and subject to change. In the recent past, an impressive amount of teaching ideas and materials has emerged in the field of teaching literature that aim precisely at changing perspectives and coordinating points of view (e.g. Nünning, 2007; Surkamp, 2007). These have usually been implemented in a discursive fashion, integrating the 'savoirs' – 'savoir comprendre' as well as 'savoir être' – dimensions of intercultural communication in classroom discourse. But how do new insights, a slightly changed perspective or a revised attitude translate into *interactions*, and how does the change show verbally as well as in body language? Those are the performative dimensions which have not yet been unlocked and used productively in language teaching. Including the dimension of body language in Byram's model means that at the level of 'savoir comprendre' the skill of interpreting and understanding needs to be complemented by the skill of understanding and interpreting the communicative value also of gestures and postures, facial expressions and body movements. At the same time, it includes the knowledge about culture-specific body language as part of the so-called 'savoirs'. Critical cultural awareness, however, needs also to integrate a critical awareness for one's own culturally predetermined body language and its limitations and the willingness to communicate, for instance, openness not only verbally but also through movements, postures and gestures. With regard to the physical dimension in communication, we will see in Part 4 that the level of interaction is the common ground where a drama approach in language teaching will develop its performative powers best (cf. Kessler & Küppers, 2008; Küppers *et al.*, 2011a).

## Intercultural Drama Teaching: Doing Diversity in the Drama Process

School is apparently a place for learning. Yet, all too often, children and adolescents experience school as a place of instruction and testing but not necessarily as a place where first-hand experience takes place. For a long time, classical school research has criticized the learning processes at school as overly intellectual, too academic in nature and too narrowly focused on cognitive learning (cf. Küppers *et al.*, 2011b). By contrast, intercultural education deliberately integrates the affective dimension of learning and also opens the door to more holistic learning experiences on the level of interaction. Physicality, movement and emotion are likewise at the heart of the drama approach. In the drama process, meaning is not only negotiated verbally through discourse but also in a cooperative way through body language and using the classroom space. The more overloaded curricula become with academic content, the stronger the chances are that schools reduce learners to thinking-revising-and-talking heads. Students are usually unaccustomed to experiencing their bodies or emotional reactions while learning. The same applies to university students, who are taken even more by surprise if, in a context which epitomizes intellectualism and cognitive powers, they are exposed to activities that are deliberately designed to let them experience learning holistically. Discomfort and uneasiness often accompany the first learning experiences in the drama process when university students embark on a training course which integrates holistic learning and drama teaching. It usually does not correspond with their expectations, nor can they relate it to previous experiences. Schewe (2011) quite rightly calls for a performative turn in foreign language teaching – and argues that this paradigm shift is especially necessary in initial teacher training courses at the higher education level (Schewe, 2013; cf. also Haack & Surkamp, 2011). On the one hand, students can explore their learner/teacher identities and experiment with their future roles as instructors in the safe space within the classroom walls. On the other hand, the seminar room can provide the stage for genuine intercultural experience as an important reference point for their future work as language teachers. Hence, dealing with differences and coping with uneasiness and discomfort triggered by hitherto unexperienced learning processes are deliberately intended objectives in my teacher training courses and can be seen as a fundamental part of understanding intercultural learning (cf. Küppers, 2015).

### The snag in changing behavior

In order to raise awareness of the invisibility of habits and routines as well as of automated behavior and thinking as described at the outset of this chapter, I employ a very simple activity which is called 'the other hand experiment'.[4] Its purpose is at least threefold: (a) it initiates the development of observation and critical self-monitoring skills, both of paramount importance in the drama process and teaching profession; (b) it ploughs the field for an appreciation of the basic principles in learning and especially in learning a foreign language; and (c) it can be used as a metaphorical equation in order to address automation in behavior and perception.

The 'wrong-hand activity', which asks students to write their signatures with the hand they usually do not use, also focuses on one of the two main principles in drama teaching: next to empathy, this is reflection. The drama process in general consists of two phases: the active, holistic, cooperative drama process in the group, and afterwards the reflection phase, a discourse among the group members in which observations and experiences are shared. Self-awareness and learning often take place in the second phase of the drama process, not necessarily the first. The following section will now focus on the two aforementioned drama teaching units, both of which were based on an appreciation of Byram's model of ICC in a more classical academic discourse. Moreover, both units involve critical incidents either experienced or written by the students themselves.

## Critical incidents and intercultural learning

Germans seem to have a harder time than some others in dealing with compliments. Sometimes, their responses can even appear blunt or flippant to the ears of the person paying the compliment. Remarks like 'You must be joking!' or 'Impossible!' are not an exception, and they point to the underlying cultural standards that show the way compliments that are dealt with by many Germans. In return, the payer of the compliment may be irritated, because the intention was almost certainly not to mock the German interlocutor. A situation like this is referred to as a 'critical incident'; it can make both interlocutors feel uneasy or annoyed, but will probably not lead to an end to the relationship. However, critical incidents are realistic episodes or small 'everyday dramas' based on misunderstandings due to different underlying values or beliefs, whether cultural, social, religious, gender or lifestyle based in nature. A critical incident can lead to astonishment and irritation; the consequence can be discomfort, frustration or anger. Bertallo *et al.* (2004: 26) call them 'a focal point in communication processes in which the interlocutors involved become aware of their intercultural differences' (translation by A.K.). Thus, critical incidents can have the quality of a moment of epiphany with a deep emotional resonance. As a text genre, however, they are very short and concise fragments, linguistically easy to understand but always pointing to divergent underlying value systems. As such, they seem ideal for educational purposes (cf. Küppers *et al.*, 2009) and have been used in studies (e.g. in Deutsch-Englisch-Schülerleistungen-International, DESI, for a critical review cf. Küppers & Trautmann, 2008) as well as in intercultural training programs and psychology courses (cf. Schmidt & Thomas, 2003, and for a critical account Bredella, 2010).

## German–English perspectives: 'Hitler's daughter' and 'Hitler salute'

The first teaching unit I will discuss took place in an initial teacher training course at Frankfurt University, and aimed to prepare students for a foreign language teacher assignment at one of the institute's partner schools in England. Although a preparatory course, it has at the same time been a wrap-up course for student teachers who have just returned from a one year stay abroad. Hence, the fresh impressions and experience the returnees bring to the course and critical incidents reported by students from previous courses have been a valuable source of learning for the whole group.

One of the frequently experienced stereotypes that student teachers from Germany are confronted with is the so-called historical German-stereotype. Some of the questions they were asked by pupils in class included e.g. 'Miss, are you a Nazi?' or 'Miss, do you like Hitler?' These were perceived as 'irritating' if not 'weird' by the students. 'Shocking' was the word Claudia used for a critical incident she experienced at an after-work party in a local pub, where she was approached by the school's history teacher who said, 'Hiya Claudia, I'm sure Hitler would have loved to have you as a daughter!' A critical incident of similar emotional quality was Timo's encounter with the librarian. He had wanted to ask the name of another colleague and got the following answer: 'Why do you want to know this, Timo? Do you want to subject her to a Hitler salute?' Both incidents represented a focal point in the communication process with colleagues; but due to the powerful emotional resonance, these incidents also marked the end of the relation to these persons. Claudia, who apparently fits the stereotype of a very blond, blue-eyed German, seemed vividly to re-experience strong emotions stirred up by the incident: 'I was so horrified and furious, I just turned round and walked away'. Timo, for his part, had managed to remain calm on the surface but could only stutter a weak response. He recalls, just like Claudia, that he had no idea how to react appropriately. In a discussion with the group, it became clear that others had experienced similar situations, which had contributed to a reinforcement of their stereotypical thinking about 'the English' rather than challenging it. 'Many English people still believe Germans are Nazis' was a statement shared by many in the group – even those who had spent a year in the country.

Studies show that the development of intercultural competencies is actually not an automatic side effect of a stay abroad (cf. Ehrenreich,

2004; Kristensen, 2015). Intercultural learning is much rather a wearisome struggle on the way to new insights, and it requires considerable self-reflective powers. Although a stay abroad provides a wealth of intercultural encounters, there is often no institutionalized place for foreign language assistants where these can be transformed into intercultural competencies. Hence, these two incidents lend themselves to being explored by means of drama in order to challenge, modify and adjust the underlying auto- and hetero-stereotypes of 'the Germans' and 'the English' with the aim of challenging thinking in 'national stereotypes' and to show the multitude of individual perspectives in critical encounters.

The unit was started with a warm-up activity called 'silent dialogue', in which the students are asked to comment on a provocative or open statement just by writing a response on a poster. 'In the eyes of the English, Germans are ...' and 'In the eyes of the Germans, English people are ...' were the two statements intended to generate the group's ideas on the two respective national stereotypes. The emerging hetero-stereotypes were clustered in groups and their origin and everyday relevance discussed against the backdrop of the group members' knowledge and experience. One of the most popular clichés for the Germans (driving a fast car) and for the English (standing in a queue while it rains) was then presented in a freeze frame and its validity scrutinized by the group. In a next step, the groups worked on the two critical incidents 'Hitler's daughter' and 'Hitler salute' with the aim of developing an improvisation using dialogue to represent the situation before the conflict arose and eventually leading to the moment the English colleague uttered the irritating statement. The final critical moment was then presented in a 'freeze frame' in order to show the moment of the students' shock as well as their and their interlocutor's body language. With the drama activity 'thought-tapping',[5] the participants were now asked to explore the two persons' private thoughts, emotions and irritations. This activity proves to be very productive as feelings and inner conditions can be shown in a linguistically reduced fashion. Just a word or two or a stream-of-consciousness might be enough to express surprise, anger, shame and embarrassment. In this phase, one contribution can trigger another thought in another participant, and it can often be observed how the minds of individuals and the thinking in the group become connected in a truly cooperative way. The teacher, too, is a participant in this phase. Quite understandably, it seemed much easier for the students to explore the inner worlds of the two German students. The librarian as well as the history teacher got only a few comments, their perspectives being much harder to imagine with empathy. At this point, it is crucial that the drama teacher – as an important participant in the drama process – opens up new perspectives and provides contributions which lead in a new direction. Whereas from Claudia's perspective, the participants pictured the history teacher as a drunkard and mostly qualified his statement as a cheap chat-up line, I suggested a perspective in which the history teacher could have meant to approach Claudia in a humorous way and that the way she reacted fully confirmed the cliché of the 'dry, humorless Germans'. In both, the improvisations as well as the thought-tapping activities, the librarian as well as the history teacher were predominantly presented as insensitive, mean colleagues who took pleasure in deliberately provoking the German students with a taboo topic. In the reflection phase afterwards, students compared the seeming contradiction between the clichés which emerged in the warm-up, namely the proverbial English politeness and friendliness with the image of the librarian and history teacher. It also became clear that as follow-up activities emerging from these incidents, it would be worth repeating the scenarios showing the range of different possible intentions of the history teacher or the librarian. Likewise, it would be valuable to use follow-up drama to focus on different versions of (a) the incidents as *experienced* by the recipients and (b) as *intended* by the protagonists.

Whereas until then the drama unit had been required to work mostly with Byram's ICC fields of 'savoir être' and 'savoir comprendre' – in other words dealing with attitudes, emotions and interpreting, understanding and coordinating various perspectives – it was now important to provide the students with further background information intended to develop their socio-cultural knowledge, or simply 'savoir'. A passage was taken from Schmidt and Thomas (2003: 127–141), who use critical incidents for intercultural training.[6] In this extract, the authors deal explicitly with taboo topics as part of the national stereotype of the Germans in England. According to the authors, most young Britons do not know that in Germany the Third Reich and the Holocaust are taboo topics and that Germans do not employ Nazi gestures or expressions. 'Don't mention the war!' is, however, a widespread admonition in England when it comes to dealing with Germans.[7] From an English point of view, remarks about the Second World War are usually not meant as an allusion to the fact that it epitomizes the cruellest chapter in German history or that the Holocaust can be seen as unique in the history of mankind. Instead, it is apparently often meant to remind the 'war sensitive' Germans of the fact that they 'lost the war'. Apparently, illusions to Germany's history are sometimes even intended in a humorous fashion to establish contact (cf. Schmidt & Thomas, 2003: 138).

One does not have to agree with this – maybe somewhat questionable – elaboration of the two national stereotypes, and it is certainly not wise to claim that they represent a common understanding of the Germans or English or how they see each other. But they do open up an unknown perspective for the German students and can serve as a new orientation in order to better understand the critical incident they experienced – and suffered from. Against the backdrop of the Schmidt and Thomas text extract, the students were now asked to develop a new improvisation integrating the critical incident in the pub and/or library, but this time Claudia or Timo should be shown with a variety of possible reactions. In a brief discussion beforehand, attention was drawn again to social and cultural determinations in behavior patterns, which are also much influenced by character traits. It might, for instance, be much easier for a rational and 'cool' type of person to deal with an incident like the ones in question as opposed to a very emotional and compassionate person who quickly feels uncomfortable. In line with Byram's ICC model and intercultural learning objectives, the students were asked to develop possible interactions which should take into consideration an understanding approach to diversity. The results showed a multitude of different reactions. In one, Timo openly showed the librarian how angry he was and afterwards lectured her about how Germans deal with their national history. In another, Timo took it a lot more light-heartedly, laughed at the remark and left performing a Hitler salute as a goodbye gesture. A similar variety of reactions were shown for Claudia. Whereas one, Claudia bluntly replied, 'What do you mean?' and pretended she had not understood the history teacher's remark, a good-humored Claudia picked up on the provocation and said 'Thanks for the compliment! But you should see my mom, she's an Eva Braun look-alike!' In the follow-up reflection phase, some students clearly pointed to the difficulties they had to 'act in an understanding way' in interactions which turn out to be highly emotional. The real Claudia, however, remarked at the end that she was probably not cut out for acting in contradictions: 'How can I act cool and amused when deep down I am upset and furious?' Slightly disillusioned, she concluded that she would need a lot more training in order to perform 'better' in critical incidents. As Claudia's remark ties in with the above-mentioned challenges of changing one's own behavior, the point was made that drama is a way of showing the openness of such critical incidents and the absence of a 'correct' understanding/reaction due to the multitude of perspectives and possible reactions. Moreover, it was discussed that drama provides the means to explore different responses and to help each group participant to judge for himself/herself which reaction was more desirable and whether his/her intellectual judgment accords with how he/she would be able to respond in the given circumstances.

## German–Turkish perspectives: 'Noodle salad' and 'surprise visits'

The next drama unit took place as part of an initial teacher training course at Marmara University, Istanbul, and was designed for prospective teachers of German as a foreign language. The course was similar to the

Frankfurt course in its focus on intercultural learning and the use of the target language in class, but larger in size[8] and more concerned with literary texts. Another difference can be seen in the mix of course participants. Whereas the Frankfurt groups had been slightly more homogeneous in terms of socio-economic background and ethnicity, the Istanbul group was more diverse, involving many Turkish students with some kind of biographical connection to Germany.[9] In both courses, the drama unit was integrated in an otherwise (more or less) academic schedule; both groups had worked in detail with the advanced version of Byram's model of ICC (cf. Kessler, 2008; Kessler & Küppers, 2008) as a theoretical basis for the exploration of critical incidents.

The text 'Eine deutsche Leidenschaft namens Nudelsalat' (*A German Passion Called Noodle Salad*) written by Rafik Schami (2011) formed the literary basis for the drama unit.[10] In this text, exaggerations, irony and especially stereotyping are used as literary devices in order to create humor for the exploration of the different ways of dealing with visitors in different cultural contexts. In a very subtle manner, Schami employs the right to not like German noodle salad as an allegory for the freedom to not be completely assimilated into another culture. The text is a comparison of how people visit each other in Germany and how visiting and hospitality are dealt with in Arabic culture.

Due to the nature of the overall course topic ('literature in foreign language teaching'), the text was first approached in a classical analytical way (analysis of the literary devices and narrative situation etc.). During the discussion in class, a number of issues were raised, and in particular, hospitality in German and Arabic culture was explored in more detail. It was generally agreed that in Arabic culture, similar to Turkish culture, guests are always revered as saints, even if they stop by without previous notice, since paying a visit means honoring the host. The host would not ask how long the guests intend to stay, and would always make sure they feel welcome and are offered food. Arriving late and bringing along other people is not considered a problem in Arabic culture. In Germany, by contrast, a visit is usually thoroughly planned and both parties know the duration of the visit and the number of people invited. A guest usually adapts very much to the rules set by the German host, and any changes would be communicated beforehand. A surprise visit could be perceived as an interference with the host's plans or daily program. In the critical appreciation of this comparison afterwards, the German Erasmus students in particular embarked on a very heated debate on the improper and illegitimate way of generalizing and stereotyping cultures in the text. Apparently, they argued, visiting each other without planning is common among young people also in Germany. To illustrate the multitude of perspectives inherent in a critical incident was the aim of the follow-up drama unit.

'Arabic guests usually turn up without notice. Now, what about the host? When he hears the doorbell, he gets up – unwillingly – because he has been watching a crime film on TV, or because he needs to chill a bit but what he certainly does not need are guests' (Schami, 2011: 34; translation by A.K.).

This short passage was the basis for a creative writing activity in which the students were asked to write a short dialogue from the perspective of a German host and an Arabic host, respectively. One of the students' responses from the perspective of a German host was then used for a detailed analysis by means of drama activities.

*(Lisa, the German host, opens the door and sees her Arabic friend Samira as well as five other people.)*

**L**: Ohhh, Samira! Hello!
**S**: Hi Lisa!
**L**: *(while she steps out of the flat and into the corridor, she leaves the door ajar behind her)* Yes?
**S**: I was passing by with my sisters who are visiting and we just wanted to say hello.
**L**: *(Lisa welcomes the sisters warmly)* Listen Samira ... that's really very nice of you ... but honestly, I have no time right now.
**S**: O come on! We could just have a coffee together and then we'll be on our way. Promise!
**L**: No, honey, honestly! Please don't be cross with me. We can meet up in a café another time, ok? Let's phone before that, alright?
**S**: *(gives up)*

Among the many realistic and enlightening dialogues written by the students, the above example was chosen for its palpable performative dimension in the evolving critical incident. The students were asked to discuss the physical aspect of this situation in groups and to be ready to act out the little scene. It was agreed that a special focus had to be put on Lisa's body language. A number of versions were improvised in front of the classroom door, and the moment in which Lisa opens the door and leaves the flat to welcome the guests with the door ajar was re-enacted by different Lisas in slower motion in order to explore the various ways in which the Lisas communicated with their body language. The feelings explored ranged from surprise, annoyance, dilemma, shock, indifference. The end of the scene was eventually 'freeze-framed' and the emotional state of Lisa and Samira explored through 'thought-tapping'. In the reflection phase afterwards, a large range of perspectives emerged, which showed, on the one hand, that initially underlying culture-bound behavior accounted for the conflict between Lisa and Samira. On the other hand, a number of students stressed the influence of other factors such as context (which was missing) or the duration and degree of intimacy in the friendship between Lisa and Samira as well as character traits. Some contributions suggested that this could be the end of the relationship between the two girls, while others argued that their friendship would be sound enough to cope with a crisis like this. The group arrived at the conclusion, however, that the conflict could not be attributed to a cultural misunderstanding only.

It is often argued that appropriate test formats are missing for the evaluation of intercultural competencies. Yet, drama work in class can be complemented with more analytical tasks in written assignments. The group of Marmara students were given the critical incident 'At the door' again for their semester finals. First they had to briefly discuss Byram's extended model of ICC. Next, they were given a creative writing task in which they had to imagine a future encounter between Lisa and Samira in the university cafeteria and develop a dialogue in which the girls talk about the encounter at the door. Afterwards, they had to comment on the way the two students had dealt with their conflict by making use of Byram's model of ICC and by referring to the physical dimension of it as well. There is no space here to present the test results in detail, but a number of examples of students' work should serve to illustrate the multitude of ways in which (a) the conflict was either resolved or aggravated and (b) the depth of students' analysis as shown by their comments.

In all of the dialogues between Lisa and Samira, the conflict was still noticeable. In some texts, Samira ignored Lisa in the café, in another she had not replied to text messages and not answered the phone, while in others she was offended. If they had not met accidentally in the café, it was usually Samira who initiated the talk with Lisa. In one case, Samira approached Lisa with a very sly and biting remark 'Hello, Ms. Superbusy! How are you doing lately?' Sometimes, Lisa was unaware of the impact the situation had had on Samira. As a response to the question 'Hey, what's up, Samira?' she answers: 'I'm still angry with you because you just left us in front of your door the other day. That was really appalling!' In many texts, it was shown that Samira had suffered embarrassment due to the fact that she had had her sisters with her. These were at best astonished (or 'irritated', 'shocked', 'offended') by Lisa's behavior at the door. In one case, the door was explicitly named as a symbol for openness and hospitality in the Arabic culture, and according to Samira her sisters had been shocked at the fact that they had been left outside. Due to this incredible unfriendliness, they had left Germany with a totally negative impression.

In most of the texts, the girls endeavored to solve their conflict and to develop empathy for the situation of the friend. Only in one case did the dialogue end with Samira walking out of the unresolved situation. Lisa's perspective was often also developed well with references to the bad feelings caused by rejecting her friend and a situation which did not allow her to ask the friends into her flat (no food to offer, rooms not tidy, washing machine broken). In some situations, Lisa had just had a hard day with lots of work for exams, in others she had experienced some other problems and in a few she was just not ready for visitors. In almost all of the work on Lisa's role, it was mentioned that the friend should have called her in order to make the visit less unexpected. In some texts (written by female students) the two girls depart at the end hugging each other warmly to show their happiness at the fact that they had talked it over and, thus, understood each other's behavior better. Some Samiras even apologized for having made Lisa feel bad. In a few dialogues, explicit references were made to the different cultural approaches to surprise visits.

In their analysis, many students were quite successful in explaining their dialogues on the grounds of Byram's extended ICC model. In a number of tests, it was mentioned that heavy emotions had accompanied the conflict at the door, especially for Samira, who had to cope with anger and shame (because she had e.g. spoken very highly of her good friend Lisa in front of her sisters but was rejected by her). Some others remarked that the talk in the café was also a situation loaded with emotions. One student argued that his Samira was so overwhelmed by her emotions that this was the reason why she was not able to act appropriately. In the café talk afterwards, his Samira was e.g. still attacking Lisa for being selfish, which proved that she had neither a well-developed self-critical cultural awareness nor enough background knowledge to understand Lisa's behavior better. This student even accused his Samira of not being able to overcome her ethno-centrist point of view. Another student had developed a dialogue between the two friends who were both very interested in overcoming their conflict. In her comment, she attributed well-developed intercultural competencies to them both, as they had both shown a lot of respect and tolerance for each other's behavior and were open enough to deal with criticism. In this case, Samira had shown a lot of willingness to critically reflect upon her own behavior, and had thus come to the realization that Lisa's behavior at the door was culturally determined and not personal. She understood that Lisa had felt overwhelmed by Samira's surprise visit. However, in this dialogue the student criticized her Lisa for being slightly less willing to develop empathy for Samira's perspective and to understand that Samira's visit was intended as an honor and not as a test-case.

## Conclusion

The world has developed into a unified space of communication, yet 'more communication means at first above all more conflict' (Sloterdijk, 2006: 84 in Žižek, 2009: 50). And as new forms of communication (e.g. shaming and blaming) in social networks and media become more disembodied, faster and more volatile, empathy seems to be getting lost on the communication highways.[11] Employing a performative approach in language teaching not only enables us to slow down, to focus and look at conflicts in slow motion, to rewind and analyze dilemmas in more detail, but drama also opens up spaces to the inner worlds of modern protagonists who are at home on the urban dancefloors of hybridity. This can provide us with rich perspectives on new worlds – as if standing in somebody else's shoes. Some – like Richard Sennett (2013: 274) – argue that 'a lack of mutual understanding should not keep us from engaging with others', especially if we want to achieve something together. Others however, – like the philosopher Slavoj Žižek (2009: 51) – suggest that a dose of alienation seems indispensable for peaceful coexistence, and that 'sometimes alienation is not a problem but a solution'. With reference to Sloterdijk, it might in fact be right to claim that the widespread urge to 'understand each other' needs to be supplemented by the attitude of 'getting-out-of-each-other's-way' by maintaining an appropriate distance and by implementing a new 'code of discretion' (cf. Žižek, 2009: 50).

Understanding can never be more than an approximation, as it aims to negotiate meaning from at least two perspectives. The two drama units described in this chapter were designed to explore the diversity of possible perspectives in small, everyday dramas called 'critical incidents'. Linked to Byram's extended model of ICC, foreign language students experienced cognitive, physical and emotional dimensions in difficult everyday encounters by means of small-form drama activities. The realization that misunderstandings can derive from a multitude of sources and predeterminations and can never be explained by a 'culture-clash' alone (cf. Sen, 2007) has been an important insight for the future language teachers. In drama, language is conceptualized as performative experience; hence, a 'drama in education' approach proves especially valuable for the exploration of emotions and their impact on behavior in critical incidents. Moreover, drama creates awareness of the fact that dilemmas and conflicts are part of the human condition and that sometimes mutual understanding is simply not possible, because life often remains a multilayered and unresolvable mystery.

## Notes

(1) I am indebted to Regina Davies and Ben Andersen for their comments and proofreading this text.

(2) There is no room here for a lengthy critical appreciation of the ongoing academic debate on the term 'intercultural' as opposed to 'transcultural', 'cross-cultural' or others. For a detailed account see Hu (2007) as well as Freitag-Hild (2010a, 2010b).

(3) 'Our shared humanity gets savagely challenged when the manifold divisions in the world are unified into one allegedly dominant system of classification – in terms of religion, or community, or culture, or nation, or civilization' argues Nobel laureate and philosopher Amartya Sen, who sees the hope of harmony in a clearer understanding of the pluralities of human identity namely that we are 'diversely different' (cf. Sen, 2007: 8ff).

(4) The task is straightforward. First, I take a piece of chalk or a pen and jot down my signature on the board. Over the years, both parts, my first and second name have

transformed into something our children call a seismic triggered doodle. Next, I tell the group that they are now supposed to also write their own names as signatures on a piece of paper and next to it a word which stands for one of their secret passions like 'chocolate', 'music' or 'bungee jumping'. Afterwards, the group is told to repeat the task but this time with the 'wrong hand'. It is now important to also tell students to closely monitor what is happening during this activity (a) in class and (b) to them. Important observations that are usually named include time (it takes so much longer to write the name wrong-handedly), achievement (the outcome of trying to 'sign' with the other hand is not nearly as acceptable as the real signature; it is much easier to write a 'normal' word like the secret passion with the wrong hand), repetition (it needs a lot of practice to achieve a better looking result), concentration (it takes much more cognitive effort to accomplish a seemingly simple task like this), emotional reactions like feeling embarrassed or clumsy (there is usually a giggle running through the class during this activity compensating uneasiness with comic relief). In the next phase, I ask the group to reconsider what this activity has in common with learning a new language and to find similarities and differences. The students are usually quick in making the connections with basic principles of learning: At the beginning of learning something new, let us assume a new language, it takes a lot of time to string words together and to form a sentence. Even simple sentences are not expressed flawlessly and it needs a lot of practice until they flow more correctly and fluently. Beyond the much slower speech/language production time, a lot of repetition is necessary to also approximate pronunciation and intonation. Cognitive mobilization is much higher at the beginning and especially when learning a new language it includes overcoming inhibitions to perform in public. Coming to terms with the feeling of clumsiness and uneasiness when dealing with one's own linguistic limitations is often stated as another principle of learning and which leads nicely into the next phase, namely the more general question about what this activity has to do with the way we do things and look at things in general. It may need a couple more prompts to take the students to the realization that many of the routines and operations we perform daily are highly automated activities and that automation is not only a natural way of being more efficient in actions but also in interactions, in behavior as well as in thinking and perception. Hence, learning a foreign language can encompass the empowering experience to deal with our own linguistic as well as cultural limitations.

(5) The participants step behind one of the actors in the freeze frame and establish a symbolic contact to the person's mind by putting a hand on his/her shoulder.

(6) These intercultural training sessions are designed to prepare for job assignments abroad and focus on a cognitive approach to dealing with cultural differences in intercultural encounters. Critical incidents are presented in a narration, followed by a variety of possible explanations in a multiple-choice fashion and finally the situations are explained with references to cultural determinations. Such an attribution seems like an over simplification as it entails the danger of perpetuating collective national identities instead of challenging them. For a more detailed critique, see Küppers (2015: 158ff.)

(7) This phrase was made popular through the episode 'The Germans' of the British TV series *Fawlty Towers*, which was broadcast in the 1970s and later became an international success.

(8) Frankfurt groups usually consist of 10–18 students; the Istanbul group had 60 participants.

(9) Whereas in the Frankfurt groups almost all the courses between 2000 and 2010 usually consisted of students whose families belonged to the German middle classes and only in rare exceptions to a family who had once immigrated to Germany

('migration background'), the Istanbul group consisted of students whose families had once migrated from the countryside to Istanbul or who were born in Istanbul, another group whose relatives had lived in Germany for a considerable amount of time and had re-migrated to Turkey between the 1980s and 2010s, another group who had migrated to Germany themselves with their families or were born there – but had decided to study in Turkey after school ('Abitur'). Last but not least, a large group of Erasmus students took part in this course, too. The majority were Germans without previous contact with Turkey and a few so-called 'Almanci' students usually with German passports with a family background of migration from Turkey to Germany in their third generation.

(10) Rafik Schami is a well-known and very popular German-Syrian author and narrator who was born in Damascus and has been living in Germany ever since he emigrated from Syria when he was 25 years old. Schami is internationally praised for his humorous flow of narration which merges oral Arabic traditions of storytelling with the European tradition of literary essay writing. The perception of the Arabic world in the past and present and migration are the two huge life-topics in Schami's work.

(11) Cf. 'The empathy deficit. Even as they become more connected, young people are caring less about each other'. See http://www.boston.com/bostonglobe/ideas/articles/2010/10/17/the_empathy_deficit/?page=4 (accessed 20 November 2015).

## References


Bertallo, A., Hettlage, R. and Perez, M. (2004) *Verwirrende Realitäten. Interkulturelle Kompetenzen mit Critical Incidents trainieren*. Zürich: Pestalozzianum.

Bonnet, A. and Küppers A. (2011) Wozu taugen kooperative Lernen und Dramapädagogik? Vergleich zweier populärer Inszenierungsformen. In A. Küppers, T. Schmidt and M. Walter (eds) *Inszenierungen im Fremdsprachenunterricht* (pp. 32–52). Braunschweig: Bildungshaus Schulbuchverlage.

Bredella, L. (2010) Interkulturelles Lernen. In C. Surkamp (ed.) *Metzler Lexikon Fremdsprachendidaktik* (pp. 123–126). Stuttgart/Weimar: Metzler.

Byram, M. (1997) *Teaching and Assessing Intercultural Communicative Competence*. Clevedon: Multilingual Matters.

Ehrenreich, S. (2004) *Auslandsaufenthalt und Fremdsprachenlehrerbildung. Das Assistant-Jahr als ausbildungsbiographische Phase*. München: Langenscheidt.

Freitag-Hild, B. (2010a) Transkulturelles Lernen. In C. Surkamp (ed.) *Metzler Lexikon Fremdsprachendidaktik* (pp. 308–309). Stuttgart/Weimar: Metzler.

Freitag-Hild, B. (2010b) Interkulturelle Kommunikative Kompetenz. In C. Surkamp (ed.) *Metzler Lexikon Fremdsprachendidaktik* (pp. 121–123). Stuttgart/Weimar: Metzler.

Haack, A. and Surkamp, C. (2011) Theatermachen inszenieren – Dramapädagogische Methoden in der Lehrerausbildung. In A. Küppers, T. Schmidt and M. Walter (eds) *Fremdsprachenunterricht inszenieren* (pp. 53–66). Braunschweig: Schulbuchverlage.

Hu, A. (2007) Kulturwissenschaftliche Ansätze in der Fremdsprachendidaktik. In W. Hallet and A. Nünning (eds) *Neue Ansätze und Konzepte der Literatur- und Kulturdidaktik* (pp. 13–30). Trier: Wissenschaftlicher Verlag Trier.

Hu, A. (2010) Interkulturelle Kommunikative Kompetenz. In W. Hallet and F.G. Königs (eds) *Handbuch Fremdsprachendidaktik* (pp. 75–79). Seelze-Velber: Klett-Kallmeyer.

Kessler, B. (2008) *Interkulturelle Dramapädagogik. Dramatische Arbeit als Vehikel interkulturellen Lernens im Fremdsprachenunterricht*. Frankfurt am Main: Peter Lang.

Kessler, B. and Küppers A. (2008) A shared mission. Dramapädagogik, interkulturelle Kompetenz und holistisches Fremdsprachenlernen. *Scenario* 2 (2), 3–22. See http://research.ucc.ie/scenario/2008/02/kesslerkueppers/02/de (accessed 20 November 2015).

KMK – Kultusministerkonferenz/Sekretariat der ständigen Konferenz der Kultusminister der Länder in der BRD (ed.) (2004) *Bildungsstandards für die erste Fremdsprache (Englisch/Französisch) für den Mittleren Schulabschluss*. Neuwied: Luchterhand.

Kristensen, S. (2015) Measuring the un-measurable: Evaluating youth mobility as a pedagogical tool for intercultural learning. In A. Küppers and Ç. Bozdağ (eds) *Doing Diversity in Education Through Multilingualism, Media and Mobility* (pp. 31–34). Istanbul: Istanbul Policy Center.

Küppers, A. (2015) Interkulturelle Kompetenzen, Dramapädagogik und Theaterwissenschaft. In W. Hallet and C. Surkamp (eds) *Handbuch Dramendidaktik und Dramapädagogik im Fremdsprachenunterricht* (pp. 145–164). Trier: Wissenschaftlicher Verlag Trier.

Küppers, A. and Trautmann, M. (2008) Kerstin Göbel: Qualität im interkulturellen Englischunterricht. Eine Videostudie. Waxmann: Münster 2005 (review) *Zeitschrift für interkulturellen Fremdsprachenunterricht* 13 (2). See http://tujournals.ulb.tu-darmstadt.de/index.php/zif/article/view/242/234 (accessed 20 November 2015).

Küppers, A., Trautmann, M. and Wolf, T. (2009) Interkulturelle Konflikte inszenieren mit Critical Incidents. *Praxis Englisch* (5), 18–22.

Küppers, A., Schmidt, T. and Walter, M. (eds) (2011a) *Inszenierungen im Fremdsprachenunterricht. Grundlagen, Formen Perspektiven*. Braunschweig: Bildungshaus Schulbuchverlage.

Küppers, A., Schmidt, T. and Walter, M. (2011b) Inszenierungen – Present tense incarnate im Fremdsprachenunterricht. In A. Küppers, T. Schmidt and M. Walter (eds) *Inszenierungen im Fremdsprachenunterricht* (pp. 5–17). Braunschweig: Bildungshaus Schulbuchverlage.

Küppers, A. and Bozdağ, Ç. (2015a) Introduction. In A. Küppers and Ç. Bozdağ (eds) *Doing Diversity in Education Through Multilingualism, Media and Mobility* (pp. 5–8). Istanbul: Istanbul Policy Center.

Küppers, A. and Bozdağ, Ç. (2015b) Conclusion/outlook/recommendations. In A. Küppers and Ç. Bozdağ (eds) *Doing Diversity in Education Through, Media and Mobility* (pp. 41–49). Istanbul: Istanbul Policy Center.

Lippmann, W. (1956) *Public Opinion*. New York: Macmillan.

Mall, R.A. (2003) Interkulturelle Verständigung. Primat der Kommunikation vor dem Konsens? *Erwägen, Wissen, Ethik* 14 (1), 196–198.

Nünning, A. (2007) Fremdverstehen und Bildung durch neue Weltsichten: Perspektivenvielfalt, Perspektivenwechsel und Perspektivenübernahme durch Literatur. In W. Hallet and A. Nünning (eds) *Neue Ansätze und Konzepte der Literatur- und Kulturdidaktik* (pp. 123–142). Trier: Wissenschaftlicher Verlag Trier.

Schami, R. (2011) *Eine deutsche Leidenschaft namens Nudelsalat und andere seltsame Geschichten*. München: Deutscher Taschenbuch Verlag.

Schewe, M. (2007) Drama und Theater in der Fremd- und Zweitsprachenforschung. Blick zurück nach vorn. *Scenario* 1 (1). See http://publish.ucc.ie/journals/scenario/2007/01/schewe/08/de (accessed 20 November 2015).

Schewe, M. (2011) Die Welt auch im fremdsprachlichen Unterricht immer wieder neu verzaubern – Plädoyer für eine performative Lehr- und Lernkultur! In A. Küppers, T. Schmidt and M. Walter (eds) *Inszenierungen im Fremdsprachenunterricht* (pp. 20–31). Braunschweig: Bildungshaus Schulbuchverlage.

Schewe, M. (2013) Taking stock and looking ahead: Drama pedagogy as a gateway to a performative teaching and learning culture. *Scenario* 7 (1). See http://publish.ucc.ie/journals/scenario/2013/01/Schewe/02/en (accessed 20 November 2015).

Schmenk, B. (2010) Intercultural speaker. In C. Surkamp (ed.) *Metzler Lexikon Fremdsprachendidaktik* (pp. 117–118). Stuttgart/Weimar: Metzler.

Schmidt, S. and Thomas, A. (2003) *Beruflich in Großbritannien. Trainingsprogramm für Manager, Fach- und Führungskräfte*. Göttingen: Vandenhoeck & Ruprecht.
Sen, A. (2007) *Identity and Violence: The Illusion of Destiny*. London: Penguin.
Sennett, R. (2013) *Together: The Rituals, Pleasures and Politics of Cooperation*. London: Penguin.
Surkamp, C. (2007) Handlungs- und Produktionsorientierung im fremdsprachlichen Literaturunterricht In W. Hallet and A. Nünning (eds) *Neue Ansätze und Konzepte der Literatur- und Kulturdidaktik* (pp. 89–106). Trier: Wissenschaftlicher Verlag Trier.
Žižek, S. (2009) *Violence: Six Sideways Reflections*. London: Profile Books.

# 7 Staging Otherness: Three New Empirical Studies in *Dramapädagogik* with Relevance for Intercultural Learning in the Foreign Language Classroom

John Crutchfield and Michaela Sambanis

## Overview

If, in recent years, performative approaches have found increasing use in foreign language (FL) pedagogy, this is largely due to the interest generated by individual FL teacher/researchers who have published persuasively on their experiences. In the European context, Manfred Schewe's ground-breaking 1993 study, *Fremdsprachen inszenieren* ('Staging Foreign Languages'), is perhaps the best-known work of this kind, and since then many others have followed, including contributions by Elektra Tselikas (1999) Susanne Even (2003) and Benedikt Kessler (2008). Meanwhile, on the more theoretical side, Wolfgang Hallet (2010), for example, has adapted the social philosopher Judith Butler's concept of *performativity* to make a strong case for seeing the FL classroom itself as an ineluctably performative space, and hence for orienting FL pedagogy toward the training of what he calls 'performative Kompetenz'. In certain respects, these practical and theoretical explorations build upon earlier work in the Anglo–American context by (again to name just a few) Alan Maley and Alan Duff (1978), Gavin Bolton (1979), Stephen Smith (1984) and Elliott Eisner (1985).[1]

Thus, we might very well speak of a 'paradigm shift' in pedagogical theory and practice that directly parallels, albeit at a remove of some 30 years, the more general shift in the fine arts and humanities from an interest in text and artifact to performance, event, happening, etc. (Crutchfield, 2016a).[2] In the field of pedagogy, this has meant above all an interest in *drama*, or more precisely, in *embodied action before witnesses*. Often, these actions are of an 'aesthetic' nature, i.e. they are framed as 'play' and emphasize creativity using artistic means. Hence, one can also understand this shift as a move toward *aesthetic* or *arts-based education*; though here we would have to lay the emphasis on the *performing arts*: drama, dance and music. In other words, the focus is now on techniques that engage the learner's sensuous and kinesthetic body, his/her emotions and imagination, his/her spontaneity and intuition and his/her moral intelligence no less than his/her more familiar cognitive or intellectual faculties. A performative pedagogy is thus *holistic* in intention; and the claim is that it supports deeper, more sustained and more sustainable learning than does the traditional 'frontal' approach, in which students typically remain immobilized at their desks while the only one really 'performing' is the teacher.

In the midst of this enthusiastic hubbub of performative theory and practice, however, one has begun to hear calls for filling in the middle term, i.e. for new empirical research that would (1) connect theory more explicitly to practice and hence lay the scientific basis and justification for what is already being done; (2) correct that practice in areas where it is perhaps less (or differently) effective than is believed; and (3) open up new areas for both practice and theory that might not have been imagined before.[3]

As we have argued elsewhere (Sambanis, 2016), the need for such 'translational research' is particularly urgent now, given the recent efflorescence of neuroscientific studies dealing precisely with the brain structures and mechanisms that underlie learning. Such findings would appear to have direct relevance for the classroom; yet it is important to remind ourselves that the classroom is an infinitely more complex, differentiated, aleatory, unstable and, in a word, messy environment than the laboratory in which neuroscientists typically gather their data. Thus, while the insights of neuroscience into the brain as the 'organ of learning' are both powerful and highly relevant for educators, there is also a high risk of misinterpretation and misapplication. In order to bridge this gap, educators must undertake their own rigorous empirical research to test the postulates of neuroscience in an educational environment. Only then can such postulates be appropriately and sustainably adapted for practical application in teaching.

In short, what is needed is an *evidence-based approach* to new education research. Among the many possible entry points for such research, the current neuroscientific view of the *interplay of emotion and cognition in learning* holds particular interest for FL education, especially where *intercultural learning* is an explicit pedagogical concern. As we will see in what follows, it is no accident that this is also an important area in which performative methods, and above all *drama pedagogy*, can have positive effects.[4]

## Current empirical research in English didactics at the Freie Universität Berlin

Among several empirical studies recently conducted in the Department of English Didactics at the Freie Universität Berlin, three masters theses stand out as particularly relevant to the theme of the present chapter. The first study, 'Dramapädagogische Methoden und affektive Dimension fremdsprachlicher literarischer Kompetenz'[5] (Schuh, 2014; unpublished), comprises a qualitative investigation of the effectiveness of performative approaches in teaching literary texts (in English) to a group of Berlin-area 11th graders, a large proportion of whom had immigrant backgrounds.[6] The second, 'Förderung des Perspektivenwechsels im Englischunterricht durch Dramapädagogik'[7] (Sellin, 2014; unpublished), investigates the extent to which performative approaches can support or encourage the 'shifting of perspectives' in the English as a foreign language (EFL) classroom, and is likewise based on a qualitative study of a group of 11th graders in the Berlin public schools. The third study, 'The effects of self-verbalization on foreign language anxiety' (Redondo, 2014; unpublished), combines qualitative and quantitative methods to assess the levels of anxiety about speaking English among students in three advanced EFL classes in Berlin, and to measure the effects of using self-verbalization exercises as warm-up to an in-class speaking activity.

Taken together, these three empirical studies shed light on the effectiveness of drama pedagogy in the FL classroom, particularly for purposes of intercultural learning. They also exemplify the interdisciplinary, evidence-based approach that is the primary mode of both scholarly research and teaching practice in the Department of English Didactics at the Freie Universität Berlin: an approach in which the fine arts (especially theatre, but also creative writing), FL teaching and learning, and the neurosciences are seen to converge.[8]

# Drama, Affect and Literary Competence

In her unpublished 2014 master's thesis, 'Dramapädagogische Methoden und affektive Dimension fremdsprachlicher literarischer Kompetenz', Nathalie-Anne Schuh investigates the use of a drama-pedagogical approach to handling literary texts in the EFL classroom. The key factor, as Schuh's title suggests, is the 'affective dimension': the emotions. While the overarching concern here is *literary competence* and its relation to the learner's personal development [Persönlichkeitsbildung], Schuh's study offers useful hints as well for the related question of intercultural learning.

Schuh's conceptual framework for understanding literature is Paul Ricoeur's 'Reader Response Theory' or *Rezeptionsästhetik*, albeit as adapted by Bredella and Burwitz-Melzer (2004) for pedagogical purposes. In this hermeneutic framework, the meaning of the text is considered to be the co-creation of author and reader, much as, in contemporary performance theory, a performance is seen as the co-creation of performer and audience (e.g. Fischer-Lichte, 2004; Schechner, 1988). Moreover, this process is both open-ended and, to varying degrees, ambiguous, polysemous, dialectical, even self-contradictory. Because the text is viewed as engaging a non-linguistic reality beyond itself, one can also speak here of a truth-claim as *representation of reality*. As will be seen, this is important for the question of literature's relation to intercultural learning: there too, the assumption is not only that a cultural Other exists outside or exterior to our representations of it, but that an open-ended communicative exchange is both desirable and possible, which would bring our representations closer to that reality, and hence to enable understanding – however limited, provisional and subject to constant revision. Thus literary understanding turns out to be analogous to intercultural understanding, and might in fact be seen as a kind of propaedeutic for it:

> In the engagement with the literary world, the reader's preconceptions are subjected to a transformation that brings about new insights and that accordingly deepens the understanding of his or her own world. (Schuh, 2014: 11)

Of crucial importance for Schuh is the fact that the medium or 'link' [Verbindungsglied] between the world of individual experience and the world of aesthetic/literary experience is furnished by the emotions (Schuh, 2014: 22). Quoting Surkamp (2010: 46), she writes, 'The ability to feel for and empathize with literary characters leads to "the taking of engaged positions, precisely under the aspect of intercultural learning", and in the long term, enables students to take part in social and cultural discourse and to develop an openness toward other points of view' (Schuh, 2010: 24).

All the more so when dealing with literary texts in an FL. In a way that closely parallels the *shifting of perspectives* necessary to intercultural understanding (see below), 'the reader of a foreign-language literary text shuttles constantly between two worlds; he interacts between the world of the foreign language and the world of the mother tongue, between the fictional world and the real, extra-textual world' (Schuh, 2010: 11–12). In the FL classroom, this shuttling activity is merely one aspect of the larger picture: the other is the 'authentic speech situation' of class discussion. 'While the students are testing their linguistic skills in a meaningful context – the discussion of literature being an authentic speech situation – they are also communicating their thoughts about both the literary text and about themselves, their own emotions and the emotions of others' (Schuh, 2010: 12). The result is a perceptual and conceptual widening of horizons.

As emphasized above, the entry point for Schuh is *affect*, which, in Bredella and Burwitz-Melzer's view, plays an essential role in the hermeneutic process.[9] Given the growing body of evidence to suggest that the affective dimension is where a drama-pedagogical approach can be particularly effective, it stands to reason that such an approach could offer advantages for the development of literary competence in the FL classroom. The results of Schuh's qualitative empirical study, conducted using an action research model involving a small group of Berlin-area 11th graders, indicate that this is indeed the case.

## Research methods

The experimental and data-collection phase of Schuh's study consisted of a series of three 90-minute teaching units, in which a randomly selected group of 11th graders (9 boys and 13 girls) at a public school in Berlin were taught English literature using drama-pedagogical activities. For the purposes of the present report, it is important to note the ethnic composition of the class: 10 of the students had Turkish backgrounds, 5 Arabic, 2 African, 3 Asian and 2 German. It is these students' subjective experiences that stand in the foreground of the study.

While the literary texts in question were generically related (both were poems), they were of widely differing types and historical periods: First, the 'Vogon Poem' ('Oh freddled gruntbuggly ...') from Douglas Adams's popular 1979 novel, *The Hitchhiker's Guide to the Galaxy*; and second, William Shakespeare's 'Sonnet 18' ('Shall I compare thee to a summer's day?'). At the end of the drama-pedagogical work on these texts (which involved creative interpretation, rudimentary staging and performance), qualitative data were obtained from the participants via open interviews using the 'Thinking Out Loud' technique.[10] Because the students were divided into five groups (of four or five each), these interviews were likewise conducted in groups and, in an effort to encourage free and spontaneous expression, in the students' first language (German). The interviews were transcribed in accordance with Mayring's (2002) method of literal transcription.

Schuh's study takes as its categorical basis the emotional taxonomy developed by Ulich and Mayring (1992), in which emotions are distinguished according to valence (positive or negative), intensity, frequency, temporality (present, prospective or retrospective) and personal reference (Self or Other). The data analysis procedure is likewise based upon Mayring's (2000) 'Structuring Content Analysis'. Because the students' comments were 'open' i.e. not directed through specific questions, the precise taxonomy of analytic categories arose inductively: (1) Acceptance of Individual Mental Associations; (2) Capacity to Suspend Disbelief and Participate Emotionally; (3) Capacity to Manage Speech-Emergency Situations; and (4) Positive Emotions in the Teaching/Learning Context.

## Research findings

What emerges from Schuh's data is a fairly consistent picture: the drama-pedagogical methods she used had a positive effect on the students in all four categories, regardless of the individual's ethnic background.[11] As she puts it, 'The catalyst of texts and emotional impulses immediately drew the students in on both an affective and cognitive level, and prompted them to spontaneous reactions in their thinking and feeling' (Schuh, 2000: 58). Schuh goes on to conclude that 'drama pedagogy creates a connection between elements of the Self and the literary text, activates the affective memory and opens a space for reflection' (Schuh, 2000: 60).

Although Schuh's study does not concern itself directly with intercultural learning, the structural parallel between literary competence and intercultural competence becomes clear as soon as we see the analogy between *textual* and *personal/cultural* forms of Otherness. Understanding a foreign person or culture and understanding an FL literary text are both, finally, hermeneutic processes: they require *suspension of disbelief* (or 'co-ordination of perspectives'), *emotional engagement* (or 'empathy') and a *tolerance for ambiguity, open-endedness and transformation*. To the degree that drama pedagogy develops these capacities in FL learners, it can be seen as a suitable method for the purposes of strengthening both literary and intercultural competence. As Kessler and Küppers (2008: 17ff) have rightly pointed out, it would remain for the individual teacher to make this connection explicit in class (through choice of materials, exercises and guided reflections), and hence to optimize it as a pedagogical tool.

# Drama Pedagogy and the Shifting of Perspectives

Aurelia Sellin, in her unpublished 2014 master's thesis, 'Förderung des Perspektivenwechsels im Englischunterricht durch Dramapädagogik', directly addresses one of the key components of intercultural learning. She follows Surkamp (2010: 238) in defining *perspective* as 'the subjective view of reality' that 'determines a person's picture of the world', and that is 'influenced by biographical background, psychic disposition, values and norms, internalized conventions, culturally marked schemata of perception and understanding, wishes and needs, knowledge and skills'. The *shifting of perspectives* is thus understood as the ability to 'place oneself into the life situation of another person', and thus to 'reconstruct his or her motive, intention and view with respect to a particular event'. This ability, or rather, this 'complex bundle of cognitive-affective abilities' (Surkamp, 2007: 136) is considered 'essential for all social action', and Sellin (2014: 5) correctly places it at the center of what we have come to call 'intercultural communicative competence'.

Drawing upon the theoretical framework proposed by Byram (1997) and elaborated by Kessler and Küppers (2008), Sellin goes on to note, however, that intercultural communicative competence consists not merely in the ability to place oneself cognitively and emotionally 'in the shoes' of a cultural Other, but also in the ability to critically reflect upon such processes and experiences: 'In the encounter with the realities of a foreign culture, we are dealing with a perspective that is both interior and exterior [...] a dialectical relationship between understanding the Self and understanding the Other' (Kessler & Küppers, 2008: 6). By its very nature, the FL classroom would appear to be especially well-suited to staging such dialectical, self-reflective encounters with Otherness, and hence to encouraging intercultural learning. There, students confront not only an FL, but the foreign culture of which it is both part and expression (Sellin, 2014: 9). Making the most of this potential, however, requires a suitable FL pedagogy, and the growing consensus seems to be that *drama* should have a place there – perhaps even a central place. As Sellin puts it (here paraphrasing Kessler and Küpers, 2008: 9), where intercultural competence is an important educational goal,

> the holistic approach to learning that is characteristic of drama pedagogy offers among other things the possibility of making the abstract – and hence, for school children, difficult to grasp – concept of culture experienceable. (Sellin, 2014: 3, here paraphrasing Kessler & Küppers, 2008: 9)

Sellin points out that in theoretical discussions of intercultural competence and drama pedagogy, despite the emphasis placed on the ability of drama to support the shifting of perspectives, there has been surprisingly little research into how and under what circumstances, if at all, such shifting actually occurs:

> Most articles and studies mention the shifting of perspectives as an essential element of intercultural competence that can be stimulated by drama-pedagogical methods, but few examine it more closely. (Sellin, 2014: 16)

The notable exception, as Sellin mentions, is Jäger (2011). Sellin's project thus represents an attempt to address this gap in research.

## Research methods

The study itself was designed as action research (with Sellin herself as teacher/researcher), comprising a series of eight classes (of 45 minutes each) structured around drama-pedagogical activities. The subjects consisted of

11 girls and 4 boys in an 11th-grade 'Leistungskurs' (advanced course) in English. The level of competence with English was accordingly high.

For the primary drama-pedagogical activity, the 15 participants first divided themselves into 3 groups of 5 persons each. Each group received the same packet of texts, which included brief (five–seven page) encyclopedic biographies plus portraits of four British monarchs: Henry VIII (1491–1547), Elizabeth I (1533–1603), Mary I (1516–1558) and Mary Queen of Scots (1542–1587), chosen for the historical complexity of their familial and political relations with each other. A fifth text was labeled 'Talk Show Host'. (These five texts served as the basis for the *dramatis personae* of the subsequent performance.) The three groups were then each given the assignment of creating and rehearsing, over the course of the following five class meetings (i.e. five instructional hours) as well as outside of class, a drama of approximately five minutes in the style of a contemporary TV talk show and based upon a common conflict among the four 'monarchs'. These three mini-dramas were then to be performed in class.

Sellin's reasons for structuring the activity in this way are worth noting. She justifies the use of factual (biographical) texts rather than, for example, literary texts, on the grounds that they

> [...] portray events and persons with relative objectivity and free of moral judgment, and thus they stop short of providing an interior perspective [Innenperspektive] of character [...] such that personal motives, intentions and the relevant cultural circumstances are hardly perceptible. The task of performing as these characters forces the students, with nothing but their own reality-concept [Wirklichkeitsmodell] to draw upon, to put themselves into the interior perspective of the characters by interpreting, through dialogical confrontation with their own perspective (the exterior perspective [Außenperspektive]) those characters' known actions. (Sellin, 2014: 20–21)

Moreover, insofar as we are dealing here with public figures from a relatively distant historical period, 'the students feel free to dispense with 'political correctness' (Sellin, 2014: 20–21).

The genre of the performance, the popular entertainment format of the TV talk show, was likewise chosen for specific pedagogical reasons: it is both 'a familiar format for students' and one in which typically 'conflicts are elucidated from different perspectives' (Sellin, 2014: 22). Furthermore, for purposes of supporting the shifting of perspectives, the talk show has the specific advantages of (1) including all participants (performers plus audience) in the aesthetic reality of the performance; (2) encouraging an open and 'dramatic' style of presentation, which is not experienced as embarrassing, since it belongs to the genre; (3) encouraging each actor to consider carefully the facts relating to his/her character in order to fully embody and pursue that character's interests; and (4) encouraging the audience to participate spontaneously, which in turn requires the actors to react i.e. improvise.

The data were gathered during a reflection phase that followed the students' dramatic performances. The reflections occurred in the form of 10 minute 'semi-open' group interviews (according to role, i.e. all three 'Elizabeths' were interviewed together, etc.), which were conducted with a list of questions on hand, written by the researcher in advance, but only referred to as seemed desirable in the given situation. The interviews were documented using an audio recorder, fully transcribed and anonymized, and subsequently organized in table-format as Question and Answer, with additional columns for Comment, Categorization and Interpretation. This division of the data served the important purpose of clearly separating the subjects' actual utterances from the researcher's subjective interpretations. The data analysis phase proceeded both deductively (according to the conceptual framework that also guided the formulation of the interview questions) and inductively with a view to gaining new and potentially useful conceptual hints from the participants themselves.[12]

## Research findings

Due to absences on the day of the final performance, only one of the three groups was fully represented and hence able to perform their play. This apparently unfortunate circumstance nevertheless had the experimental benefit of enabling Sellin to distinguish in her data analysis between students who actually *performed* their prepared roles and students who prepared their roles but did not perform them. This turned out to be a difference that made a difference, especially with regard to the question of the shifting of perspectives:

> The encounter between one's own perspective and that of another takes place above all in the experience of performance [Aufführung]. (Sellin, 2014: 38)

One key factor turns out to be the quality of emotional engagement. It is perhaps no accident that this finding is in line with what Schuh discovered in her study of literary competence (see above). On the one hand, certain aspects of performance that are also present in rehearsal (movement, voice, gesture, etc. in short: *embodied action*) are shown to be advantageous for the affective dimension of the ability to shift perspectives: 'Because it also supports the affective dimension, embodied action must thus be seen as a particularly helpful strategy for the shifting of perspectives' (Sellin, 2014:

47). Nevertheless, the difference between *performing* (before an audience, albeit in this case only one's classmates and the teacher) and merely *rehearsing* remains marked, especially when dealing with an Other whose 'behavior is subjectively perceived to be unusual or bizarre' (Surkamp, 2007: 136; quoted in Sellin, 2014: 48), as for example with the historical figure of Henry VIII. This is an important point for the question of intercultural learning, since it is not, finally, the *near* Other who poses the greatest and most urgent challenges for understanding, but the *distant* or, if one prefers, *radical* Other, the Other whose behavior is truly 'foreign', 'bizarre' or, in extreme cases, antithetical to one's own deepest values. What is it about *live performance* (i.e. before an audience) that makes it particularly powerful as a way of approaching this kind of intercultural challenge – at once emotional, imaginative, cognitive and moral?

The answer has to do with the nature of 'liveness' itself. As Sellin points out, the moment of live performance evinces characteristics of a 'speech emergency' [Sprachnotsituation] as described by Tselikas (1999). Because of the unpredictability of live performance, especially where audience participation is involved (as for example in the talk show), the actor is forced to some extent to *improvise in character.* This can only succeed through an act of intercultural/intersubjective imagination that is both 'linguistic-cognitive' and 'corporeal-emotional' (Jäger, 2011: 130; quoted in Sellin, 2014: 47). What is involved is not simple identification, but a dialectical encounter or coordination: an *as if*, in which the perspective of the Other is imagined, embodied and *staged* in its distinctness from the perspective of the Self without supplanting it. As Sellin writes,

> The gain in experience is owing above all to [the effort of] maintaining the *as if*-level. Through this seriousness in play, which forced [the performers] to act out of the reconstructed interior perspective of their characters, they were able to gain experiences they would not otherwise have had. Their emotional investment, moreover, was revealed in the fact that their comments often referred to specific moments, whereas those who didn't perform spoke much more generally of the rehearsals. [...] According to my observations, when they do not perform, the likelihood of a superficial and, on the cognitive level, limited shifting of perspectives is much greater. (Sellin, 2014: 49–50)

For this reason, among several recommendations she makes for optimizing the benefits of drama pedagogy, Sellin (2014: 52) emphasizes the importance of actual performance [Aufführung]: whenever possible, it ought to be a part of drama-pedagogical work, 'despite the orientation toward process'. As her findings show, this is especially true where the larger educational goal of intercultural learning is in focus. Performance provides the affective heat, so to speak, that transforms factual knowledge into lived (and living) understanding.

## Anxiety and Self-Verbalization

As point of departure for her unpublished 2014 master's thesis, 'Speak it out loud! The effects of self-verbalisation on foreign language anxiety', Natascha Redondo notes the widespread phenomenon of anxiety about speaking an FL – even (or perhaps especially) in an FL classroom, where speaking would seem to be an indispensable aspect of the learning process.

In a cogent introductory survey of the scientific literature on anxiety, Redondo (2014: 30) points to Hans Jürgen Eysenk's famous characterization of anxiety as a form of 'cognitive interference' in which 'distracting, self-related cognition such as excessive self-evaluation, worry over potential failure, and concern of the opinions of others' means that the anxious person's attention is 'divided between task-related cognition and self-related cognition, thus making cognitive performance less efficient' (Eysenk 1979). Anxiety is particularly destructive in FL learning, moreover, because it interferes with all three stages of cognitive activity: input, processing and output.[13]

Foreign language speaking anxiety (FLSA) is thus qualitatively different from the conventional 'fear of public speaking', and is best understood as one form of foreign language anxiety (FLA), which can manifest itself in both productive skills (speaking and writing) and receptive skills (listening and reading), and which, as Redondo (2014: 6) notes with reference to recent research, fully one-third to one-half of FL learners report having experienced at debilitating levels. Given the key role that emotions are now recognized as playing in learning processes, it is no surprise that a highly negative emotion such as anxiety would have detrimental effects on learning.[14] Nor is this all, for anxiety not only undermines performance in the particular learning situations where it arises, but also tends to become associated with learning as such, and hence to have negative effects that are more long term (cf. McGee, 1999: 24; Spitzer, 2003: 161). Anxiety is thus understood to present a major disruption to any kind of learning process.

But the case of FL learning would appear to be especially fraught due to the very nature of the task itself. FL learners are being asked to speak a language they are by definition still in the process of learning, in other words: *to perform a role they cannot possibly have mastered yet*. Seen in this way, any anxiety they feel is a natural human response to a situation in which one is exposed to embarrassment and doomed to (at least partial) failure. The real question, then, is not how to dispel anxiety altogether, but how to make it less debilitating, more manageable or (ideally) even productive for the task of FL acquisition (Crutchfield, 2016b). This last possibility is worth considering, since research has shown that 'a certain modicum of stress actually stimulates learning and leads to the release of dopamine in the brain, thereby making it ready to receive new information' (Hoegg, 2011: 94). This is also true of the stress associated with what sociologists call the 'demonstration effect' [Vorführeffekt], whereby the presence of observers (as is usually the case in a classroom) affects performance either positively or negatively, again depending on the 'dose' of stress involved (Hoegg, 2011: 94).

One answer is to look for ways to change the culture of the FL classroom itself, to make it a place in which embarrassment and failure are acceptable, a place where learners feel 'safe'. Precisely this has often been pointed to as one of the great strengths of drama pedagogy: by embracing playfulness and by framing classroom activities in aesthetic terms (e.g. the 'as-if' situation of role-play), it dissolves the conventional boundary between failure and success, and renders both experiences useful for the purposes of learning. Indeed, in the context of a drama activity, particularly one involving improvisation, the 'failure' associated with risk-taking can be more fun – and more fruitful for learning – than 'success' where no risk is involved.

Redondo approaches the matter differently. Drawing on Süleymanova (2011), she hypothesizes that learners' FLSA itself can be directly reduced through the technique of 'self-verbalization'. Seen from the perspective of drama-pedagogy, this technique could be considered a kind of personal 'warm-up' or 'rehearsal' prior to an assignment or activity involving oral presentation.

Redondo (2014: 33) follows Smolucha (1992) in using the term 'self-verbalization' to refer to the practice of speaking to oneself: 'a communicative technique in which the usually hidden mental processes [...] are spoken out loud'. Redondo goes on to note that, in John Hattie's comprehensive meta-analysis of evidence-based education research, self-verbalization and self-questioning strategies – especially when employed to retrace or organize one's own learning process – produce significant positive effects on learning outcomes (Hattie, 2009).[15] Taking this cue, Redondo's study represents an attempt to obtain empirical data on the effectiveness of self-verbalization in reducing FLSA within the specific context of the EFL classroom.

## Research methods

Redondo used a mixed (qualitative-quantitative) design based upon a questionnaire, and gathered her data in three different advanced EFL classes at two different secondary schools in Berlin. Participation was voluntary and anonymous. The participating students, of which there were 56 (30 female and 26 male, all between 14 and 17 years old), were asked to give two spontaneous oral descriptions (in English) of two different picture-puzzles, the first without and the second with a prior self-verbalization exercise.[16] Each of the two phases of this procedure was followed by a questionnaire with a total of 23 items, many of which were multiple choice or involved a Likert scale. The first part of the questionnaire asked for biographical data and for a self-assessment of FLA levels.[17] The second focused on the participant's subjective experience of the self-verbalization exercise. The questions were composed in the subjects' native language (German) in order to avoid difficulties of comprehension. (Three of the participants, however, did report a first language other than German; but as their competence in German was fluent, this was not seen as a prohibitive factor.)

## Research findings

In her subsequent analysis, Redondo divides her data into four categories: Language Attitudes, Motivation, Learner Strategies and Foreign Language Speaking Anxiety, in accordance with the categories covered by the items that constituted the questionnaire. Of particular interest are the data on FLSA, which fall into a classic Gauss distribution or 'bell curve': most students report feeling either 'relaxed' (41.07%) or 'not very relaxed' (39.29%), as opposed to the two extremes of 'very relaxed' (8.93%) or 'not relaxed at all' (10.71%), when speaking English in front of the class. Taken at a glance, this would indicate that fully half of the participants (50%) experience FLSA either mildly ('not very relaxed') or intensely ('not relaxed at all').

The part of the questionnaire that dealt with the experience of the self-verbalization exercise revealed, somewhat surprisingly, that the participants at either extreme ('very relaxed' and 'not relaxed at all') experienced the exercise most positively, particularly in terms of its use as a strategy for warming-up, organizing thoughts and finding phrases. In terms of its effectiveness for motivation and for reducing FLSA, however, the results were inconclusive. Nevertheless, Redondo reasons that, if indeed self-verbalization is effective in helping learners warm up and organize their thoughts before speaking in front of the class, it should also help motivate students to do so, and reduce the anxiety that impedes them. Establishing a direct link, however, between self-verbalization and FLSA reduction would require more extensive research, likely over a longer period of time.[18]

Although Redondo's study does not directly connect drama-pedagogical (or other performative) methods to the question of intercultural learning, the connections are there to be made. As with the other two empirical studies discussed in this chapter, Redondo's work points toward the crucial role that emotions play in learning – especially FL learning. If those emotions are 'negative' or unpleasant, as is generally the case with anxiety, the quality of learning will likely suffer as a result. Furthermore, to the degree that learner anxiety in the FL classroom condenses around the issue of *speaking in front of others*, we are dealing with a version of something well-known to actors, namely, *stage fright*. Just as an actor can 'know his lines cold' and yet still 'go up' (i.e. forget his text) in the moment of performance, so an FL learner can memorize his/her vocabulary, grammar, idioms, etc. and yet seem to forget it at the moment he/she opens his/her mouth to speak in the 'live situation' of the classroom.[19] A single experience of this kind can plant the seed of anxiety about future performances. Repeated experiences will quite literally change the structure of the brain, such that performance anxiety becomes 'hardwired' and therefore all the more difficult to alleviate (Spitzer, 2003: 172).

The long-term consequences of this for FL acquisition could be quite debilitating: Not merely a retardation and superficialization of the learning process, but also (and for our purposes here, perhaps even more significantly) a subjective 'staining' of both the FL *as material* and the foreign culture *as idea* with negative emotional associations. It would require a different sort of investigation to discover to what degree such affective marking impacts future behavior with respect to the foreign culture, or rather, *vis-à-vis* the actual individuals who represent it. But it is not difficult to imagine that if, for example, I have highly negative emotional associations with the French language as a result of years of 'failing' in French class, those associations will be activated whenever I encounter actual French people or hear them speak. Regardless of how well or poorly I may have 'acquired' their language, my anxiety will continue to haunt my interactions with them, and may indeed, by blocking or drying up the flow of empathy necessary for a shifting of perspectives, prevent me from reaching any kind of intercultural understanding. This would be a double loss: not only would my interactions with French people remain superficial and externalized, lacking in the internal dimension by which I might imaginatively inhabit their point of view and come to understand it, but a part of myself would remain in darkness as well.

Thus, from the earliest possible stage of FL education, the learning environment and the learning process itself ought to be infused with positive emotions. A performative pedagogy – one that draws upon aesthetic practices in the performing arts – would seem to offer a strong possibility for achieving this. By embracing an ethos of creativity and play, performative approaches de-claw the very idea of 'failure', and hence potentially reduce learners' anxiety about it. Redondo's study draws attention to one simple technique – self-verbalization – which could very easily be introduced into a classroom setting, and which could serve as an effective warm-up to any kind of in-class speaking activity. If integrated in a systematic and consistent way, this technique could have an important anxiety-reducing function within a broader performative pedagogy.

And even beyond the classroom, anecdotal evidence suggests that self-verbalization could be an effective tool for 'warming-up' before real-world encounters: in essence rehearsing in private, like an actor in front of a mirror. In fact, when one considers the fundamentally performative aspect of all social interaction (cf. Goffmann, 1959; Turner, 1974), the idea of rehearsing seems not merely metaphorical but entirely practical and appropriate.

## Conclusion

Whatever else they may be, cultures are 'made things': made by actual people over the course of long, complex but traceable histories. They could have been made differently, and they could be unmade or remade. Perhaps now more than ever before, these histories are intertwined – economically, politically and ecologically – and increasingly inter-dependent. To remain 'in one's own world' is to turn a blind eye to the other worlds that impact it and shape it in the profoundest ways. Thus, it is no longer enough simply to recognize the legitimate existence of other cultures and to grant them, from an ethical point of view, their sovereignty. (This was the 'multicultural' moment of the 1980s and early 1990s.) Now we must endeavor to engage other cultures (and the other cultures within ourselves) in meaningful dialogue, or rather, in *intercultural meaning-making*. The call for an increased emphasis on intercultural communicative competence in FL teaching and learning is not primarily a matter of instrumentality or economic interest, i.e. understanding the cultural Other in order better to sell him our products. It is a matter of existential urgency: understanding the Other so that we can peaceably coexist, learn from each other and cooperate on solving problems that affect us all. This is predicated upon mutual respect, which in turn depends upon mutual understanding: a perception and appreciation of the Other not as mirror image, inversion or negation of the Self (the imperialist view) and not even simply in the dignity of his/her Otherness (the multicultural view), but in a dynamic exchange in which Self and Other are seen to be inextricably intertwined, woven of diverse threads, and like Penelope's shroud, constantly woven, unraveled and re-woven. This is the ultimate meaning of interculturality.

The FL classroom is indispensable in this intercultural process, since for many young people, even for those living in culturally diverse communities, it is one of the few places in which they can be supported in practicing a *conscious, empathic and self-reflected engagement with another culture*. As the three new empirical studies we have reviewed here show, there is strong evidence to suggest that a performative approach to FL teaching not only supports language acquisition, but also (and in many cases simultaneously) exercises and strengthens those personal aptitudes or 'savoirs' (Byram, 1997) that are essential for the development of intercultural communicative competence.

## Importance for FL teaching and learning

While drama pedagogy, because of its holistic approach, can be seen to support learning in general, its effectiveness is particularly strong where the educational aim involves competences dependent upon empathy and imagination. Intercultural communicative competence is certainly one of these, and the FL classroom is the setting *par excellence* for its training (Aden, 2014; but cf. also Chapter 4 in this volume). More than in other subjects, even those in which a cultural or historical Other is addressed as an object of understanding (such as History, Geography, Anthropology, Sociology or Literature), the FL classroom lends itself to being structured as a zone of authentic encounter with Otherness. In certain respects, the FL classroom is already part-way within the Other's territory: we are learning to speak the Other's language, and that means learning to embody it, to think and feel through it and to imagine the complex of values, practices, histories and dreams – in short, the *way of life* – of which it is an expression. The FL classroom, in other words, is the ideal space for staging intercultural learning. By addressing the learner's sensuous and kinesthetic body, emotions, imagination and moral intelligence in addition to his/her rational and analytical mind, drama pedagogy provides a powerful set of tools for making this happen.

Thus, while it is certainly better than nothing at all, it is also far from sufficient simply to 'expose' students to other points of view, whether cultural, historical, political, etc. Whatever knowledge is gained through such purely cognitive processes remains, so to speak, 'on the outside', like pictures in a book of foreign places and foreign faces. Within the context of education, it is above all in the crucible of *performance* – embodied action for and in the presence of witnesses – that this external knowledge is transmuted into a deep, inner understanding of other lives, an understanding infused with empathy, imagination, curiosity and respect.

Nor should we forget that intercultural learning is hardly a one-way street. The cultural Other to our Self is in turn a Self to whom we are a cultural Other. Intercultural communication is not only about, for instance, German schoolchildren learning to communicate with cultural sensitivity in English, French, Chinese or Arabic. As of this writing, the massive influx into Germany of refugees from the Middle East means that, in short order, many thousands of children will be entering German schools who have no knowledge of the German language, and only the vaguest idea of German culture. For them and their parents, the German as an SL classroom will be the single most important place where they learn who their hosts – and now fellow citizens – actually are. In many ways, the stakes are significantly higher for such learners: German is not merely a subject they need to learn for academic and professional success, but something that will be essential to their well-being as new members of a transcultural German (and European) society. FL and SL classrooms will be, to a large extent, the place where this encounter occurs. Whether it succeeds or not will depend on whether that environment is experienced as a place of recognition and address of the whole person, and whether the intercultural potential of the classroom itself is fully realized through a pedagogy oriented toward the performativity of culture.

## Importance for FL teacher education

For such a performative pedagogy to be practiced successfully, it must first be successfully taught and learned as part of teacher training – and not in the traditional manner, but on its own terms. That is to say: unlike the teaching of other pedagogical methods, *the teaching of performative pedagogy must be an exemplary instance of itself*. Teachers in training must themselves experience the aesthetic/holistic processes of performative teaching and learning before they can be expected to practice it effectively in their future classrooms (Crutchfield, 2015). It goes without saying that this experiential training must be of the highest quality, taught by people with a great depth of experience, knowledge and skill both in the performing arts and in the classroom.[20]

On the surface, then, we would appear to be caught in an infinite regress: How can we begin to educate differently until we have educated the educators differently? And how and by whom will the educators of the educators be educated? But change does happen – even in education – and there's no reason to abandon all hope. Despite the proverbial inertia of institutions, there is much that teacher training programs can do on their own to foster an interest in performative approaches. On the one hand, performative techniques are always available to individual instructors; one need only try them out.[21] This sort of experimentation ought to be encouraged. Concurrently, education faculty should be actively motivated to seek additional 'in service' training in performative pedagogy or even in the performing arts themselves – especially drama.[22]

Most education programs will also have some modicum of curricular flexibility, for example in selecting themes for 'special topics' courses or electives, or in determining a proportion of the syllabus content for an otherwise standard course. In these cases, the focus should be on performative pedagogy, even if this amounts to no more than alerting students to its existence, having them read an article or two from *Scenario* or exposing them to a sample of exercises. Better still would be the devotion of one or two entire courses to performative pedagogy, courses which would themselves be taught performatively, so that future teachers gain first-hand experience of its benefits and challenges.[23]

One additional step deserves mention, and it is the one exemplified by the three masters theses presented above: in programs where a bachelor's or master's thesis is required or optional, students should be encouraged to do empirical research into performative pedagogy, ideally using some form of 'action research'. Apart from the scientific value of (and current need for) such research, it has the added educational value of offering future teachers the opportunity to experience performative techniques in action, to observe them closely in real time and to evaluate their effectiveness on a scientific basis. As the three masters theses presented in this chapter show, the results, though modest in scope, are convincing in themselves, and they make an important contribution to the creation of a performative teaching and learning culture.

## Notes

(1) For a summary of this history from two different perspectives, see Lutzker (2007) and Schewe (2013).

(2) This shift has its historical origins in the 1950s: in the arts with John Cage's experimental 'happenings' at Black Mountain College beginning in 1952, and in the social sciences and humanities with the philosopher J.L. Austin's 1955 William James Lectures at Harvard University (later published as *How To Do Things With Words*), the anthropologist Victor Turner's 1957 dissertation, *Schism and Continuity in African Society* and the sociologist Erving Goffman's 1959 study *The Presentation of Self in Everyday Life*. All three point toward the idea that human behavior is best understood as *performance*.

(3) Schewe (2011) calls for this in a programmatic way. Were one to listen-in at academic conferences relating to these topics, however, one would also have to conclude that the current emphasis on empirical research is at least in part motivated by the perceived need to 'justify' aesthetic education to the governmental agencies and private foundations that either determine education policy or fund its implementation. Since these are often the same agencies and foundations that also fund education research, the rhetorical problem is not an easy one to solve.

(4) We use the term *drama pedagogy* (and the adjective *drama-pedagogical*) to cover the same semantic field as the term *Dramapädagogik* in the German-speaking context: The use of drama, often in the form of isolated classroom activities, to support learning in a variety of school subjects. It is thus not synonymous with *performative pedagogy*, but might be considered a major subset of it.

(5) 'Drama-Pedagogical Methods and the Affective Dimension of Foreign Language Literary Competence'. Unless otherwise noted, all translations from German to English are the present authors'.

(6) In the German school system, these students would be approximately 17 years old. The schools in question would be of the *Gesamtschule* type (known in the Berlin system as *Integrierte Sekundarstufe* or ISS), i.e. a non-selective secondary school, similar to a U.S.-American public high school or to what in Great Britain would be called a 'comprehensive school'.

(7) 'Promoting the Shifting of Perspectives in English Class through Drama Pedagogy'.

(8) cf. Sambanis (2013). In conjunction with this emphasis on empirical research, the Department of Didactics co-hosted the first Global LangEduConference 'Focus on Evidence' in December 2015, at the Catholic University of Eichstätt (Germany). The speakers included neuroscientists David Poeppel, Friedemann Pulvermüller, Rita Franceschini, Steffi Sachse and Manfred Spitzer. For more information, see http://www.foe2017.de. For conference proceedings, including transfer discussions and interviews, see Böttger and Sambanis (2016).

(9) As Schuh puts it, drawing on Bredella and Christ (2007) and Nünning and Surkamp (2006), 'The reader is addressed and challenged as thinking and feeling subject [...] and directly involved in the meaning-making process' (Schuh, 2006: 10). This claim takes its place within the larger context of the discussion of the significant (and now scientifically evidenced) role emotions play in learning, in terms of both cognition and motivation. cf. Spitzer (2002), Wolff (2004) and Sambanis (2013).
(10) cf. Doff (2012: 185): 'Thinking Out Loud [Lautes Denken] involves the unfiltered verbalization of a subject's thoughts immediately following a mental, active or interactive process' (quoted in Schuh).
(11) Be it noted, however, that since there was no control group in the study, it is impossible to say anything definite about the precise degree to which these methods are more effective than, for example, the more traditional 'frontal' approach.
(12) Here, Sellin refers to Mayring's (2000) 'Qualitative Content Analysis'.
(13) Here, Redondo refers to the 'Three Stages Model of Cognitive Processing in Second Language Acquisition' (cf. Tobias, 1986).
(14) For empirical evidence, Redondo draws here primarily upon the work of Robert C. Gardner. See especially Gardner (2010). Likewise, her theoretical framework for understanding FLA is the 'Socio-Educational Model' proposed by Gardner and MacIntyre (1993).
(15) The effect size that Redondo refers to is $d=0.64$, significantly higher than Hattie's 'hinge point' $d=0.40$.
(16) A different picture-puzzle was used for each phase; both, however, were Berlin themed and taken from Drews (2010).
(17) It is important to note that, in the questionnaire, Redondo does not use the word 'anxiety' or any of its synonyms, but instead formulates her questions positively, e.g. 'I like to participate in discussions in English', with answer options on a Likert scale from 'applies completely' to 'not correct at all'.
(18) This makes sense on a purely intuitive level as well, since anxiety – even situational anxiety like FLSA – does not generally disappear 'overnight'. A study in which self-verbalization was made a regular part of FL class activities over the course of a longer period of time and with a larger and/or more diverse sample would be necessary to determine its true effectiveness.
(19) One must be careful, however, not to push the analogy between acting and learning an FL too far. Acting is in many respects much more circumscribable. But for our purposes here it is worth pointing out that both the actor and the FL learner are tasked with speaking words which are quite literally *someone else's*. Anxiety about performing is thus interpretable as a fear of failing to 'do justice to the role', and hence of appearing incompetent. The answer (and the goal) in both cases is to *make the words one's own*, i.e. to embody them in an authentic way.
(20) Such individuals are, admittedly, difficult to find. But one has to start somewhere; and one plausible solution – though far from ideal – would be to bring professional performing artists as experts into collaborative partnerships with university teacher training programs. The result might look something like the 'artist-in-residence' concept one sees at North American universities; the difference being that, instead of 'residing' in their respective aesthetic department (of Dance, Theatre, Music, Creative Writing, Visual Arts, etc.), they would be part of the School of Education.
(21) This is essentially what happens in many school classrooms, as well as in university classrooms in other subjects – wherever the individual teacher happens to have an interest in performative approaches. In the context of teacher education, however, it would also be of crucial importance to make sure that students are made

consciously and critically aware of these techniques *qua* techniques, and of their justification and purpose.

(22) See for example Peter Lutzker's (2007) study of a series of workshops in which a group of Waldorf School teachers learned the art of clowning.

(23) A comprehensive survey of performative approaches to French FL teacher training at universities in the German-speaking area is to be found in Fleiner (2016).

## References

Aden, J. (2014) Theater education for an empathic society. In C. Nofri and M. Stracci (eds) *Performing Arts in Language Learning* (pp. 52–57). Rome: Edizioni Novacultur Rome.

Bolton, G. (1979) *Towards a Theory of Drama in Education*. London: Longman.

Böttger, H. and Sambanis, M. (eds) (2016) *Focus on Evidence: Fremdsprachendidaktik trifft Neurowissenschaften*. Tübingen: Narr Francke Attempo.

Bredella, L. and Burwitz-Melzer, E. (eds) (2004) *Rezeptionsästhetische Literaturdidaktik*. Tübingen: Gunter Narr.

Bredella, L. and Christ, H. (eds) (2007) *Fremdverstehen und interkulturelle Kompetenz*. Tübingen: Gunter Narr.

Byram, M. (1997) *Teaching and Assessing Intercultural Communicative Competence*. Clevedon: Multilingual Matters.

Crutchfield, J. (2015) Creative writing and performance in EFL teacher training: A preliminary case study. *Scenario* 9 (1), 3–34. See http://www.ucc.ie/en/scenario/scenariojournal/ (accessed 22 June 2016).

Crutchfield, J. (2016a) Brief encounters: Reflections on the performative integration of creative writing in the foreign language classroom (with a workshop for teachers). In O. Metz and M. Fleiner (eds) (in preparation) *The Arts in Language Teaching. International Perspectives: Performative – Aesthetic – Transversal*. Berlin: LIT Verlag.

Crutchfield, J. (2016b) Fear and trembling: The role of 'negative' emotions in a performative pedagogy. *Scenario* 9 (2), 101–114. See http://www.ucc.ie/en/scenario/scenariojournal/ (accessed 22 June 2016).

Doff, S. (2012) *Fremdsprachenunterricht empirisch erforschen: Grundlagen, Methoden, Anwendung*. Tübingen: Gunter Narr.

Drews, J. (2010) *Berlin Wimmelbuch: Ausbruch aus dem Zoo*. Berlin: Wimmelbuch Verlag.

Eisner, E. (1985) *The Educational Imagination: On the Design and Evaluation of School Programs* (2nd edn). New York: Macmillan.

Even, S. (2003) *Dramagrammatik: Dramapädagogische Ansätze für den Grammatikunterricht Deutsch als Fremdsprache*. München: Iucidium.

Eysenck, H.J. (1979) *Intelligenz: Struktur und Messung*. Berlin: Springer.

Fischer-Lichte, E. (2004) *Ästhetik des Performativen*. Frankfurt am Main: Suhrkamp.

Fleiner, M. (2016) *Performancekünste im Hochschulstudium: Transversale Sprach-, Literatur- und Kulturerfahrungen in der fremdsprachlichen Lehrerbildung*. Berlin: Schibri.

Gardner, R.C. (2010) *Motivation and Second Language Acquisition: The Socio-Educational Model*. New York: Peter Lang.

Gardner, R.C. and MacIntyre, P. (1993) A student's contributions to second language learning: Part 2: Affective variables. *Language Learning* 26 (1), 1–12.

Goffmann, E. (1959) *The Presentation of Self in Everyday Life*. Garden City, NY: Doubleday Anchor.

Hallet, W. (2010) Performative Kompetenz und Fremdsprachenunterricht. *Scenario* 4 (1), 5–18. See http://www.ucc.ie/en/scenario/scenariojournal/ (accessed 22 June 2016).

Hattie, J. (2009) *Visible Learning: A Synthesis of 800+ Meta-Analyses on Achievement*. London: Routledge.

Hoegg, G. (2011) *Wie Schüler denken*. Berlin: Cornelsen Verlag.

Jäger, A. (2011) *Kultur szenisch erfahren. Interkulturelles Lernen mit Jugendliteratur und szenischen Aufgaben im Fremdsprachenunterricht*. Frankfurt am Main: Peter Lang.

Kessler, B. (2008) *Interkulturelle Dramapädagogik. Dramatische Arbeit als Vehikel des interkulturellen Lernens im Fremdsprachenunterricht*. Frankfurt am Main: Peter Lang.

Kessler, B. and Küppers, A. (2008) A shared mission: Dramapädagogik, interkulturelle Kompetenz und holistisches Fremdsprachenlernen. *Scenario* 2 (1), 3–22. See http://www.ucc.ie/en/scenario/scenariojournal/ (accessed 22 June 2016).

Lutzker, P. (2007) *The Art of Foreign Language Teaching*. Tübingen: Francke Verlag.

Maley, A. and Duff, A. (1978) *Drama Techniques in Language Learning*. Cambridge: Cambridge University Press.

Mayring, P. (2000) Qualitative Inhaltshanalyse. In U. Flick, E.v. Kardoff and I. Steinke (eds) *Qualitative Forschung. Ein Handbuch* (pp. 468–475). Reinbek: Rowohlt.

Mayring, P. (2002) *Einführung in die Qualitative Sozialforschung* (5th edn). Weinheim: Beltz Verlag.

McGee, A. (1999) *Investigating Language Anxiety through Action Inquiry: Developing Good Research Practices. Göteburg Studies in Educational Sciences*. Göteburg: Acta Universitatis Gothoburgensis.

Nünning, A. and Surkamp, C. (2006) *Englische Literatur unterrichten: Grundlagen und Methoden*. Seelze-Velber: Klett, Kallmeyer.

Redondo, N. (2014) The effects of self-verbalisation on foreign language anxiety. Unpublished MA thesis, Freie Universität Berlin.

Sambanis, M. (2013) *Fremdsprachenunterricht und Neurowissenschaften*. Tübingen: Gunter Narr Verlag.

Sambanis, M. (2016) Drama activities in the foreign language classroom: Considerations from a didactic-neuroscientific perspective. In S. Even and M. Schewe (eds) *Performatives Lehren, Lernen, Forschen: Performative Teaching, Learning, Research* (pp. 206–221). Berlin: Schibri Verlag.

Schechner, R. (1988) *Performance Theory*. London: Routledge.

Schewe, M. (1993) *Fremdsprache inszenieren: Zur Fundierung einer Dramapädagogischen Lehr- und Lernpraxis*. Oldenburg: Didaktisches Zentrum, Carl von Ossietzky Universität.

Schewe, M. (2011) Die Welt auch im fremdsprachlichen Unterricht immer wieder neu verzuabern: Plädoyer für eine performative Lehr- und Lernkultur! In A. Küppers, T. Schmidt and M. Walter (eds) *Inszenierungen im Fremdsprachenunterricht: Grundlagen, Formen, Perspektiven* (pp. 20–31). Braunschweig: Diesterweg.

Schewe, M. (2013) Taking stock and looking ahead: Drama pedagogy as a gateway to a performative teaching and learning culture. *Scenario* 7 (1), 5–23. See http://www.ucc.ie/en/scenario/scenariojournal/ (accessed 22 June 2016).

Schuh, N.-A. (2014) Dramapädagogische Methoden und affektive Dimension fremdsprachlicher literarischer Kompetenz. Unpublished MA thesis, Freie Universität Berlin.

Sellin, A. (2014) Förderung des Perspektivenwechsels im Englischunterricht durch Dramapädagogik. Unpublished MA thesis, Freie Universität Berlin.

Smith, S. (1984) *Theater Arts and the Teaching of Second Languages*. Reading, MA: Addison-Wesley.

Smolucha, F. (1992) Social origins of private speech in pretend play. In R. Diaz and L. Berk (eds) *Private Speech: From Social Interaction to Self-Regulation* (pp. 123–142). Mahwah, NJ: Erlbaum.

Spitzer, M. (2003) *Lernen, Gehirnforschung und die Schule des Lebens*. Heidelberg/Berlin: Spektrum Akademischer Verlag.

Süleymanova, R. (2011) *Abbau der Sprechangst im Unterricht Deutsch als Fremdsprache. Eine empirische Untersuchung am Beispiel der Integrationskurse*. Berlin: Verlag Dr. Köster.

Surkamp, C. (2007) Fremdes spielerisch verstehen lernen: Zum Potenzial dramatischer Texte und Zugangsformen im Fremdsprachenunterricht. In L. Bredella and H. Christ (eds) *Fremdverstehen und interkulturelle Kompetenz (Giessener Beiträge zur Fremdsprachendidaktik) (pp. 133–147)*. Tübingen: Narr Francke Attempo.

Surkamp, C. (ed.) (2010) *Metzler Lexikon Fremdsprachendidaktik*. Stuttgart: Metzler Verlag.

Tobias, S. (1986) Anxiety and cognitive processing of instruction. In R. Schwarzer (ed.) *Self-Related Cognition in Anxiety and Motivation* (pp. 35–54). Mahwah, NJ: Erlbaum.

Tselikas, E. (1999) *Dramapädagogik im Sprachunterricht*. Zürich: Orell Füssli.

Turner, V. (1974) *Dramas, Fields, and Metaphors. Symbolic Action in Human Society*. Ithaca, NY/London: Cornell University Press.

Ulich, D. and Mayring, P. (1992) *Psychologie der Emotionen. Grundriß der Psychologie (5)*. Stuttgart: Kohlhammer.

Wolff, D. (2004) Kognition und Emotion im Fremdsprachenunterricht. In W. Börner and K. Vogel (eds) *Emotion und Kognition im Fremdsprachenunterricht* (pp. 87–103). Tübingen: Gunter Narr Verlag.

# Part 4

# Focus on Specific Performative Approaches: Process Drama and Playback Theatre

# 8 Using Process Drama to Engage Beginner Learners in Intercultural Language Learning

Julia Rothwell

Until relatively recently, intercultural communication in a school context was largely theorised as a bilingual project, an attempt to compare the communicative behaviours and cultural beliefs and mores of the learners' first language (L1) with those of the classroom target language (TL). Although this approach is still integral to much contemporary intercultural theorising, it is now widely perceived as insufficient (e.g. Pennycook, 2012). It is based on the outdated assumption that learners can use a shared L1 such as English as a basis for reflecting on language and culture of self and other; yet, in Australia, for example, around 30% of students have an L1 other than English. As Scarino and Liddicoat (2009: 5) note, 'In developing a contemporary stance, language teachers must consider and respond to notions of complexity and change'. Moreover, in today's culturally and linguistically hybrid nations, the bilingual approach increasingly contains at least the seeds of stereotypical 'us and them' thinking (Kramsch & Whiteside, 2008). This is particularly true when most students have very limited exposure to additional language learning, as is the case in countries such as Australia, New Zealand, the UK and the USA. They therefore have little time to explore the nuanced diversity of socio-cultural groupings within countries which officially use a specific language. This lack of time on task can also have implications for learner engagement in terms of their perception of actual language outcomes and of the purpose of language study. A further impediment to engagement in language learning can be the classroom pedagogy itself, so often out of step with adolescent learners and their times.

A contemporary intercultural approach therefore needs to focus on three interwoven outcomes: intercultural understandings beyond the English/TL nexus, specific TL knowledge and skills in use and, crucially, the engagement of students in language learning through meaningful content and stimulating 21st-century orientated pedagogy. Without this engagement, the other two projects are largely doomed. The process drama-languages research study underpinning this chapter was an attempt to confront these three interconnected issues simultaneously – the need for both a bicultural and a multicultural approach to intercultural work, the need to make limited language learning outcomes seem worthwhile and 'usable' and the need to explore engaging 21st-century ways of teaching languages in an intercultural context. In this chapter, the impact of process drama on each of these issues is explored, using classroom and interview data from an 18-week action research doctoral study in an urban Australian school. I show how process drama as languages pedagogy laid the groundwork for an effective intercultural approach to language learning in the 21st century.

## The Study

In what follows, I draw on data which emerged from work with a class (12- to 13-year-old males and females) in its first year at an Australian public secondary school. As teacher-researcher, I taught the class German for 18 weeks, using two connected process dramas, interviewing and questioning students as we went along. The students came from multiple feeder primary schools. Some were absolute German beginners, some had between one and three years of prior learning. However, the language learnt/retained was extremely variable due to the diversity of primary programmes. The data are drawn from transcripts of classroom video-recordings and from student focus interview and questionnaire material collected throughout the study. All students completed questionnaires and most of them participated in voluntary interviews at some stage.

## Intracultural Meets Intercultural Learning

In the early 20th century, Bakhtin (1981) described the creation of any text as a struggle to make meaning with another. Even within native speaker groups, using a particular word or phrase does not guarantee it will conjure up the same images and meaning for another native speaker. Today's school students live in a time of massive global migration, and the struggle to make meaning is far greater as the diversity of L1s in many communities makes communication a minefield of potential misunderstanding and cross purposes. At the very least, without intercultural experience through language learning, contact with the culturally 'other' can be superficial or labelled as 'too hard' and avoided completely.

One of the attributes of an intercultural competence according to Byram (2006) is a critical cultural awareness – citizenship education as part of language learning and, in the 21st century, citizenship involves multilingual and multicultural subjects (Kramsch, 2009). As the present study suggests, the language learning experience has the potential to pay more localised as well as international dividends for students living in multicultural communities; more generic intracultural understandings can develop alongside more bilingual intercultural ones. Even if students never travel overseas, this approach could better equip them for their future lives in Australia. Therefore, in the process drama described below, I wanted to provide both generic and bilingual contexts for learning about language and culture. As I explain, the structure of process drama is particularly suitable for developing this kind of approach.

## Process drama and intercultural language learning

Process drama is an improvisatory style of drama in education and is a performative pedagogy approach rather than a means to a theatrical end performance. The pedagogical emphasis falls predominantly on improvised or spontaneous interaction in role, although written tasks can also be integrated, as they were here. The adoption of role is often more sustained than in a typical language role play, involving relationships, varied contexts and texts, and slips across time and space. In fact, process drama involves three key elements of intercultural work identified by Kramsch (1993): imagination, time and space. By exploring life as another, living across time and space, learners can better acquire a sense of language and culture as evolving over time in a co-constructive way.

Many of the tasks undertaken for this drama-languages sequence of work (Appendices A and B), whether focused more on dramatic or linguistic experience, are adapted from established process drama activities (e.g. Neelands & Goode, 2000) including Pretext, Teacher in Role, Shoulder Tap, Conscience Alley, Freeze Frames, Gossip Mill, Whole Class Role Play, Inside-Outside Circles, Body Sculpting. In the first nine-week unit of the drama in the study (Appendix A), students become forced migrants aboard a ship. The drama explores the personal language challenges of the migration experience common to so many Australians. In the second nine-week unit (Appendix B), the migrants are in Berlin in 1961 as the Berlin Wall goes up. They 'experience' a key historical period and event which still has strong cultural reverberations for German peoples and German life. These two narratives encompass the *action of the plot* (Morgan & Saxton, 1985). Every process drama also has an underlying central question which becomes the *action of the theme*, in this case, 'What is it like to leave your homeland for ever and live in a new country using a new language?' The intention in both units was to extend students' understanding of the influence of different personal and cultural histories on language group membership; in Bakhtin's (1981) terms, to explore with learners the concept of *heteroglossia* or many voices in our heads which influence our meaning-making. In Kramsch's (2009) terms, I wanted to lead students to a perception of language as:

> ... not just an instrumental activity for getting things done but as a subjective experience, linked to a speaker's position in space and history, and to his or her struggle for the control of power and cultural memory. (Kramsch, 2009: 190)

However, it is also necessary to counter the possibility of creating stereotypical images of migrants as helpless victims, and to encourage learners to embrace rather than shy away from intercultural encounters. Therefore, although the drama highlights the lack of everyday power which accompanies limited language proficiency, learners are also able to rediscover the resources we almost all have to make meaning, despite language difficulties.

## Phases of process drama

A process drama is loosely structured round three interwoven kinds of activity: *enrolment, experiential* and *reflective* (O'Toole, 1992). These phases of the drama represent a physically, cognitively and affectively *active* approach to intercultural language learning (Piccardo, 2013; Rothwell, 2013). The drama phases are initiated by a *pretext* (O'Neill, 2006) which serves as an orientation both to the dramatic narrative and, sometimes indirectly, to the theme behind the drama. It can be anything; a verbal text such as a story or poem, realia such as a pile of clothing, a photograph or video clip and so on. The way the pretext is interrogated and presented by the teacher can be used to influence the initial direction of the drama (O'Neill, 2006). In language terms too, it can be a more exciting hook into the language content of the unit than, for example, a series of flash cards.

### *Enrolment phases*

Enrolment can be a gradual process, and this development of role means learners become more deeply involved in the dramatic context and relationships than in a brief and often scripted role play, typical of the beginner language classroom. The drama for the present study began as learners pondered the possible story behind an illustration of a man departing his family from the picture book, *The Arrival* (Tan, 2006). They then read an original ship's passenger list from the *Sophie*, a ship which came to Brisbane, Australia, from Hamburg, Germany, in 1865. Each group of students went into role as a family from this ship, now going back to Germany, and a range of early activities built their belief in their roles and family relationships (see Appendix A). They then posed for archival government photographs, expressing their family relationships and feelings on departure, both physically for the camera and verbally in German. Language drills and focus activities, contextualised by the dramatic world, are interspersed through this work. The students also adopted other roles intermittently, such as immigration officers, residents of Hamburg and job centre staff. The teacher's roles across the units included ship's captain, immigration officer, a cook in a hostel and a bus driver.

### *Experiential phases*

Once the students/migrants have their family photographs taken, the enrolment phase of the drama is already interwoven with the *experiential* phase which advances the action of the plot. Appendix A provides further examples of the experiential tasks that learners undertook as part of these phases in Unit 1, culminating in their immigration interviews, in which they had to satisfy the immigration officers (teacher and rotating students in role) that they can speak enough German to enter the new country. In this task, the dual tensions of the classroom requirement to speak German and the dramatic need to enter the country led to what O'Toole (1992: 132) calls 'emotional disturbance' related to frustration and power relations in the classroom and the imaginary world. This is affectively stimulating for the students; as Jake[1] put it, 'I was in the zone!'

In the second unit of the drama (Appendix B), the students were still migrants, firstly disembarking from the ship to a mixed welcome from locals, then seeking work in Berlin. They had crossed space and time and were living in a migrant hostel in Berlin in 1961 just before the Berlin Wall went up. Examples of key tasks are a 'coffee and cake' session, where the migrants are invited to meet the locals, and a written job application. Students learnt about the post-war politics of Germany via the internet (in English), applied for jobs (in German) and travelled to work in different suburbs. Their families were then separated by the erection of the Wall. By transporting the learners over time to Germany and then having them live there in 1961, we (teacher and students) were able to explore more fully the migration process and the language challenges it can bring to individuals who don't share the cultural knowledges and referents of native speakers or long-term residents.

It can be seen from the units of work that the drama offers opportunities for a wide range of genres and modes to be experienced by learners, including photographs and captions, a protest meeting, an interview, meeting people on the ship, a job application, a cake recipe as well as many simpler dramatic strategies used to drill vocabulary and focus on form (Appendix A). In Halliday's (1978) terms, the variety of field, tenor and mode available through these genres, combined with the way drama brings students 'out of their seats', is a significant contributor to learners' energy and sense of realness and their consequent engagement and sense of purpose in the learning as the student commentary in Figures 8.1–8.17 shows.

Moreover, several oral tasks differ from those more commonly used with beginners; they require spontaneous use of language by teacher and students in role without the use of personal palm cards. As the data discussion below demonstrates, the dramatic enrolment encourages learners to risk this kind of interaction and use what little German they have to participate. Authentic texts and realia such as a passenger list in Gothic script, 1945 documentary footage from the internet, a migrant's suitcase, a map of Berlin suburbs in 1961, a 1960s poster of a soldier at the Wall, also make contact with the other culture more tangible, imaginable and 'do-able'. They help students realise that, as Warriner (2011: np) puts it, history 'weighs on words'. The learners' sense of purposeful learning and authentic meaning-making, through connections to the discursive world beyond the classroom, is exemplified by Tom's statements at interview (Figure 8.1).

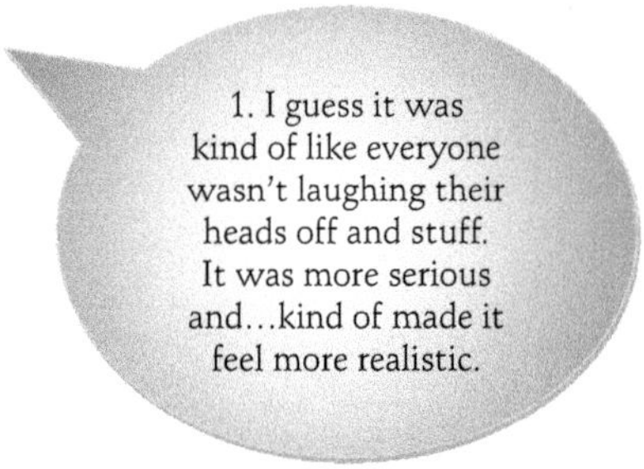

1. I guess it was kind of like everyone wasn't laughing their heads off and stuff. It was more serious and...kind of made it feel more realistic.

**Figure 8.1**

## *Reflective phases*

The third type of phase in a process drama (as in Figure 8.1) is reflective. It is probable that the opportunities for reflection incorporated into the drama and through the interviews enhanced the sense of a serious, worthwhile project for learners. The reflective tasks offer a focused thinking experience at various 'distances' within and beyond the drama (Eriksson, 2011). These tasks can be undertaken in the TL or in English. For example, 'freezing' a scene from the drama to convey an emotional moment is further removed from the drama and the German language than actually role playing an afternoon tea; watching a (teacher-generated) German news video allows students to view the immigrants from a different time and place, from another's perspective; allowing learners to discuss (in English) migrant language testing policies or a video of their own performance in their immigration interview are even more distanced tasks. As many suggest (Liddicoat, 2007; Turnbull & Dailey O'Cain, 2009), this kind of abstract cognitive work, integral to an intercultural approach, cannot be fully achieved through the TL by beginner or even intermediate learners. The integration of reflection with enrolment and experiential work is the key to process drama as a pedagogy for intercultural language learning.

## Target language in use

The structure and forms of process drama also lend themselves to the development of the other two contributing factors for intercultural language, learning highlighted in the introduction: developing confidence and skills to interact in a foreign language (FL) and engaging learners in language learning. In this section, classroom video data are used to show how the drama provides the space where learners can *and want to* risk using a new language in imaginary but life-like spontaneous interaction. This opportunity to create a dramatic interaction through their role as playwright seems a more useful preparation for unpredictable intercultural encounters than the often formulaic and decontextualised exchanges of many beginner classrooms. As Kramsch and Whiteside (2008) suggest, successful intercultural communication involves the ability to approximate someone else's language *and* to shape the context in which one learns and uses the language. Here, learners are *shaping* the classroom talk.

Particularly in the beginner classroom, teacher/student talk is regularly composed of simple, three-part turns, often referred to as initiation-response-feedback (IRF) (van Lier, 2001), for example:

**T**: What colour is your jumper?
**S**: My jumper is brown.
**T**: Yes, it's a brown jumper.

At its most reduced, this IRF model of talk can lead to monotonous interaction which requires little cognitive or affective engagement on the learner's part, beyond remembering the word for brown. Researchers (e.g. van Dam, 2002) demonstrate that limited and thoughtfully implemented IRF can have a beneficial place in language classrooms; but it is always teacher controlled and dominated and, used exclusively, can be an obstacle to 'the creation of contingent discourse and coherent discussion' (Donato, 2004: 292).

This kind of classroom talk can be what Bakhtin (1981) terms *authoritative*. The interaction is predetermined by the authority of the speaker/s or their text and by the authority of the limited focus on a specific topic or form. It is interaction wherein the learner is listening to and fitting into someone else's script without the opportunity to innovate or personalise the text. Consequently, such speech is 'sharply demarcated, compact and inert' (Bakhtin, 1981: 343). However, analysis of data from the drama languages classroom demonstrates that enrolment in the drama can change the nature of the language classroom talk. Authoritative discourse can be disrupted by responding to or bypassing it with *internally persuasive* speech (Bakhtin, 1981: 345). This occurs 'When thought begins to work in an independent, experimenting and discriminating way' (Bakhtin, 1981: 345).

Such speech is *double-voiced* (Bakhtin, 1981), running in two channels: one where the speaker is thinking about the situation and the relationships of the speakers to decide what to say, and another where the body is actually producing the words to make meaning. Rather than a rote response, interaction involves a (usually imperceptible) consideration and realisation of the situation, purpose, relationships and communicative medium/s of the interaction (Halliday, 1978), and the cultural or intercultural context in which they are realised. Dervin and Liddicoat (2013) note that such pragmatic understandings are significant for a deepening understanding of the relationship between language and culture, yet traditional versions of classroom talk inhibit this exploration. The restrictions relate to: who says what when; acceptable gestures, behaviours and signs to accompany speech; what topics are discussed; and which aspect of one's identity it is permissible to reveal.

By defining classroom talk as a genre, the potential for change – over time and with intent – is apparent. As Bakhtin (1986) writes, genres are relatively stable, but since they emerge from all possible human activities, they are also boundless in their ultimate diversity, subject to change and innovation in response to social history itself. Others, such as Diamond (2000) and Halliday (1993), also highlight the contradictory aspects of genre as persistent but open to challenge. Halliday states that they are, of themselves, normative and limiting structures, a regulatory framework which guides our social interaction, but their relationship with culture means they also contain the seeds of change.

The traditional form of the classroom talk genre requires learners to perform simply as 'willing student'. Yet, as Burns (2001) and Norton (2013) note so clearly, personalised conversation beyond the classroom is shot through with more than one discursive version of ourselves. Our many discursive memberships allow us to connect with each other as we perform and recognise different discourses *and* to realise that people's discourse memberships vary within and between countries and cultures. By working through a drama in contexts where different linguistic, social and historical and language discourses might pertain (such as being a migrant, perspectives on the Berlin Wall division or collapse), the learners can begin to understand the potential for intra- and intercultural understandings and misunderstandings.

## Learners as playwrights in the target language

The transcript extracts which follow are from a video recording of a whole 64-turn class role play where the students were in role as migrants on board a ship. There had been a storm at sea, and one of the consequences envisaged by the students was that most of the food boxes had been washed overboard. The migrants were protesting the lack of food to the captain of the ship (teacher in role).

In this whole class role play, the context for the interaction was pre-established, as well as the participants' roles, the time and the place, but the trajectory of the conversation and the development of roles and relationships were unscripted and unprepared. This means that each turn was contingent on what came before (van Lier, 1996). According to O'Neill (2006), this sense of unpredictability and mystery develops the dramatic tension and hence the depth of student enrolment. Contingency also mirrors intercultural encounters far more accurately than continuous teacher-scripted performance. This kind of spontaneous interaction also serves to take students well out of their 'comfort zone' as inexperienced users of the TL, adding a frisson of excitement to the proceedings.

This was the students' first attempt at such an extended role play, and I have listed the phrases which I had introduced, explained and written up on the board earlier in the session to support them if they wished. These phrases are highlighted in the transcripts. Significantly, several students in role moved beyond this language or used it in creative ways.

(German only written on the board)

(1) Wir sind hungrig! *We are hungry!*
(2) Wir brauchen Essen! *We need food!*
(3) Wieviele Kisten sind übrig? *How many boxes are left?*
(4) Was essen Sie, Herr Kapitän? *What are you eating, Captain?*
(5) Meine Kinder werden hungrig. *My children will go hungry.*
(6) Meine Familie wird krank. *My family will get sick.*
(7) Kein Essen und das Wasser ist braun! *No food and the water is brown.*
(8) Was für eine Katastrophe! *What a catastrophe!*
(9) Das reicht doch jetzt! *That's enough!*
(10) Wer kriegt das Essen? *Who is getting the food?*

The words on the board represented a limited, authoritative script for learners to reuse, but they were already using what Bakhtin (1981) might call *internally persuasive speech* – making the script their own through their choice of phrase and use of their bodies and voices to convey anger and frustration. By adopting a conscious, *double-voiced* process, they chose different ways to express hunger, using gesture, loud volume and facial expression to emphasise their emotional commitment to the drama and the oral protest. Interestingly, I had to practise my (the captain's) 'entry' with them beforehand to encourage them to raise their voices as I approached – a classroom talk boundary which one can cross in the drama.

Learners also chose *when* to insert the phrases, overlapping almost every turn as they took on the conventions of the protest meeting genre. This gave them far more control over the text than an IRE model of interaction where learners wait to be called or are chosen to speak, and it is meaningful preparation for the initiative which has to be taken in intercultural encounters. Indeed, across the 64-turn transcript, there were four examples of a turn sequence where, rather than teacher–student–teacher, the exchange goes T–S–S–T; the students did not wait for me to speak. Even when I did speak, the turn was often part of a much longer, meandering sequence of meaning-making rather than the tight, tripartite rhythm of an IRF pattern. When students were engrossed in the dramatic situation, their role as passengers often overrode their more passive student interaction habits.

## Adopting the playwright functions

In the original classroom study, several (interrelated) reasons for students' willing participation in the drama-languages experience were identified, such as the physicality of the drama (Rothwell, 2011), the connectedness to worlds beyond the classroom (Rothwell, 2015) and the affective tensions generated by the drama-languages work (Rothwell, 2013). The present focus is on the effects of the opportunity to contribute to the unfolding narrative of the drama, via enrolment in an imagined world. Throughout the drama-languages experience, it appeared that the teacher and the learners were expressing their new roles by adopting several *playwright functions* (Dunn, 2011). During the study, it became clear that using the playwright functions as an analysis tool can serve two purposes for the language teacher and researcher. It can highlight how the dramatic roles, relationships and settings led students to productively override traditional classroom interaction rules: how they can become 'brave'. Intercultural conversation is often limited by a fear of the unknown, of losing face, of embarrassment when one doesn't understand, whereas these learners took risks with language. The analysis of playwright functions also helps to clarify the value of the playwright role to language learning in terms of extending the language in use and engagement in learning.

In her work with a middle school drama club, Dunn drew on O'Neill's (1995) original definition of four playwright functions to identify nine functions in the club participants' dramatic play. In this discussion, I focus on Functions 1–5 below:

(1) Maintaining the narrative.
(2) Extending the narrative.
(3) Intervening (positively) to advance the narrative.
(4) Reinforcing an extension or advance (actively integrating the advance or interruption to the text through a relevant contribution).
(5) Intervening to interrupt the narrative (comedic or non-comedic).
(6) Resisting an advance (reacting to the advance by actively resisting or contradicting it).

(7) Reviewing the narrative.
(8) Ignoring (passively ignoring the advance).
(9) Sabotaging (blocking that may include denying the existence of the dramatic frame entirely). (Adapted from Dunn, 2011: 18)

## Maintaining, extending and advancing functions

In Table 8.1, the student use of the provided phrases *maintains* the narrative to great effect – passengers loudly and physically protest their hunger and the captain denies responsibility. The annotated Table 8.2 illustrates student and teacher use of the *maintaining and extending* functions.

**Table 8.1** The role play begins

**Preparation phase transcript** *(all names are pseudonyms)*

**2.09** Claire is already thumping fist as I am talking about the process

**2.14** As we move into the activity, Kit is already playing with language to get into role:

**Kit:** Wer ist der Essen? *Who is the food?* (shaking spread, upturned hands for emphasis)

**T/R:** Wo *(Where)* – there are your question words (points to wall)

**Kit:** Wo ist der Essen? *Where is the food?*

**2.49** David is 'warming up' his fists

**3.09** Hamish, Imogen and Anna also gesticulating (can't see rest of class at this stage)

**3.17** After one abortive entry as captain of the ship, I re-enter and all students respond animatedly and together, protesting with their chosen phrase from board. Then:

| *Turn* | *Original transcript* | *Translation* |
|---|---|---|
| **1** | **T/R:** Was ist mit euch? ... Was ist denn das? Was ist all diese Br ... ouhaha auf dem Schiff? Was ist passiert mit euch? Was ist das Problem? ///slight overlap | *What's the matter with you? What's all this commotion on board? What's happened to you? What's the problem?* |
| **2** | **Imogen:** Meine Kinder si ... (then other sts join in, repeating phrases) | *My children are ....* |
| (One student is thumping the air in protest; Hamish is pointing energetically at me; Imogen raises herself lightly out of the chair as she speaks; Anna bounces her hand on her lap.) | | |
| **3** | **T/R:** Ok. Ihr habt kein Essen. Wir haben kein Essen. Alles ist wegflotiert/// | *Ok you have no food. We have no food. Everything has floated away.* |
| **4** | **Nick:** Wir sind hungrig!/// | *We are hungry!* |
| **5** | **T/R:** (Defensive) Die Kisten sind umgekippt/// | *The boxes have been knocked over.* |

*(Continued)*

**Table 8.1** Continued

| *Turn* | *Original transcript* | *Translation* |
|---|---|---|
| **6** | **Nick:** Wir sind hungrig! | *We are hungry!* |
| **7** | **Kit:** Meine Kinder werden hungrig/// ... indistinguishable simultaneous student speech. | *My children will get hungry!* |

Note: /// indicates overlapping speech; **TR indicates** teacher-in-role (as ship's captain). Highlighted phrases are taken verbatim from whiteboard.

**Table 8.2** Maintaining, extending and advancing the narrative

| *Turn* | *Original transcript and translation* | *Playwright function and annotation* |
|---|---|---|
| **25** | **T/R:** Ihr kriegt alle Wasser<br>*You're all getting water* | Extend<br>Captain is extending the food issue to say there's plenty of water |
| **26** | **Kit:** Keine Essen *No Food* | Reinforce<br>Extracting a phrase from a sentence on the board, Kit reuses language to contradict the captain and so, indirectly, reinforces the captain's extension. |
| **27** | **T/R:** Viel Wasser (other students starts to mutter)<br>*Lots of water* | Maintain<br>Captain keeps his defensive strategy going, maintaining the food/water theme. |
| **28** | **Kit:** Wasser ist braun!<br>*Water's brown* | Extend<br>Using the rest of the longer sentence on the board, Kit integrates the teacher's T25 extension and in doing so, extends the narrative further. |
| **29** | **T/R:** Wasser ist? *Water is?* | Maintain<br>Teacher either didn't hear or is playing for time as she seeks new ways to maintain the interaction. |
| **30** | **Kit+another St:** Braun!///<br>*Brown* | Maintain<br>Students forcefully maintain Kit's extension into the water theme. |
| **31** | **Nick:** Ich bin bose!///<br>*am angry!* | Advance<br>Nick introduces an expression of feeling into the argument and thus advances the narrative into territory beyond the physical loss of food. |

**Table 8.2** Continued

| *Turn* | *Original transcript and translation* | *Playwright function and annotation* |
|---|---|---|
| **32** | **T/R:** Das Wasser ist braun. Das ist ok; ein bisschen ... (Sts mumbling – inaudible whether L1 or FL) *The water is brown. That's ok. A bit ... .* | Maintain<br>Here the teacher is obviously fumbling and the parallel student mumbling could represent disengagement which distracts her. |
| **33** | Hamish: ?Rosa *[?Pink]* | Barely audible<br>The water, perhaps, is pink?? An attempt to enter the fray at all costs perhaps. |
| **34** | David & Nick: (banging fists onto knees but also smirking) Wir sind hungrig! *We are hungry!* | Maintain<br>Trying to keep the talk going perhaps, the boys chant in unison – unable to find new speech they revert to maintaining the original theme with strong gestural emphasis. This is one of three occasions when the flagging interaction was resurrected by a student using the FL (a different student each time). |

*Extending* and *advancing* the narrative are the most adventurous playwright functions. As can be seen from Table 8.3, in the protest meeting role play they were used by students as much as by the teacher.

Table 8.4 demonstrates the use of the *advancing* function by Kate and Kit. I interpreted the advancing function to mean that the speaker broke with the theme or style of the previous few turns to switch the content and often the tenor and linguistic function of the narrative interaction. As the teacher in role held back, this most powerful function was taken up almost solely by learners (Table 8.3). Table 8.4 indicates that this function often took the form of a question which, in an authoritative IRF model of classroom talk, is the domain of the teacher. This kind of interaction pattern was also noted by Kao and O'Neill (1998) in their teaching English to speakers of other languages (TESOL) drama work with university students, but is perhaps more surprising in a classroom of learners who have minimal language proficiency and are relatively young.

In this sequence, Kate initiated an advance by using a phrase off the board (T14). In doing so, she turned the tone from one of anger to one of suspicion and resentment – and managed to revive a flagging interaction. She made a coherent move from the issue of the passengers' lack of food to imply that the captain perhaps wasn't suffering in the same way.

In an adventurous switch to a pleading role at T16, Kit asked, 'Kann[st] du nicht sehe[n]?' (Can you not see?). This utterance, intensified by Kit's

**Table 8.3** The distribution of the playwright functions across teacher and student turns

| *Playwright functions (Dunn, 2011)* | *Student turns* | *Teacher turns* |
|---|---|---|
| Maintaining: Maintains the narrative with no attempt to redirect | 11 | 9 |
| Extending: Extends the narrative with no attempt to redirect it | 4 | 6 |
| Intervening to advance the narrative in a new direction | 7 | 1 |

hand gesture, indicated an affective engagement with not just the anger but also the potential frustration of the passengers. This apparent engagement led to the most complex language work attempted in this activity. Kit correctly assembled a question by reversing the verb and pronoun, a form he had heard endlessly but had so far had no formal instruction in. He had noticed that *kann* is phonetically the same word as the English (but we did not focus on this as a form until the following term), although he used the first-person form instead of the second person. To complete his meaning, he used the verb *sehen* which we focused on at the start of the unit to describe what we could see, hear, taste, etc., on deck. Again, he used the more familiar first-person *sehe* instead of the correct infinitive form *sehen*. Despite us and even within this error, the question was comprehensible and carried a strongly emotive interpersonal emphasis. Moreover, Kit managed to complete this compound sentence, begun in T16, at T19 with 'Dass keine Essen', so that in total he said, 'Can you not see ... that no food?' Subordinate clauses in German, even with a missing verb in the second clause, are not commonly used by beginners and, even when focused on in later years, it is a form which can take a while to become embedded for English L1 speakers as the word order is so very different.

Although Table 8.4 illustrates that the advancing function can be effected through the simplest strategy of using a sentence from the board (T14), in the role play as a whole, *only* the advancing function elicited language such as that created by Kit at T16 and T19. This is language which is transformed – without a specific model, the learner has drawn on passive exposure to multiple forms and hypothesised, *á la* Swain (1985), how to make meaning by putting them together in new ways. Learners used different playwright functions to participate in the drama using the FL, but it seems that the freedom to initiate narrative can drive the willingness to 'go out on a limb' and, in so doing, exploit learner agency in a linguistic sense. Moreover, they can find headspace to hypothesise despite the contingent nature of the talk. All playwright functions are useful in maintaining and elaborating the text, but the advancing function can be seen as the core of what O'Neill (1995: 148) describes as the 'animating current' of the playwright functions. It appears that it can also provide a concurrent animating effect in the language learning process.

**Table 8.4** Advancing the narrative

Was ... Teacher-supplied phrase from the board used

| *Turn* | *Original transcript (all names pseudonyms, T/R=teacher/ researcher)* | *Translation* | *Playwright function* |
|---|---|---|---|
| **12** | **Tom:** Ich bin krank. | *I am sick* | Extending |
| **13** | **T/R:** Du bist krank? Also. Dann w ... als wir in Deutschland sind kannst du Medizin haben. | *You're sick. Good. Then w ... when we're in Germany you can have some medicine.* | Extending |
| **14** | **Kate:** Was essen Sie, Herr Kapitän? | What are you eating, Captain? | Advancing |
| **15** | **T/R:** Ich? Ich esse nichts. Ich ... ich habe ein bisschen Brot. Nichts anderes. Ein bisschen Brot. | Me? I get nothing to eat. I ... I get a bit of bread. Nothing else. A bit of bread. | Reinforcing the advance |
| **16** | **Kit:** Kann du nicht sehen? | Can you not see? | Advancing |
| **17** | **T/R:** Se ... Was? Was? Sehen - was?// | What? See what? | Resisting an advance |
| **18** | **St ?:** D ... Gewitter// | Storm ... | Reinforcing the advance |
| **19** | **Kit:** ... dass keine Essen | ... that no food | Reinforcing the advance |

Intervening to advance the narrative is, moreover, a controlling function (Dunn, 2011), and hence student appropriation of it marks a significant change in the classroom talk. In its potential to initiate questions, to challenge the teacher (albeit in role) and to control and change topic, this particular playwright function can be a medium for language and narrative choice. Rather than the talk being a passive adoption of the teacher's script, there is intentionality in the interaction which van Lier (1996) claims is an important element of learner motivation to participate. Moreover, owning the agency to switch topic, tenor or function of the language in use is a necessary skill for the speaker who is trying to maintain or develop an intercultural conversation. Agency is crucial to what Warriner (2011) and Kramsch and Whiteside (2008) refer to as 'shaping' or 'reframing' the interaction.

The use of the extending and advancing functions in particular also enriched the narrative beyond merely sustaining it. It is probable, therefore, that they also played a part in developing an artistic response to the dramatic interaction in students (Winston, 2010), a sense of co-creating the drama alongside the language, a creative purpose to the language use. This combination of belief in role, creative license and practical learning appeared to contribute much to learners' positive responses to the drama-languages experience.

## Engagement in Intercultural Language Learning

Learning a language is a challenging cognitive activity. Therefore, high-level outcomes will be more likely if a satisfying engagement in the experience persuades learners to participate willingly and energetically in language creation and reflection. If successful language learning is defined by an intercultural approach, then it can be argued that the cognitive demands of a more critical pedagogy are even greater and engagement even more necessary. Apart from deepening the scope of the learning by providing context, situation and relationships for interaction, the dramatic connection to a wider narrative can help to avoid the boredom and limitations associated with the recycling of mundane early learner topics, such as shopping, hobbies and family members. Drama can also help place more emphasis on oral work, which, according to many in this class, is often superseded by excessive focus on writing the TL.

Questionnaires and interviews throughout the study highlighted the learners' approval of the experience in general and the reasons they gave for this approval. The comments offered below are necessarily limited but could readily be augmented by many others collected during the study. Several themes emerged from this evidence which relate to learner engagement in the linguistic and intercultural aspects of the learning.

### Engagement through language in use

Almost all learners found the drama language experience *preferable to any prior language learning experience*, and none of them did not enjoy it. Commentary at the beginning and end of the study made it possible to compare learners' past experiences with this one, which they did in these terms (Figures 8.2–8.4):

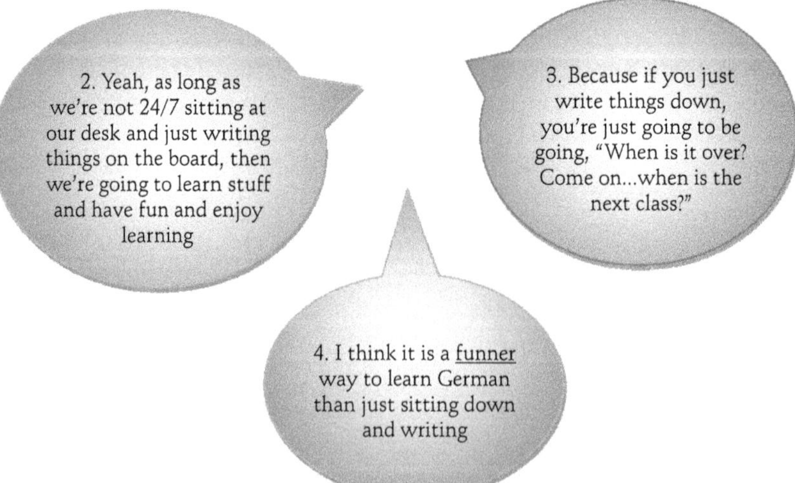


**Figures 8.2 to 8.4**

As Tom's comment about 'seriousness' cited earlier indicates, the experience was not just a light-hearted romp; students also felt it *made the learning easier and more recognisable*. They 'learnt a lot', 'learnt more', 'learnt heaps'. They were also able to identify various reasons for their positive response, including the opportunities for varied interaction and the fact that the language became easier to remember due to the 'hands on', playful nature of the experience (Figures 8.5–8.7).

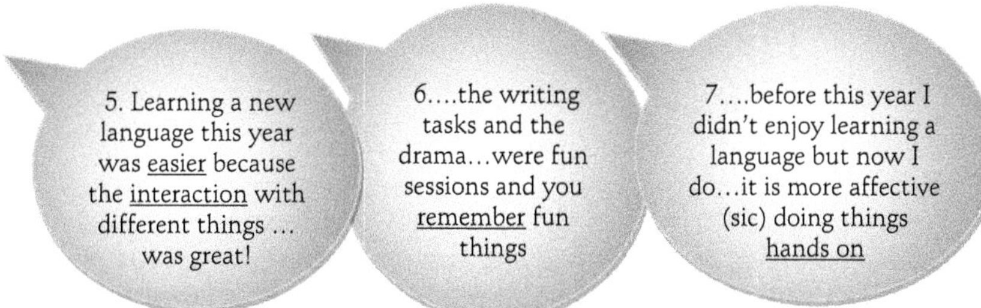


**Figures 8.5 to 8.7**

The enrolment in another role, place and time has a stimulating effect on their *willingness to participate* orally (Figures 8.8 and 8.9).

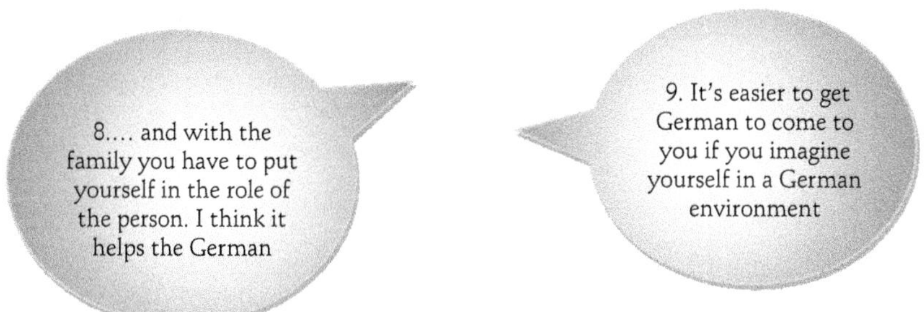


**Figures 8.8 to 8.9**

As well as the practical and physical nature of the work, explored in more detail in Rothwell (2011), learners identified *cognitive benefits* from the dramatic elements and context. One such benefit was the necessity of mentally revisiting all that they had learned to find a way to make meaning in a spontaneous exchange (Figure 8.10).

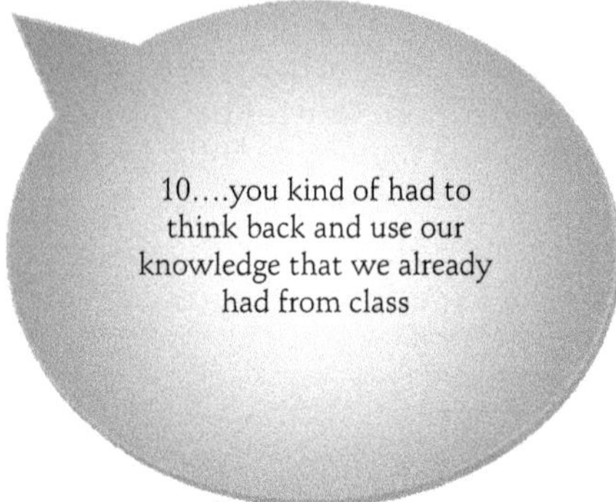


**Figure 8.10**

The content and nature of the classroom talk seemed *more meaningful* to learners. One learner compared the language classroom in his primary school to the drama-languages classroom, highlighting the decontextualised nature of much vocabulary acquisition in primary school in what was perhaps a more grammar-based pedagogy. This experience was then compared with the way the drama *widens the language scope beyond normal classroom topics* (Figures 8.11 and 8.12).

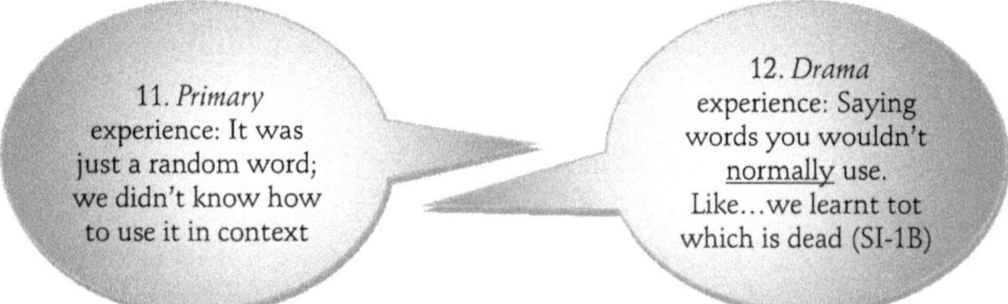


**Figures 8.11 to 8.12**

This move into language more obviously connected to language and socio-cultural life beyond the classroom was enhanced by the *learners' agency* to use it as playwrights (Figure 8.13).

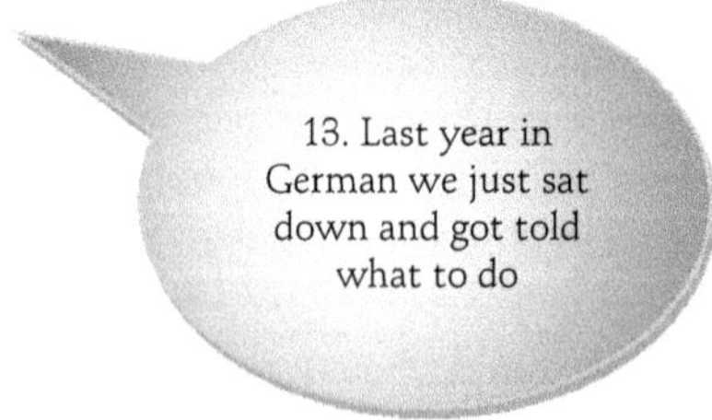


**Figure 8.13**

Learners were able to describe the *layers of thinking* which were introduced by the dramatic duality of their classroom roles as students/migrants and that of their audience such as teacher/ship's captain. Here, the family had to suddenly deal with a stowaway at the immigration point (Figure 8.14).

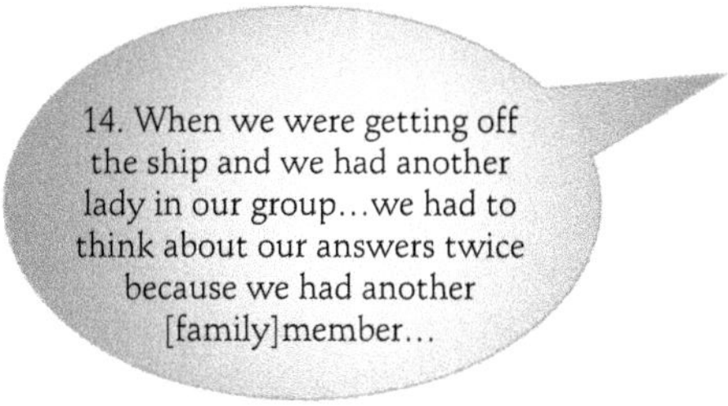

14. When we were getting off the ship and we had another lady in our group...we had to think about our answers twice because we had another [family]member...

**Figure 8.14**

## Engagement in intercultural and intracultural reflection

There is also much food for thought in learners' comments in individual interviews around the cultural context and personal effects of the drama, and it is in these reflections that the deeper intracultural and intercultural understandings can be identified. (For further student comments and analysis see Rothwell [2015].) Since the reflections below emerged not from the classroom but from the research interviews, they also confirm the importance of integrating more reflective tasks into the actual unit of work (Liddicoat & Scarino, 2013).

Much of the commentary and student work suggested that the drama has given these learners pale memories of historical and social events which have provided what Warriner (2011: np) refers to as an 'entrée into the referential world of others'. Some of them were looking at the lives and experiences of others with new interest, some were relating the experiences to their own lives in new ways. For example, the German word Mauer (wall) has deep and diverse significance for many German-speaking people; the dramatic experience of Berlin in 1961 led Ben to enhance his own understanding of the significance of this event. I asked him if he'd seen or heard anything since the study (five months earlier) which had stirred memories of the experience; he told me he had recently seen and noticed anniversary footage of the Wall coming down (Figure 8.15).

15. Yeah, like on the TV they showed the Berlin Wall being knocked down

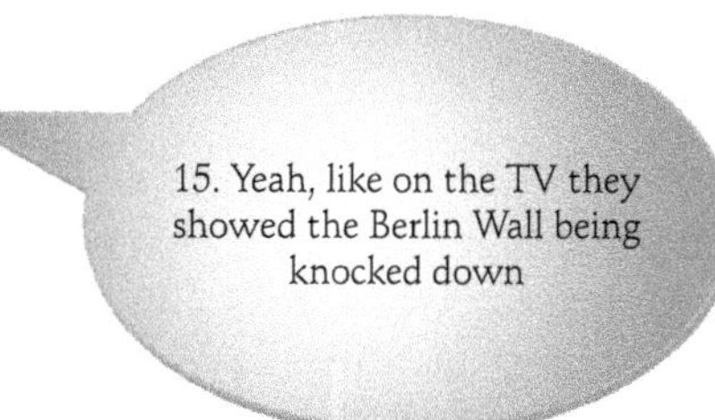

**Figure 8.15**

The event has become significant for him in that he has realised its significance for others.

In a more reciprocal response, Ali turned her new eyes onto her own sense of self and her real experiences. Herself a migrant, she gave several striking explanations (Rothwell, 2015) of how the drama had caused her to reflect in a layered, reciprocal way about not just her own immigration experience but how others experienced her arrival. In one interview, I asked her if the drama experience on the boat had changed who she was or how she thought about herself, and she replied (words in brackets are hard to hear but gist is clear) (Figure 8.16). In a process of defamiliarisation (Pennycook, 2012), Ali was imagining how others might have seen her. She was looking back at herself across time and space from the distance of others, recognising that her perspective is not the only one.

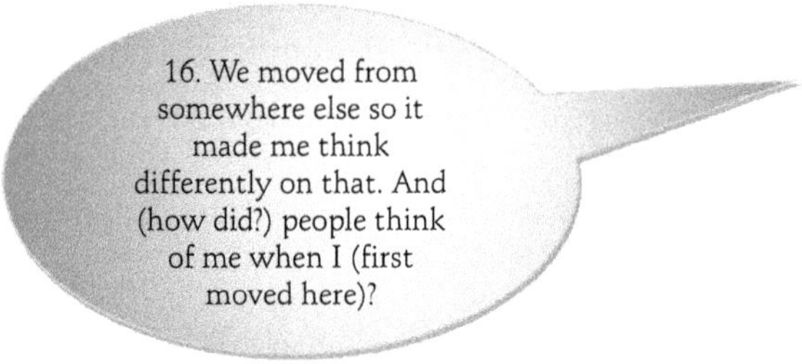

**Figure 8.16**

## Conclusion

As teacher feedback to the draft Australian languages curriculum demonstrated, the concept of interculturality is often seen as difficult to integrate into language learning. However, this study suggests that process drama can provide the groundwork for an engaging intercultural approach. It does this through

- exploiting the dramatic opportunities for imagining and reflecting on the experience of what it is to be the other, both in a home community and away from home;
- changing the nature of classroom talk so that learners can experience purposeful but difficult, unpredictable language encounters;
- employing the elements of drama such as role, relationship, time, place and physical performance to provide a stimulating learning experience.

The shift in role and classroom talk means that the availability of identity positions from which to speak (Norton, 2013) is broadened. Learners can move beyond their 'ascribed identities' (Warriner, 2011: np) of passive students listening, writing and repeating language, often mindlessly, and have permission to skim along the boundaries of other identities, other communities. All this was engaging for these learners and provoked an attitude to learning which led to a performative consciousness as learners reflected on the layers of dramatic/classroom experience. Through the drama, the language in use became what Pennycook (2008) calls an 'emergent social act' rather than a body of knowledge to be learnt and regurgitated. The learners become accustomed to negotiating an interaction in a new context with an audience they were not quite sure of. They had to listen carefully to the TL and negotiate meaning. This was a step towards what Byram (1997: 38) refers to as the intercultural skills of 'establishing relationships, managing dysfunctions and mediating'.

The relative freedom of the playwright function meant that learners had to adopt internally persuasive speech (Bakhtin, 1981) which required them to create personalised text and to carefully monitor what they dared to voice in terms of their dual student/migrant identity and dual teacher/captain audience. This personalisation challenged the entrenched genre of authoritative language classroom talk. The classroom and interview/questionnaire data in this study support the definitions of genre as both culturally persistent *and* inherently unstable, referred to earlier (Diamond, 2000; Halliday, 1993). The student comments suggest that, in many classrooms, the genre of language classroom talk is particularly unstable, and therefore vulnerable, because it is out of step with the times. The study, therefore, supports international educational research (e.g. Alexander, 2010) which suggests that classroom talk can indeed be performed differently. As Warriner (2011) states, analysis of small, localised stories relating to language experience and identity can show how it is possible to evoke and contest ideologies of language in circulation, in this case the ideology of what classroom talk *should* be.

In this drama-languages classroom, the talk more closely modelled unpredictable everyday intercultural encounters, at home or abroad, and provided opportunities for distanced reflection on the implications of what students were experiencing and learning through the drama and language in use. Learners responded with enthusiastic participation and TL use. Equally significantly, learners clearly articulated strong approbation for the pedagogy. As one Final Questionnaire respondent wrote (17):

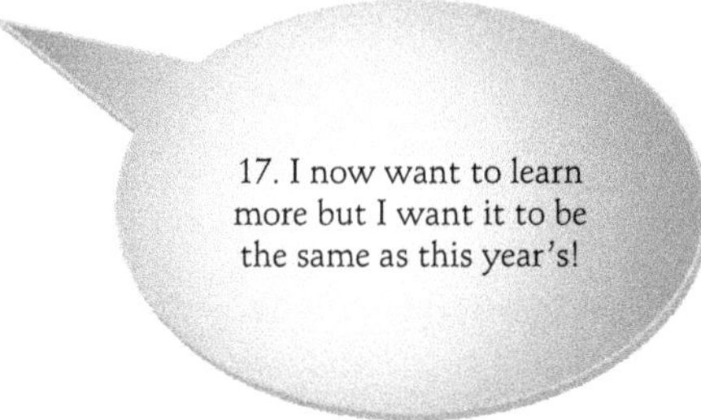


**Figure 8.17**

## Note

(1) Pseudonyms have been used throughout the chapter.

## References

Alexander, R. (2010) Reform, retrench or recycle? A curriculum cautionary tale. Paper presented at the National Curriculum Symposium, University of Melbourne, 25–27 February 2010.

Bakhtin, M.M. (1981) *The Dialogic Imagination* (trans. C. Emerson and M. Holquist). Austin, TX: University of Texas Press.

Bakhtin, M. (1986) *Speech Genres and Other Late Essays* (trans. V.M. McGee). Austin, TX: University of Texas Press.

Burns, A. (2001) Genre-based approaches to writing. In C. Candlin and N. Mercer (eds) *English Language Teaching in its Social Context* (pp. 200–207). London: Routledge.

Byram, M. (1997) *Teaching and Assessing Intercultural Communicative Competence*. Clevedon: Multilingual Matters.

Byram, M. (2006) Developing a concept of intercultural citizenship. In G. Alred, M. Byram and M. Fleming (eds) *Education for Intercultural Citizenship: Concepts and Comparisons* (pp. 109–129). Clevedon: Multilingual Matters.

Dam van, J. (2002) Ritual, face and play in a first English lesson: Bootstrapping a classroom culture. In C. Kramsch (ed.) *Language Acquisition and Language Socialization: Ecological Perspectives* (pp. 237–265). London: Continuum.

Dervin, F. and Liddicoat, A.J. (2013) *Linguistics for Intercultural Education*. Amsterdam/ Philadelphia, PA: John Benjamin Publishing Company.

Diamond, E. (2000) Performance and cultural politics. In L. Goodman and J. de Gay (eds) *The Routledge Reader in Politics and Performance* (pp. 66–69). London/New York: Routledge.

Donato, R. (2004) Aspects of collaboration in pedagogical discourse. *Annual Review of Applied Linguistics* 24 (1), 284–302.

Dunn, J. (2011) Developing an extended playwright function framework for analysing dramatic structuring within improvised forms. *NJ: Drama Australia Journal* 34 (1), 21–34.

Eriksson, S. (2011) Distancing at close range: Making strange devices in Dorothy Heathcote's process drama: 'Teaching political awareness through drama'. *Research in Drama Education: The Journal of Applied Theatre and Performance* 16 (1), 101–123.

Halliday, M.A.K. (1978) *Language as Social Semiotic*. London: Edward Arnold Publishers.

Halliday, M.A.K. (1993) *Language in a Changing World: Occasional Paper Number 13*. Deakin, ACT: Applied Linguistics Association of Australia.

Kao, S-M. and O'Neill, C. (1998) *Words into Worlds: Learning a Second Language Through Process Drama*. Stamford, CT: Ablex.

Kramsch, C. (1993) *Context and Culture in Language Teaching*. Oxford: Oxford University Press.

Kramsch, C. (2009) *The Multilingual Subject*. Oxford/New York: Oxford University Press.

Kramsch, C. and Whiteside, A. (2008) Language ecology in multilingual settings: Towards a theory of symbolic competence. *Applied Linguistics* 29 (4), 645–671.

Kohler, M. (2010) Intercultural language teaching and learning: Policy and practice. In A.J. Liddicoat and A. Scarino (eds) *Languages in Australian Education: Problems, Prospects and Future Directions* (pp. 179–192). Newcastle-on-Tyne: Cambridge Scholars.

Liddicoat, A.J. (2007) Language choices in the intercultural classroom. *ILTLP Project Discussion Paper 5*. See http://www.iltlp.unisa.edu.au/papers.html (accessed 24 March 2016).

Liddicoat, A.J. and Scarino, A. (2013) *Intercultural Language Teaching and Learning*. Chichester: John Wiley & Sons.

Lier van, L. (1996) *Interaction in the Language Curriculum: Awareness, Autonomy and Authenticity*. London/New York: Longman.

Lier van, L. (2001) Constraints and resources in classroom talk. In C. Candlin and N. Mercer (eds) *English Language Teaching in its Global Context* (pp. 90–107). Sydney/London: Routledge.

Morgan, N. and Saxton, J. (1985) Working with drama: A different order of experience. *Theory into Practice* 24 (2), 211–218.

Neelands, J. and Goode, T. (2000) *Structuring Drama Work* (2nd edn). Cambridge: Cambridge University Press.

Norton, B. (2013) *Identity and Language Learning: Extending the Conversation*. Bristol: Multilingual Matters.

O'Neill, C. (1995) *Drama Worlds: A Framework for Process Drama*. Portsmouth, NH: Heinemann.

O'Neill, C. (2006) Drama and the web of form. In P. Taylor and C.D. Warner (eds) *Structure and Spontaneity* (pp. 57–72). Stoke-on-Trent/Sterling, VA: Trentham Books Limited.

O'Toole, J. (1992) *The Process of Drama: Negotiating Art and Meaning*. London: Routledge.

Pennycook, A. (2008) English as a language always in translation. *European Journal of English Studies* 12 (1), 33–47.

Pennycook, A. (2012) *Language and Mobility: Unexpected Places*. Bristol: Multilingual Matters.

Piccardo, E. (2013) Plurilingualism and curriculum design: Towards a synergic vision. *TESOL Quarterly* 17 (3), 600–614.

Rothwell, J. (2011) Bodies and language: Process drama and intercultural language learning in a beginner language classroom. *Research in Drama Education: The Journal of Applied Theatre and Performance* 16 (4), 575–594.

Rothwell, J. (2013) Let's eat the Captain! Thinking, feeling, doing: Intercultural language learning through process drama. Unpublished PhD dissertation, Queensland University of Technology. See http://eprints.qut.edu.au/63847/ (accessed 18 June 2017).

Rothwell, J. (2015) Laying down pale memories: Learners reflecting on language, self and other in the middle school drama-languages class. *The Canadian Modern Language Review Special Edition* 71 (4), 331–361.

Scarino, A. and Liddicoat, A.J. (2009) *Teaching and Learning Languages: A Guide*. Melbourne: Curriculum Corporation.

Swain, M. (1985) The output hypothesis: Just speaking and writing aren't enough. *The Canadian Modern Language Review* 50 (1), 158–164.

Tan, S. (2006) *The Arrival*. Melbourne: Lothian Books.

Turnbull, M. and Dailey O'Cain, J. (eds) (2009) *First Language Use in Second and Foreign Language Learning*. Bristol: Multilingual Matters.

Warriner, D. (2011) Symbolic competence as strategic performance: Narratives of displacement, contested identities, and transformative practices. *Applied Linguistics Speaker Series ASU Tempe Campus*. See https://vimeo.com/20708783 (accessed 6 January 2016).

Winston, J. (2010). *Beauty and Education*. London/New York: Routledge.

# Appendix A: Unit Plan – The *Sophie*

**Unit Plan The *Sophie***

| **TERM 1 TASK SEQUENCE (further focus on language form activities integrated in context of drama)** |
|---|
| ***All activities in TL unless stated*** |
| 1. Imagine who the family in Tan's illustration is and what is happening. |
| 2. Read Ship's List as a group and take a family name for enrolment |
| 3. Decide what 4 things you most want to take. |
| 4. Government family photo |
| 5. Shoulder tape motion at time |
| 6. Fill out ticket with name, family and age |
| **7. Give name and age to Captain as board ship** |
| 8. Gossip mill: imagine what can see, hear, taste and see on the old ship |
| 9. Freeze frame of family on deck. Imagine and say how might feel |
| 10. Follow captain's instructions to scrub deck etc. |
| 11. Find your character in Tan's illustration of families on deck and sculpt body to match |
| 12. Shoulder tap to say what can see, hear etc. |
| **13. Gossip mill the state of the ship** |
| **14. Fill in speech bubbles for a member of the family on freeze frame photo** |
| 15. Scripted soundscape practised for 'A storm is coming". |
| 16. Interview students about language learning (in English) |
| 17. Freeze frame an incident resulting from the storm |
| 18. Discuss each other's frames (in TL and English) |
| 19. Tell 'child overboard–food gone' story using freeze frame photographs and discuss |
| **20. No Food whole class role play confronting Captain about lack of food** |
| **21. Family Immigration Assessment interviews to enter the country** |
| 22. Stimulated recall interviews watching Immigration Assessment task (in English) |
| 23. Freeze frame expressions of anticipation as sight land from ship |

# Appendix B: Unit Plan – Berlin 1961

**Unit Plan Berlin 1961**

| **TERM 2 TASK SEQUENCE (further focus on language form activities integrated in context of drama)** |
|---|
| ***All activities in TL unless stated*** |
| Discuss necessity of language test for immigration (in English). |
| Students in role as immigrant families enter Germany down gangplank as locals shout slogans of abuse and welcome |
| Watch video recording of the 'German news' on migrant arrival. |
| Watch and comment on a series of teacher modified web extracts (photographs, documentary film, maps) on political Germany at the end of World War 2. |
| Stylised job search. 1 migrant goes round shopkeepers asking for a job; rejected in various ways. |
| Read job adverts |
| Discuss what skills are required for jobs in ads and what skills you have |
| **Written job application** |
| Read and accept in writing invitation to Kaffee und Kuchen (Coffee & Cake) with locals. |
| Attend a Coffee Cake session and make conversation. |
| Attend job centre interview |
| Interact with bus driver on journey to work |
| Listen to announcement of Wall's erection while scattered through city at work and leisure |
| Use further collection of teacher adapted web material to show/discuss how and why the Wall went up. |
| Freeze frame family reaction to division by wall and add caption. |
| Task (not undertaken in this study):<br>In pairs, students write an illustrated news report about the Wall and its effects on families.<br>Can be class or school online newsletter article. |

# 9 Intercultural/Dramatic Tension and the Nature of Intercultural Engagement

Erika Piazzoli

## Introduction

Research has shown that drama pedagogy can be an effective way to enhance intercultural language learning (Bräuer, 2002; Rothwell, 2011). Clearly, intercultural education is an important dimension in the growing field of performative teaching and learning (Schewe, 2014). In this chapter, I propose a connection between intercultural engagement and the elements of drama, particularly 'dramatic tension' – introducing the term *intercultural dramatic tension*. O'Toole (1992: 27) describes dramatic tension as a key element of dramatic form, one of the driving forces of drama, as well as 'a construct to define a set of emotional reactions which percipients of a drama experience individually and as a group'. In this sense, tension is also connected to engagement and has been defined as 'a mental excitement fundamental to intellectual and emotional engagement' (Morgan & Saxton, 1987: 3).

The seed of a connection between tension and engagement in second language (L2)/drama was planted early on. Within the anglophone research community, the first study to investigate process drama in L2 and foreign language (FL) learning was Kao's (1995) research on the impact of drama on L2/FL discourse. Kao's process drama intervention lasted 14 weeks; for the purpose of data analysis, four activities were selected and coded for turn-taking. Overall, her findings showed that when using the process drama approach, the students engaged in spontaneous communication, taking 20% more turns than the teacher. When analysing each drama activity, it appeared that one activity was less successful in encouraging student participation. Importantly, Kao realised that this drama activity carried less dramatic tension than the others. In other words, the very first study in the field already pointed to a connection between engagement (in Kao's words, 'active participation') and dramatic tension. In this chapter, I will advance this argument, sharing some reflections – based on a five-year investigation on dramatic tension – about the significance of *intercultural dramatic tension* for intercultural engagement in performative teaching and learning.

## Intercultural Engagement

Engagement as a construct can have several interpretations. In this chapter, *engagement* is defined through the Vygotskian lens of a felt-experience – in Russian *perezhivanie,* i.e. an embodied experience through which individuals perceive, feel, interpret, internalise and recreate meaning. This Russian term, which cannot be translated directly into English, was used by Vygotsky (1994) to refer to the individual's emotional and cognitive meaning-making experience in a given situation. It implies that the same situation may be 'interpreted, perceived, experienced or lived through by different [individuals] in different ways' (Vygotsky, 1994: 354). In this sociocultural perspective, the construct of engagement as *perezhivanie* can be understood in terms of the interdependence of cognitive, emotional and social aspects (Ferholt, 2014). Vygotsky used *perezhivanie* as a unit of analysis to comprehend experience across the cognitive, affective and social dimensions of learning.

Similarly, the notion of the *intercultural* is subject to many interpretations. Here, I use the term to refer to encounters where individuals are immersed in cultures other than their own and become aware of this experience through reflection. As Gupta (2003) argues, the intercultural process refers to an encounter whereby, for the individuals concerned, a change has been triggered. In this sense, 'intercultural' does not mean just being in the presence of more than one cultural system; it requires that the individual actively engage with the context, making sense of the new cultural dimension in relation to his/her own. Here, we can draw a preliminary link between Gupta's active engagement and the active involvement mentioned by Kao (1995) in relation to dramatic tension and process drama.

Alred *et al.* (2003) explore the concept of *interculturality* in relation to the active experience of operating in-between cultures. They note that there can never be a complete intercultural experience; it is an ongoing process of experience and reflection. 'Being intercultural' implies a qualitative interpretation, a shift, a questioning of preconceptions:

> Being intercultural is [...] the capacity to reflect on the relationships among groups and the experience of those relationships. It is both awareness of experiencing otherness and the ability to analyse the experience and act upon the insights into self and other which the analysis brings. (Alred *et al.*, 2003: 4)

In essence, 'being intercultural' is a process which comprises (1) experience; (2) awareness of experiencing otherness; (3) reflection, i.e. the analysis of this experience; and (4) acting upon the insights into self and other, gained through reflection. The authors argue that a consequence of this kind of intercultural experience is a challenge to one's modes of perception, thought and feeling. Thus, their construct validates not only the cognitive but also the sensory and affective dimensions of the intercultural experience. This discourse ties in well with the Vygotskian notion of *perezhivanie*, a felt-experience encompassing the cognitive, affective and social aspects. It is also a well-suited framework for drama-based learning, an experiential approach that necessarily involves both cognitive and sensory/affective domains. Significantly, Alred *et al.* (2003: 4) suggest that being intercultural leads to a 'heightened awareness' of one's identity and of the interaction between *own* and *other*. This process, they argue, can trigger a psychological shift in a person's centre, which might lead to a more integrated sense of self and greater confidence in being 'in-between' socially and culturally. They further note that the role of the educator may lie in creating the conditions for this triggering. How then can an L2/drama educator do this? Over the last five years, I have searched for answers by exploring the ways in which one can generate, harness and manage the elements of drama.

## The Elements of Drama

Aristotle identifies six basic elements of drama: plot, theme, character, language, rhythm and spectacle, defined by Pavis (1998: 15) as 'the laws of dramatic composition'. Throughout history, this definition has influenced Western dramatic structure and storytelling, creating a common framework to be followed, or rejected, according to epoch, playwrights and movements. Yet, across the centuries, drama theorists have agreed upon the existence of some identifiable dramatic elements used by playwrights and directors to create theatre or, in the case of drama in education, to create learning through drama. Haseman and O'Toole (1986) put forward a seminal model of the elements of drama, featuring: situation, role and relationships, driven by dramatic tension, directed by focus, made explicit in place and time, through language and movement, to create mood and symbol, which together create dramatic meaning. In this chapter, I have adopted Haseman and O'Toole's terminology to advance a connection between the elements of drama and intercultural engagement. As O'Toole notes, these elements are dynamic and cannot be presented in a vacuum; their manifestation is dependent on the contextual factors (Davis, 2008: 64). In other words, what is crucial is not only being aware of the elements of drama, but being able to actively manipulate them in order to create engagement. While all the elements of drama are equally important in a dramatic experience, for the purpose of this discussion, I concentrate on dramatic tension in process drama – given its central importance in L2 learning (Kao & O'Neill, 1998).

Dramatic tension can be interpreted in a two-fold way: as both a key element of drama and as an emotional response to a drama. On the one hand, dramatic tension is a key element of the art form; it is the element that playwrights, directors and drama facilitators aim to generate by sequencing and structuring dramatic episodes in a particular way. As O'Toole (1992) defines it, dramatic tension is the energy that drives a drama forward. He conceptualises tension as a propelling force: 'Tension is the spring of drama. Not the action, but what impels the action' (O'Toole, 1992: 133). On the other hand, O'Toole (1992: 133) also frames dramatic tension in relation to emotional reactions in the audience's experiences, i.e. as 'a construct to define the emotional reactions of a group of percipients'. At this point in the discussion, it is useful to note that, in process drama, participants are both audience (percipients) and actors (agents) at the same time. Therefore, dramatic tension in process drama is not only to be intended as a *response* in the participants, but also as an *agentic* quality that participants actively inject in a drama, as storytellers, together with the teacher. Thus, a dual interpretation of dramatic tension emerges, with tension holding both *receptive* and *agentic* qualities.

Furthermore, dramatic tension can be classified into narrative tension (tension generated by the relationship between characters, plot, etc.) and non-narrative tension (tension generated by the contrast of music/silence, movement/stillness, light/dark). It is the drama facilitator's task to actively manipulate some of these elements to create non-narrative tension. As for narrative dramatic tension, O'Toole (1992) has identified several subtypes of tension which have been synthesised in Table 9.1.

Among these subtypes, *metaxis* is of particular interest for this discussion. Etymologically, the Greek noun *metaxis* means 'betwixt and between' and derives from the works of Homer (Bundy, 1999: 55). In current drama discourse, the notion of metaxis is used to describe the parallel involvement between the dramatic context and the real context. Two main

**Table 9.1** Types of dramatic tension

| *Type of dramatic tension* | *Description* |
|---|---|
| Tension of the task | Tension implied in fulfilling a task, given "constraints imposed by the situation" |
| Tension of relationship | Tension arising from an *inter*personal clash (opposites attitudes, motivation) and/or *intra*personal clash (values, beliefs, i.e. tension of dilemma) |
| Tension of the mystery | A form of suspense, "anticipatory expectation" |
| Tension of surprise | Tension caused by new unexpected constraints |
| Metaxis | "A tension caused by the gap between the real and the fiction" |

Source: O'Toole (1992: 153–166).

interpretations of metaxis appear in the literature. The first, stemming from Boal (1995), refers to belonging simultaneously to two different worlds. Bolton (1984: 162, my emphasis) subscribes to this view, defining metaxis as 'the phenomena of the participant holding the two worlds in the mind simultaneously, *regardless* of the specific response'. O'Toole interprets it as a more complicated dynamic: he sees metaxis as the tension arising when events in the real context are questioned through emotional response to a paradox in the dramatic context. O'Toole (1992: 169) thus defines metaxis as being created 'by the dissonance of the fictional event within the real context'. Bundy follows this line of thinking:

> Metaxis is defined as the tension created when there is a disjunction between the way participants or spectators respond to the drama and the way they would normally respond to a similar 'real life' event – but only if they are moved/affected by the discrepancy itself. (Bundy, 1999: 55)

Here, Bundy and O'Toole are highlighting a *dissonance*, a discrepancy between the responses in the real context and in the dramatic contexts. In this discussion, I use the term *metaxis* following O'Toole and Bundy's position.

## Intercultural Dramatic Tension

I coined the term *intercultural dramatic tension* during my doctoral research (described in the section below) in an attempt to capture an aspect of teacher artistry, while reflecting-on-action after a drama experience. During the fieldwork, the expression *intercultural dramatic tension* spontaneously emerged in my note-taking, to describe a particular quality of the drama. In the coding phase of the data analysis, I noted the use of this expression in my reflective journal, and I created a memo titled 'Intercultural Dramatic Tension' to attempt to unpack its meaning. Here is my earliest attempt to define it, cited from an extract from that 2010 memo:

> So what exactly is intercultural dramatic tension? Given that 'dramatic tension' is the gap between what we know and what we don't know, that electric, invisible force that drives us forward. ... Intercultural tension is a force that engages one at an intercultural level and operates within the gap existing between two (or more) cultural systems. (Piazzoli, 2010a)

In the memo, I conclude that, rather than a type of tension in itself, intercultural dramatic tension can be seen as a frame for existing types of tension. Seen in this way, the intercultural sphere adds a nuance, a new dimension to existing forms of tension. For example, non-narrative dramatic tension, contemplated through an intercultural frame, is generated by the contrast of music/silence, movement/stillness, light/dark – where culture-specific rhythms, melodies, soundscapes, movement sequences, gestures, rituals and props are consciously manipulated. Narrative dramatic tension in all its forms, as proposed by O'Toole (see Table 9.1), can also be looked through the intercultural frame:

- Tension of relationship from an intercultural perspective may be framed as the potential tension stemming from different cultural values manifested in roles and situations.
- Tension of the task from an intercultural perspective may be framed as the potential tension of having to accomplish a cross-cultural task, given the different cultural systems and rituals associated with it.
- Tension of surprise from an intercultural perspective may be framed as the gap between two (or more) cultural worlds, generating a surprise in terms of how an event or circumstance is perceived by different individuals and how they react to it.
- Tension of the mystery from an intercultural perspective may be framed as the gap between two (or more) cultural worlds creating a mystery in terms of how an event or circumstance is perceived by different individuals and how they react to it.
- Tension of metaxis: Language learners engaged in a drama are constantly renegotiating cultural systems. In role, they might experience, and be affected by, a disjunction between how they responded in the drama and how they would normally respond in their native language/culture.

Thus, the intercultural dimension can provide a frame to analyse existing types of tension, seen as one of the key elements of drama. Moreover, intercultural dramatic tension can be construed as a set of reactions, generated in drama participants when they are engaged in an intercultural experience. Accordingly, in my reflective memo I noted:

> [The participants of the research], as Chinese international students on exchange in Italy, experience two (or more) simultaneous cultural identities, and are constantly re-negotiating, processing, handling two cultural systems. If this happens to occur when they are playing a dramatic role (e.g., a Chinese playing the role of an Italian) there could be a degree of intercultural metaxis, in terms of making choices in the drama according to the new role identity, that might involve controversial ethical/social behaviour according to their native cultural identity.

To sum up, intercultural dramatic tension can be interpreted as a key element of L2/drama, which can be woven into a process drama structure to create intercultural engagement, as well as construct a set of emotional reactions of a percipient in a drama. These concepts are pivotal to the findings of my doctoral study, described below.

## The Study

The reflective practitioner research discussed in this chapter is informed by three qualitative case studies. While the research was based in Australia, the fieldwork was conducted in Milan, Italy, in a public university (Department of Intercultural Mediation) and two adult language schools. The research focused on the impact of process drama on L2 learners' engagement levels. The intervention consisted in 45 hours of process drama, conducted in Italian (L2) with three cohorts of international students. Each case study was structured as a series of five, three-hour process drama workshops, targeted at intermediate learners of Italian (levels B1–B2 of the Common European Framework of Reference for Languages). Each process drama began with a pretext: this is a source or impulse which defines the nature of the dramatic world, implies roles for the participants and 'immediately plunges the group into an imagined world' (O'Neill, 1995: 1). After the pretext was launched, the process drama unfolded as a series of dramatic episodes, linked by narrative, temporal and/or spatial connections. These were outlined in a learning structure – an outline, or sequence of dramatic episodes, rather than a lesson plan, designed by the facilitator and negotiated by the group, in action.

For each case study, up to five teachers observed the teacher/researcher while she facilitated the L2/drama workshops. The teacher-participants were involved as participant-observers in the drama. They took notes on their perceptions of the learners' engagement based on three criteria: communicative engagement, intercultural engagement and affective engagement. The student-participants were involved as active participants in the drama. At the end of each workshop, they were asked to choose one specific moment (SM) in the drama and to self-evaluate different aspects of their engagement (communicative; intercultural; affective) from 0 (disengaged) to 10 (highly engaged). The questionnaire scores were followed by individual interviews. Data from the teacher-participants' observations, teacher and students' interviews, focus groups and engagement questionnaires were cross-referenced with classroom videos and with the researcher's reflective notes, to explore the construct of 'engagement' and its relationship to 'teacher artistry'. The mapping of the coded data culminated in the selection of three SM in the drama workshops – one per case study. Overall, the three SMs were selected according to the following criteria: (1) they stood out for their distinct aesthetic nature; (2) they were selected by the majority of student-participants in the questionnaires; (3) they were mentioned as the most vivid memory of the drama workshops by most student-participants and teacher-participants in the interviews; (4) they were singled out in the researcher's reflection-on-action as particularly significant; (5) they featured a group improvisation, with teacher-in-role strategy; and (6) the interactions had been captured clearly on video and audio devices, giving access to evidence of both verbal and non-verbal responses.

## The Process of Intercultural Engagement

The analysis revealed that intercultural engagement followed a pattern similar to that outlined by Alred *et al.* (2003), albeit adapted to the dramatic context. In an intercultural perspective, experience generated degrees of intercultural awareness. This was facilitated by various kinds of intercultural reflection which, at times, resulted in intercultural meaning-making. This cycle was fuelled by dramatic tension, occurring within a specific dramatic frame, as represented in Figure 9.1. The use of the term *fuelled* here is deliberate in evoking a propulsive metaphor to describe the effect of dramatic tension as a key element of the form. This propulsion works on a felt-experience level, igniting an emotional response. In other words, intercultural engagement is framed as a process ignited by the key element of intercultural dramatic tension and generating a series of emotional reactions – grounded in experience – and triggering intercultural meaning-making.

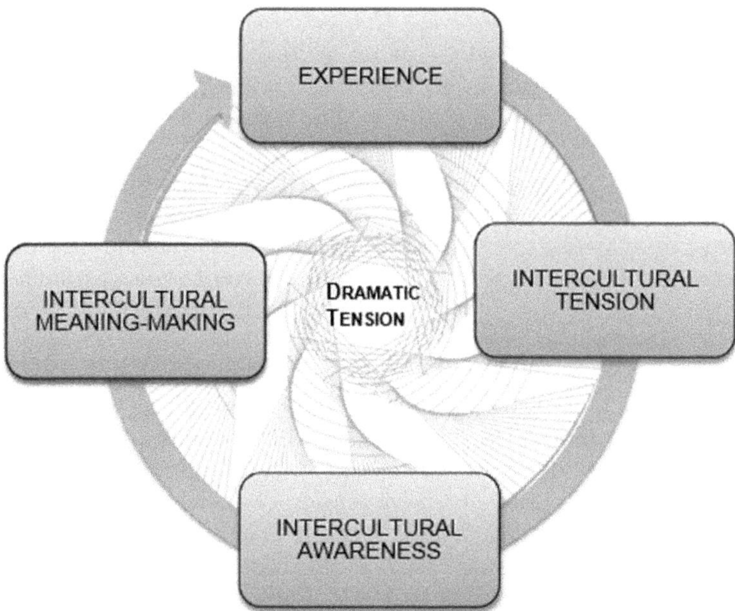


**Figure 9.1** Process of intercultural engagement

The intercultural engagement process appeared to vary considerably across the case studies. These variations resulted in the meaning-making either being acknowledged *explicitly*, or remaining *implicit* in the participants' engagement. To illustrate the argument as clearly as possible, I will follow each step of the process, discussing one case study at a time.

## Case study 1: Explicit intercultural engagement

### *Experience*

The pretext for case study 1 was a very unconventional job offer, created *ad hoc* for this drama. The job offer contained vague and somewhat suspicious information about a possible engagement with the editorial staff of the Italo–Chinese Chamber of Commerce in Shanghai – hinting at candidates having to put up with the dubious temper of the editor-in-chief. The post was specifically recruiting journalism graduates with an expertise in Chinese and Italian culture and society. This scenario was very close to the actual reality of the cohort, as all student-participants were of Chinese background, enrolled in an undergraduate degree in Italy, majoring in Intercultural Mediation and doing a module on journalism. In the drama, the teacher (in the role as the lunatic editor-in-chief), welcomed the applicants and put them on a one-week trial. The drama was initially set in Shanghai, in the editor's office; as part of their trial, the journalists were divided into groups and required to choose, from a selection of newspapers provided, an Italian current event that could appeal to the readership of the editorial. The teams had a week to pitch their ideas, travel to Italy to conduct an interview related to their topic, write the feature article and report back to their editor in Shanghai. The team with the most successful article would get the job.

The journey to Italy was of course filled with all sorts of unforeseen obstacles, peppered by the unpredictable mood of the editor-in chief. SM1, used to cross-analyse participants' experiences in the drama, was the moment when the aspiring journalists were traveling on an Italian train to get to their interviewees and, upon showing their train tickets (provided by the editor-in-chief), they were told by the ticket inspector/teacher-in-role that the tickets were fake. They then got into an argument with the ticket inspector and were detained by the local police for their association with the Italo–Chinese Chamber of Commerce. This particular moment in the drama sparked a great deal of intercultural tension of the task and tension of relationship. Intercultural tension of the task was generated as the journalists had limited time to conduct the interviews and return to China, but instead they were being detained for suspected fraud: in other words, arresting the participants was slowing down the action – when the journalists had only 24 hours to conduct the interview and go back to China to present their projects. Intercultural tension of relationship was generated as the efficient, fast-paced attitude of the journalists on an important mission was met by the indolent, slothful attitude of the Italian police force.

### *Intercultural tension of metaxis*

The analysis suggested that some participants went through a felt-experience, or *perezhivanie*, which may have involved intercultural tension of metaxis. To illustrate this concept, I draw on Teodoro[1] (21-year-old, Chinese). Below is an extract of his interview, in which he connects a past event (getting a fine on public transportation) with a significant aspect of the drama in SM1 (confronting the inspector on the train):

**Interviewer**: What moment of the workshop do you remember the most?
**Teodoro**: Yes … we have been … on the train, yes, this is more interesting!
**Interviewer**: When we were on the train; and how did you feel?
**Teodoro**: Ehm … but usually is … I did this, because but … when I've gone on the train, also on the bus I do this and … Yes, Ticket Inspector, also one time on the bus, checked my ticket, but … doesn't work [raises his voice, agitated] But I don't know why it doesn't work [protesting] and yes I have to pay … some money!
**Interviewer**: A fine?
**Teodoro [agitated]**: Yes but in that moment is very angry!
**Interviewer**: And so, in the drama, you remembered-
**Teodoro**: Yes yes!
**Interviewer**: And were you angry?
**Teororo**: Yes yes yes! [Laughs] Ohhh! (Teodoro, 2: 22–43)

In this extract, Teodoro's frustration emerges as he makes a connection with his lived-experience in the drama. In the interview, he identifies the dramatic episode of the train arrest (SM1) and offers some comments that might indicate a degree of intercultural metaxis, as the disjunction between the way he responded to the drama (playing the role of an Italian journalist) and how he responded to a similar event in his real life as a Chinese international student in Italy. At the beginning of SM1 in the drama, Teodoro behaves according to the rules of real life in the Italian cultural context: he reacts to the ticket inspector's objections by scribbling some numbers on the ticket and adding: 'Yes, yes, I've stamped it already! This one is stamped!' (This is a context-specific comment: In Italy, it is not sufficient to buy a train ticket; in order for it to be valid, it needs to be stamped. Tourists who are unaware of this often get fined.)

As the improvisation progresses, Teodoro might have experienced a disjunction between what happened to him in the real frame and in the dramatic frame. In the real frame, according to his interview above, in a similar situation, he was unable to react, although believing it was unjust, and he got fined. From how he was explaining it, he seemed disempowered in that situation. Perhaps his level of Italian was not proficient enough for him to stand his ground; he might have felt he needed to respect an older authority or he was disempowered simply because he was unfamiliar with the Italian system of validating tickets. On the other hand, in the dramatic frame, Teodoro shows a degree of empowerment in his reaction to the ticket inspector. He firmly stands his ground, contesting the authority of the inspector. It seems to be the dramatic tension within the dramatic frame (needing to get to his interviewee), resonating with a past experience, that fuels his response in the drama. A significant detail in Teodoro's reaction is the gesture he performs as the ticket inspector says, 'Shall we stop the train and let them off?' This gesture, consisting of a curled fist moving up and down, is a typical Italian expression of disbelief. In gesture studies, it is classified as an emblem: a culture-specific gesture, which completes an utterance by adding further meaning (Stam & McCafferty, 2008). By performing this emblem, Teodoro is embodying a non-verbal behaviour characteristic of the Italian language. This embodied response suggests that Teodoro is interculturally engaged through his role as an Italian journalist. This is also reinforced by the context-specific comment he makes: 'This one is stamped!' Significantly, in the questionnaire, Teodoro rated 'intercultural' as the highest value in his engagement triad (8/10). His perception of engagement in SM1 seems to be focused on the intercultural domain.

*Intercultural awareness*

The data suggest that in the SM1, some participants reached a degree of intercultural awareness. In the student-participants' focus group, when I asked whether the process drama had helped to reflect on intercultural issues, Mara (23-year-old, Chinese) shouted, 'Yes! On the train!' In the interview, Mara further expanded on this:

**Interviewer**: What is the moment that you remember most strongly, most vividly?
**Mara**: When … we catch the train! […]
**Interviewer**: In that specific moment, how did you feel?
**Mara**: Mmm … the difference between … the culture difference between Chinese and Italy!
**Interviewer**: Why? In what way?
**Mara**: Because the Chinese, they … they remain in their chair; they don't hear the … police order. But maybe Italians … go! (Mara, 2: 4–14)

Here, Mara's comment seems to indicate that during the drama she reflected on Italian and Chinese behaviour ('the difference between ... the culture difference between Chinese and Italy'). Through the drama, Mara seems to have embodied a behaviour that triggered a strong affective response. This drama experience invited Mara to reflect and analyse the situation in terms of her own culture and the Italian culture. This process resonates with Alred *et al.*'s (2003) notion of being intercultural: 'experiencing otherness' as reflection, analysis and action.

A second example of dramatic tension generating intercultural awareness is drawn from Vera (22-year-old, Chinese):

**Vera**: On the train [pause] in this, in that moment ... I thought [pause] I thought the Italian culture maybe like that, but in China this is not [...] In China people don't ... do like this very much.

**Interviewer**: They don't do that? And were you thinking this, as you were on the train?

**Vera**: I thought: hey ... this is Italy! [Laughs] (Vera, 3: 34–40)

Through this comment Vera grants us access to her inner reasoning during that specific dramatic frame. She is processing the dramatic frame, while at the same time being engaged in some degree of intercultural reflection ('Hey! This is Italy!'). This is reinforced as she states, 'In your workshop ... I've learnt, how Italians, how Italians, ehm ... how Italians think' (Vera, 4: 33). Significantly, Vera's questionnaire reveals that her intercultural value is the highest in the triad (8/10). The trigger here might have been a response to the intercultural dramatic tension, as well as role, place and space, evoked by navigating two different cultural systems.

### *Intercultural meaning-making*

Below is an account of the group discussion (out of role) that stemmed from the train arrest episode (SM1), as described by observing teacher-participant Valeria in her written observations:

> Intercultural reflection: The teacher comments about their behaviour on the train, Chun says 'We have become like Italians because the roles are Italians'. [...] To the question 'What do you think an Italian would do in a similar situation?' Huifang replies: 'He'd call mummy!' Everyone laughs. They reflect on the fact that actually they refused to notify their parents when they ended up in jail [...] In this situation, they say, they would be drawn to call someone powerful to resolve the problem, rather than a family member to be comforted. Many say the typical Italian man is mammone[2] and that Chinese people are more independent. (Valeria, OBS, 9: 35)

As Valeria's observation indicates, the discussion immediately following SM1 generated an intercultural reflection, comparing the Italian and Chinese cultural systems. Topics also emerging from this discussion ranged from reacting to injustices, dealing with emergencies overseas and acting under pressure to relationships with parents and being independent, all of which were framed comparatively across the Italian and Chinese cultures. Thus, through experience and reflection, the student-participants were able to negotiate intercultural meaning. Another point from the observation above is that, through the drama, followed by the intercultural reflection, one student-participant became an intercultural resonator for the others. In particular, Huifang's sense of humour ('he'd call mummy!') is quite poignant in portraying a stereotypical Italian way to deal with the arrest situation. This comment denotes a refined ability to pinpoint a classic Italian cultural trait (*mammone*). Indeed, Huifang stood out from the rest of the cohort: she travelled to Milan independently (before joining the university program), and she lived with Italian housemates (rather than with Chinese fellow students, like her classmates did). Her witty reply suggests a degree of sensibility, an 'engagement with otherness' and an ability to make fun of it. It also raises an important question: To what degree is humour intercultural, particularly when it turns on a cultural stereotype?

The intercultural process of meaning-making seems to be *explicit* for the participants of this cohort, in the sense that they were able to articulate, reflect and engage in the discussion. This, again, emerges from the reflective phase of the drama. Below is an entry from the teacher's journal, reporting on the discussion that followed SM1:

> I say that their refusal [on the train] intrigues me, I ask them: 'Have you become like the Italians?' General giggles (embarrassed, but also delighted) follow here. I then pin down a question: if a Chinese person that doesn't know Italy were in this situation, how would she/he react? We then start discussing the Italian habit of relying on family, and of protesting, to end up talking about what do we live for: to eat, to sleep, for my family are some of the answers. [...] Teresa says: 'I live for working', stirring everyone to react; everyone attacks her. I recall getting goose bumps when Rebecca says: 'I just live for life's sake'. (RJ, 41: 8–19)

This discussion can be contemplated in terms of the shared negotiation of meaning: Teresa's provocative statement ('I live for working') is openly questioned by others, inducing the group to reflect, analyse and negotiate new meanings related to the purpose of life. As these examples suggest, it appears that a felt-experience in the drama, followed by a semi-structured intercultural reflection, empowered the student-participants to generate intercultural awareness and intercultural meaning-making. This process, I argue, was fuelled by the intercultural dramatic tension in the drama.

## Case study 2/3: Implicit intercultural engagement

In case study 2 and 3, the process leading to intercultural meaning-making seemed to remain *implicit*: the student-participants, when asked, could identify intercultural themes, but did not appear to make explicit intercultural meaning from these. Below, I explore key data that led me to this consideration.

### *Experience*

The pretext for case study 2 and 3 was the short film, *Buongiorno* (2006) directed by Melo Primo and produced by Beka Films.[3] In the short film, a middle-aged man wakes up in the morning to find that his reflection in the mirror has a life of its own and will not reflect his own image back. A sequence of 'dreams within the dream' follows, ending in a dramatic crescendo that sees the protagonist going insane. Music has a particularly important role in the film, featuring sound by composer Ennio Morricone, famous for his Western genre soundtracks – evoking a stereotypical cowboy duel between the man and his own reflection. In the drama workshop that was structured around this short film, the protagonist was a teacher of Italian (L2) who, after having seen his own reflection come alive, was found inside the lift of his own building, in a catatonic state, refusing to talk. He would only write one sentence, over and over: 'Mirrors should stop reflecting'. Student-participants were in role as psychologists working for the Italian Association of Psychology and heard about an alleged schizophrenic case, a language teacher who had been found in a lift. The psychologists were asked to create and implement an action plan to take the subject out of the lift. After several trials, he was finally admitted to a psychiatric hospital, where the drama was peppered by several escape attempts. SM3, the SM chosen to analyse the participants' responses in case study 3, was the moment when the psychologists removed the patient from the lift. The main intercultural reflection that emerged from the drama was the cultural generalisation of the tendency of Italian families to 'cover up' mental issues within the family in order to maintain a façade of respectability. This led to the theme of mental illness perceived as taboo in Italian culture (Balboni, 2007) and on the stereotypes around this sensitive topic. The topic gave rise to a discussion in which the student-participants, who came from Brazil, Iran, Japan, Russia, Slovenia, Switzerland, Taiwan and the United States, reflected on how mental illness is perceived in their own cultures.

### *Intercultural tension*

Whereas in case study 1 the dramatic tension was explicitly intercultural, starting from the pretext to dramatic roles, situation, focus, place and mood, in case study 2/3, the dramatic tension was not explicitly tied to an intercultural domain. The pretext (short film) had no defined intercultural connotations; the setting was minimalist and did not point to specific cultural traits. Similarly, the focus and mood were not related to a particular cultural context. Consequently, in the discussion following the pretext, the intercultural dimension was not attended to. Given that the short film was devoid of specific references to the Italian cultural background, I attempted to inject a degree of intercultural tension through role-creation. For example, as the student-participants created their roles, I asked them to experiment with different nationalities. Their choice of role was eclectic: many chose to play a psychologist from a different country; some chose to play psychologists from different regions of Italy. For some participants, choosing these roles was a source of intercultural tension, as in Marika's example:

| | |
|---|---|
| **Interviewer**: | Why did you decide to come [to Italy] and study Italian? |
| **Marika [giggles]**: | Because … my grandparents were Italian, from ... Ravenna, in Emilia Romagna and … I don't know, I was born with this desire [laughs] to study Italian! |
| **Interviewer**: | In the drama, I remember you said you were from Ravenna, right? |
| **Marika**: | Oh yes, I said that, yes. |
| **Interviewer**: | Ah ah, so … |
| **Marika**: | I was looking for a name … an identity and … my grandma came up! |
| **Interviewer**: | Sure, right. Very interesting.<br>[Marika laughs] |
| **Interviewer**: | Because perhaps you identified... with an Italian part of yourself? |
| **Marika**: | Yes very much so, yes. (Marika, 1: 18–32) |

For Marika (53-year-old, Brazilian), playing a role that validated her desire to reconnect with her Italian identity might have influenced her experience of the drama on an implicit level. However, this was not discussed at any stage during the drama; its potential for intercultural awareness and meaning-making was not harnessed openly in the dramatic world and did not result in explicit intercultural discussion. Later during the drama, Marika could identify a thread for intercultural awareness, but she did not point to any explicit intercultural meaning-making. When asked whether she had learnt anything about herself and her culture, she replied, 'Not that I have learnt … about my culture, I learnt about other cultures' (Marika, 4: 45). Whatever Marika learnt about other cultures remains unspoken. Significantly, her 'intercultural' value for SM3 is as low as 1/10, while the affective is rated as 7/10 and the communicative as 9/10.

Above, intercultural metaxis was defined as the dramatic tension triggered in participants experiencing a *disjunction* between how they are responding to the drama and how they would respond in real life – when these two frames relate to different cultural systems of beliefs. Obviously, intercultural metaxis is an intangible element; as a result, it is not possible to prove its presence. However, it appears that some student-participants' comments, for example Eduarda's, indicate a degree of intercultural metaxis. During the rescue operation from the lift (SM3), Eduarda (27-year-old, Brazilian) chose not to participate actively, but to just stand outside the lift, observing. Yet, in the interview, Eduarda mentioned that she had an uncle who suffered from catatonic schizophrenia and that the drama reminded her of her uncle. From the outside, Eduarda's participation might have seemed minimal compared to other participants; she was the one who moved the least in the group. However, a closer analysis suggests that she was engaged in the drama. Her gaze was intense, fixed on the subject; her look was concerned, her head tilted, her hands clasped together in apprehension. Later, when the psychologists gathered again to discuss a new strategy, Eduarda became the centre of attention, proposing a new plan as the others gathered and listened attentively. In the interview, Eduarda stated that her engagement with this SM extended well after the workshop:

> I was inside...the character, yes. Also, the moment when I returned home [...] Even then, it was difficult to [laughs] Desconectar. (Eduarda, 3: 23–25)

For Eduarda it was difficult to disconnect (*desconectar*) with the drama; in other words, she felt deeply connected. Nevertheless, in the various opportunities for reflection following that intense moment, Eduarda chose not to share her uncle's mental illness with the group. Ironically, having a protective attitude towards family members was the very topic we were discussing. This paradox may have been quite obvious to Eduarda during our discussions on mental illness as taboo in the family unit, increasing her affective reaction. Indeed, from her interview comments it appears that Eduarda was experiencing a degree of intercultural metaxis connected to her involvement in the drama and her personal family history, as she rated her 'intercultural' engagement as 8/10 and her 'affective' engagement as 9/10. However, she chose not to open it up to the group; her meaning-making remained implicit.

### *Intercultural awareness*

Teacher-participant Rossana, following the observation of SM3 commented:

> Towards the end, [the student-participants] needed to be spoon-fed again, in the intercultural reflection... I don't think it was working very

> well because... it's not... it's not like it didn't work, but there wasn't that kind of debate that a teacher always hopes for at the end of a class. (Rossana, 13: 22–27)

Similarly, according to teacher-participant Giovanni's observation notes, the reflection following SM3 was 'stilted':

> In the last phase, the intercultural reflection, everyone replied individually to the teacher, and more because they were asked to, rather than because they really needed to talk about it. (Giovanni, OBS, 1: 46–48)

In Rossana and Giovanni's perception, the discussion following SM3 did not trigger any intercultural meaning-making. This discrepancy with case study 1 may be related to the 'intercultural/dramatic framework' of the drama: the pretext of case study 2/3 contained no explicit intercultural tension, and the dramatic structure did not encourage any intercultural awareness. In particular, the structure differed from case study 1 in terms of the elements of dramatic focus and place and their active manipulation within the intercultural dimension. While in case study 1 the intercultural focus and place were carefully framed (e.g. in the Shanghai office; at the airport in Rome; on the train from Rome to Milan; in Milan at the interview), in case study 2/3 there was no *active manipulation* of intercultural focus and place. Consequently, participants may not have become aware of such an intercultural dimension and may not have felt the need to discuss it. Although group reflection was facilitated, this discussion was structured by the teacher, rather than driven by a felt-experience fuelled by intercultural tension – as the teachers' comments above indicate.

### *Intercultural meaning-making*

When asked if she learnt anything about Italian culture compared to her own culture, Olga (27-year-old, Russian) replied:

> During the class, we spoke about … a lot about the psychological theme, thoughts, mentally disabled people; and we compared … different cultures like Italian, Russian and another student's as well, like American and Japanese, so I … kind of … had a chance to compare this, how is it in different countries. (Olga, 3: 3)

Olga was able to identify an intercultural theme that was explored during the drama, but she did not elaborate on any explicit intercultural meaning-making triggered by the drama. Olga stated that she 'had a chance to compare', but did not discuss what she reflected upon, during the drama. Again, what she felt associated with this topic during the drama remained implicit.

Catherine's comments (23-year-old, American) also seemed to imply such a discrepancy. On the one hand, Catherine stated that her intercultural perception had not shifted as a result of the experience:

**Interviewer**: Since doing the drama workshops, do you think that something has changed in your understanding of the Italian culture?
**Catherine**: I mean, I can just think of one moment, specifically when we discussed ... someone had a mental disability ... and we discussed, from each of -you know, where we come from, each of our countries ... how it's viewed, how it's dealt with. But I didn't feel ... no, I didn't feel surprised.
**Interviewer**: Did you already know about?
**Catherine**: Yeah, I mean I spend a lot of time in Italy with my dad and I would sort of listen to ... those reactions to things. (Catherine, 3: 20–39)

Catherine did not think that she had shifted her understanding or questioned her beliefs. On the other hand, significantly, in the same interview, she described process drama in terms of 'acquiring new intercultural perspectives':

> I would define [process drama] as a technique that allows the students to approach a language and leave their sort of cultural baggage ... put it aside for a moment which can allow you to sort of ... take in what you're learning ... in a less filtered way. I would describe it as that. (Catherine, 3: 49)

This remark points to Catherine's view of process drama as a medium to increase intercultural awareness, decentring from stereotypical perspectives ('taking in what you're learning in a less filtered way'). Nevertheless, while framing it this way, she was not able to apply this discourse to her own experience in the drama. Interestingly, in the questionnaire, she self-evaluated her 'intercultural' engagement for SM2 as 9/10. Yet, she was not able to articulate such engagement. Again, this suggests a discrepancy between her understanding of process drama and her self-evaluation score.

The analysis revealed that none of the interviews in case study 2/3 provided any explicit evidence of intercultural meaning-making. Clearly, meaning is an abstract, intangible concept; by acknowledging that the student-participants did not share their intercultural meaning-making with the interviewer, it cannot be inferred that they did not engage in intercultural meaning-making. This may also have been caused by the interviewer's inability to follow-up in the interview, or by the language proficiency of the interviewees (most of whom were interviewed in Italian, their second or third language). Yet, student-participants in case study 1 were asked the same questions by the same interviewer and were able to elaborate, unprompted, with lower language proficiency. Moreover, some student participants in case study 2/3 were interviewed in English (first language) and seemed to confirm this argument. In essence, what can be inferred from the data is that a *discrepancy* between high self-evaluation scores and the comments in the interviews points to intercultural meaning-making, if it occurred, remaining *implicit* in the participants' felt-experience. This might be connected to the specific 'intercultural/ dramatic framework' of the drama, in particular to the absence of explicit intercultural tension in the pretext, offering less opportunities for intercultural reflection.

## Intercultural Dramatic Framework

I identified the major points of difference between the case studies in their intercultural/dramatic framework, specifically: (1) the intercultural dramatic tension in the pretext; (2) the manipulation of the intercultural elements in the drama structure; and (3) the scope and depth of intercultural reflection generated by the drama. In Table 9.2, I compare the intercultural/dramatic structures of case study 1 and 2/3.

The differences in the intercultural/dramatic structures may have resulted in the student-participants' different degrees of engagement in the intercultural domain. In case study 1, the pretext contained *explicit* intercultural dramatic focus and tension. This resulted in roles, situation, focus, mood and all other elements of drama assuming an intercultural dimension. In case study 2, the lack of intercultural dramatic tension in the pretext resulted in a less explicit intercultural focus in the elements of drama and therefore limited intercultural reflection. Thus, an important point emerging here is the vital importance of the pretext for holding intercultural dramatic tension to generate intercultural engagement.

Moreover, in case study 1, dramatic place was manipulated and closely related to intercultural focus and mood and the various types of intercultural tension. In SM1, the element of intercultural dramatic focus was crucial (being on a train from Rome to Milan), and it was manipulated throughout the drama (having to return to Shanghai to present the article, etc.). In case study 2/3, intercultural dramatic focus was not well-defined to begin with. Importantly, the intercultural focus did not shift as in case study 1 (traveling from China to Italy and back to report the outcome of the mission). The dramatic element of mood within the pretexts also differed.

In case study 1, the pretext was related to graduates specialised in the Italian culture, applying for a job as journalists in China; in the real life

**Table 9.2** Intercultural/dramatic structures of case study, two/three

| | *Case study 1: Intercultural dramatic structure* | *Case study 2/3: Intercultural dramatic structure* |
|---|---|---|
| **Pretext** | Intercultural focus: An editor is looking for apprentice journalists for the Italo-Chinese editorial at the Chamber of Commerce in Shanghai | Intercultural focus: N/A |
| | Intercultural tension: The journalists need to write an article appealing to Chinese businessmen interested in Italian business | Intercultural tension: not specified |
| **Manipulation of dramatic elements** | Manipulation of focus: Starting from the editorial in Shanghai, travel to Italy, then back to Shanghai | N/A |
| | Intercultural dramatic tension (of the task): Journalists' arrest on the train, preventing them getting to the interview on time | Intercultural dramatic tension (of relationship): Covering of mental illness as taboo by family members |
| | Intercultural dramatic tension (of surprise): The unexpected arrest | N/A |
| | Intercultural dramatic tension (of mystery): The arrest is connected to the journalists' association with the Chamber of Commerce (their employer) | N/A |
| **Reflection** | Ongoing, stemming naturally after each episode, as well as at the end of the drama | Planned at the end of the drama |

of the participants this might have been a desirable context connected to their sense of high-achievement and business-oriented attitude. The mood associated was one of accomplishment, aligning with their motivation to learn the language and succeed in their career. In case study 2/3, the pretext was related to psychologists dealing with a schizophrenic man; setting the drama in a psychiatric ward might have been a threatening context and not aligned with their motivation to learn the Italian language. As a result, some might have chosen not to share openly, or even to resist, intercultural meaning-making. Thus, structuring a drama connected to their motivation to learn the language seemed to have an impact on their willingness to engage.

# Conclusion

As Fleming (2003) argues, drama can be a form of intercultural education. In his own words, 'Drama can provide concrete contexts and affective engagement for the participants and by its very nature can be seen as a form of intercultural education' (Fleming, 2003: 97). An important point emerging from the study is that, in a process drama structure, the nature of the dramatic elements plays a significant role in its effectiveness as a vehicle for intercultural engagement – with the intercultural dimension being implicit or explicit in the learner's experience. In this chapter, I have explored how this process unfolded in three case studies, analysing one dramatic frame in each drama structure. The construct of intercultural engagement was considered through the lens of 'intercultural experience' (Alred *et al.*, 2003) and manifested as a process of meaning-making, fuelled by dramatic tension, triggering degrees of intercultural awareness. I referred to this framework as the 'intercultural/dramatic framework' of the drama: The presence of *intercultural* dramatic *tension* in the pretext, which in turn affected the intercultural connotation of all other dramatic elements, as well as the opportunities for intercultural reflection arising from each episode.

In an earlier project, while reflecting-in-action on two different process drama sequences, I attempted some recommendations, such as 'choosing an educational objective with an intercultural potential' together with 'awareness of dramatic tension when choosing the pretext' (Piazzoli, 2010b: 10). By reflecting-on-action, I now realise that tending to these conditions is essential to generate a degree of intercultural engagement. If that is the case, then what kind of training might empower language teachers to feel confident in planning a rich intercultural/dramatic framework? Intercultural dramatic tension is not a mathematical formula. In view of current educational institutions pushing for a standardised model of education, is it possible to formulate a general intercultural/dramatic framework? These questions remain unanswered; yet, I believe that the artistry of teaching is inextricably connected to context, and attempts to over-generalise into a one-size-fits-all prescription may lose some of the educational potency intrinsic to the form. Future research stemming from this project could focus on the depth and connection between planning, intercultural engagement and artistry, to support drama educators' teaching experiences in the intercultural classroom.

## Notes

(1) All participants' names are pseudonyms.
(2) *Mammone* is a common Italian cultural trait of the grown-up man dependent on his mother.
(3) Used with permission from the director and the producers.

## References

Alred, G., Byram, M. and Fleming, M. (eds) (2003) *Intercultural Experience and Education*. Clevedon: Multilingual Matters.

Balboni, P.E. (2007) *La Comunicazione Interculturale*. Venezia: Marsilio Editori.

Boal, A. (1995) *The Rainbow of Desire: The Boal Method of Theatre and Therapy* (trans. Adrian Jackson). New York: Routledge.

Bolton, G. (1984) *Drama as Education: An Argument for Placing Drama at the Centre of the Curriculum*. Harlow: Longman.

Bräuer, G. (ed.) (2002) *Body and Language: Intercultural Learning Through Drama*. Westport, CT: Ablex Publishing.

Bundy, P. (1999) Dramatic tension: Towards an understanding of 'Tension of Intimacy'. Unpublished PhD thesis, Griffith University.

Davis, S. (2008) Coming of age: Dialogues about 'Dramawise' and the elements of drama. *NJ Drama Australia Journal* 31 (2), 59–71.

Ferholt, B. (2014) Perezhivanie in researching playwords: Applying the concept of perezhivanie in the study of play. In S. Davis, B. Ferholt, H. Grainger Clemson, S. Jansson and A. Marjanovic-Shane (eds) *Dramatic Interactions in Education: Vygotskian and Sociocultural Approaches to Drama, Education and Research* (pp. 57–78). London: Bloomsbury.

Fleming, M. (2003) Intercultural experience and drama. In G. Alred, M. Byram and M. Fleming (eds) *Intercultural Experience and Education* (pp. 87–100). Clevedon: Multilingual Matters.

Gupta, A.S. (2003) Changing the focus: A discussion of the dynamics of the intercultural experience. In G. Alred, M. Byram and M. Fleming (eds) *Intercultural Experience and Education* (pp. 155–178). Clevedon: Multilingual Matters.

Haseman, B. and O'Toole, J. (1986) *Dramawise: An Introduction to the Elements of Drama*. Melbourne: Heinemann.

Kao, S.M. (1995) From script to impromptu: Learning a second language through process drama. In P. Taylor and C. Hoepper (eds) *Selected Readings in Drama and Theatre Education: The IDEA '95 Papers* (2nd, Brisbane, Australia, July 1995). *NADIE Research Monograph Series*, 3. Brisbane: IDEA Publications.

Kao, S.M. and O'Neill, C. (1998) *Words into Worlds: Learning a Second Language Through Process Drama*. London: Ablex Publishing Corporation.

Morgan, N. and Saxton, J. (1987) *Teaching Drama: A Mind of Many Wonders*. Cheltenham: Stanley Thornes.

O'Neill, C. (1995) *Drama Worlds: A Framework for Process Drama*. Portsmouth: Heinemann.

O'Toole, J. (1992) *The Process of Drama: Negotiating Art and Meaning*. London: Routledge.

Pavis, P. (1998) *Dictionary of the Theatre: Terms, Concepts, and Analysis*. Toronto: University of Toronto Press.

Piazzoli, E. (2010a) Process drama and additional language teaching: Reflections on the Dante Alighieri immersion weekends. *Applied Theatre Researcher IDEA Journal* (11), 1–12.

Piazzoli, E. (2010b) Navigating the labyrinth: A study of engagement and artistry in process drama for additional language teaching and learning. Unpublished PhD thesis, Griffith University, Brisbane.

Rothwell, J. (2011) Bodies and language: Process drama and intercultural language learning in a beginner language classroom. *Research in Drama Education: The Journal of Applied Theatre and Performance* 16 (4), 575–594.

Schewe, M. (2014) Paving the way towards performative teaching and learning: Keynote address, 30/05/2014. Performative Teaching, Learning and Research Conference, University College Cork (UCC), 29 May–1 June 2014.

Stam, G. and McCafferty, S.G. (2008) Gesture studies and second language acquisition: A review. In S.G. McCafferty and G. Stam (eds) *Gesture: Second Language Acquisition and Classroom Research* (pp. 3–24). New York: Routledge.
Vygotsky, L. (1994) The problem of the environment. In R. Van Der Veer and J. Valsiner (eds) *The Vygotsky Reader* (pp. 338–354). Oxford: Blackwell.

# Part 5

# Focus on Performance and Biography

# 10 Enacting Life: Dialogue and Mediation in Cross-Cultural Contexts

Daniel Feldhendler

After a brief review of my 40 years practice and action-research at the Goethe University, Frankfurt (Germany), and in broader adult education (1976–2016), followed by an equally brief review of humanistic approaches in foreign language teaching designed as *relational dramaturgy*, I will focus on my current approach, *enacting life*. The creation of privileged spaces in learning and teaching contexts provides places for advanced language learners/students to tell and perform their own life stories either of language biography or of intercultural experiences. Some applications of this integration of *playback theatre* and *life stories approaches* in intercultural education will be presented. The conclusion will point out the necessity of ongoing professional development for teachers and the need for a code of ethics in lifelong learning programmes opening to dialogue and mediation in cross-cultural contexts.

The expression *enacting life* is used to describe an approach which integrates psychodrama and action methods developed by J.L. Moreno, theatre and life stories. This approach is a practical one, and its application can provide fruitful insights into questions that arise in interpersonal contexts, such as the development of social bonds when using drama-based activities in foreign/second language teaching, or how to take account of the singularities and self-expression of the individual in the context of dialogue. It helps us explore, for example, cross-cultural mediation, focusing on relationship-building and synergies between the individual, the group and the society.

Using a theatrical form catalyses the process of contextualising personal experiences. In this kind of performative approach, participants tell their personal life stories in the target language so as to talk to and see each other: participants become both agents and subjects of their story/history. The playing out of life stories in the foreign/second language counts as both dynamic anthropology and cross-cultural hermeneutics, and opens up a social and moral imagination rich in transformative dynamics.

Sharing biographical moments in a narrative form and mirroring the immediate dynamics through theatrical transformation incorporate experiences into personal resources of knowledge and perceptions of oneself and others. As an important tool in identity work, *enacting life* enables and promotes the formation of a 'narrative identity' between the individual and the community. It is also of increasing value as a tool for dynamic learning and for cultural and anthropological exploration.

## Humanistic Approaches in Foreign Language Teaching: A Personal Path

Having completed language studies at the University of Paris-Nanterre (German, French, English), I moved to Frankfurt on Main in 1969 to take up post-graduate studies in education at Goethe University and have remained in Frankfurt ever since. From 1971 on, I was involved in action-research programmes organised by the French-German Office for Youth (Paris/Berlin, http://www.dfjw.org/), where new forms of language learning (Tandem) and team-teaching were being developed, which experimented with performative approaches as modes of mediation in binational and intercultural encounter groups. During this period of intensive studies and research, I was also actively involved in teaching French as a foreign language in French and German adult education institutes that welcomed these new developments. In 1976, I took up a teaching post at Goethe University, and in 1977, I joined Marie and Bernard Dufeu in developing new approaches for language acquisition at the universities of Mainz and Frankfurt on Main, and later at the *Centre de Psychodramaturgie*, which we founded in 1983 in Mainz (http://www.psychodramaturgie.de/). By that time, we had developed three approaches: linguistic psychodramaturgy (PDL) (Dufeu, 1983a, 1990, 1994, 2003), relational pedagogy (Dufeu, 1982, 1983b) and relational dramaturgy (Feldhendler, 1983, 1993, 1999a). These procedures have in common that they stem from interdisciplinary sources. They combine basic principles and models from humanistic psychology (especially classical psychodrama), theatre/drama in education and applied linguistics.

After completing training in psychodrama at the German Moreno Institutes (1978–1983), I began to integrate what I saw as the humanistic potential of these approaches into my teaching practice at universities, in adult education and in teacher training. I used theatre-based techniques and was influenced to varying degrees by the Morenian psychodrama tradition. In 1993, I published an essay in English summarising our special contributions to the development of humanistic approaches as applied to language learning and teaching, in which I introduce the concept of relational dramaturgy, an approach derived from both dramaturgy and psychodrama (Feldhendler, 1993).

## Relational dramaturgy

Relational dramaturgy follows the principles of *drama in education*. The term 'dramaturgy' in this case draws on the original Greek meaning of drama, which is 'action'. Dramaturgy is the catalysing framework for the action and therefore also for the language. Used as an approach for foreign language instruction, it offers students greater opportunities to express themselves. It promotes a learning process in which expression of meaning, verbal and non-verbal, is integrated in a comprehensive working method. Above all, the dramaturgic models and principles of A. Boal (1980, 1989, 1990), J. Fox (1994, 1999, 2015) G. Barret (1989), J.P. Ryngaert (1985), L. Sheleen (1987), E. Souriau (1950) and K.S. Stanislavski (1988) have influenced the development of relational dramaturgy. I have deepened my knowledge of their work through participation in training courses over a long period of time, as well as through personal exchanges, especially with Augusto Boal (Theatre of the Oppressed, from 1979) and with Jonathan Fox (Playback Theatre, from 1988).

## Theatre of the oppressed

Developed by Augusto Boal in the 1970s, this dialogue-based and transitive method aims to encourage awareness, to deal with societal themes through group experience and to develop ways of resolving present or future conflicts. Many of the tools that Boal developed, such as image theatre and forum theatre, have been incorporated into current performative practice in foreign/second languages.

## Playback theatre

Developed from 1975 on by Jonathan Fox and Jo Salas, this form of improvisational theatre encompasses an accessible approach to everyday life, real experience and ambiguities or conflicts through their enactment as personal experiences, personal stories or life histories. Fox (1987) himself is trained in psychodrama. Playback theatre as community theatre constitutes above all a renaissance of oral history and transmission, moving beyond mere recounting of story to its adaptation and extension in a collective creation. Playback theatre is used as a tool in many diverse cultural and social contexts, such as social services, adult education and theatre training. This approach is also gaining significance in socio-pedagogical and pedagogical institutions, schools and universities. The training offered at the Centre for Playback Theatre (New York) and by the international network (IPTN) help to develop key social skills through the promotion of interactive, communicative and creative competencies in contexts of high diversity.

## Psychodrama

Psychodrama has been more commonly known as a therapeutic method, but today it is employed in a broad range of activities. Rooted in children's play and in theatre, psychodrama's potential for non-therapeutic applications was noted by its founder, Jacob Levy Moreno (1889–1974). He referred to these as 'action methods' (Moreno 1974, 1988), indicating spontaneous theatre (*Stegreiftheater*) (Moreno, 1923); forms such as the 'living newspaper', sociodrama (which explores groups and their problems), sociometry (which measures relationships within groups) and role play. Psychodramatic methods seek to arouse and promote creative spontaneity:

> I have always tried to show that my approach was meant as much more than a psychotherapeutic method - my ideas have emphasized that creativity and spontaneity affect the very roots of vitality and spiritual development, and thus affect our involvement in every sphere of our lives. (Moreno, in Blatner, 1973: VI)

According to Leutz (1974), psychodrama is an 'invitation to an encounter – in play'. Schützenberger (1970) sees psychodrama as a tool for exploring and modifying one's own attitude faced with that of the Other; as a training in spontaneity and creativity, and thus as a means of liberating conflicts. These practices are based on the philosophy of encounter and dialogue. A theory and practice of action was developed to this end, a praxeology of qualitative development of human relations. The qualities that facilitate this encounter with the Other are:

- empathy (*Einfühlung*) to develop an aptitude to communicate
- greater awareness of the Self and the Other
- role flexibility (through the experience of changing or reversing roles)
- handling and resolving conflicts
- developing attitudes that allow openness

## Psychodrama as pedagogy

To work psychodramatically means to bring about an interpersonal encounter. In the acquisition of a foreign language, encounter implies all interactions in the learning group – that is, the relation to oneself, to others and to the environment – and it is the driving force of language production and of speech itself. The process of foreign language acquisition then depends on the participants' relational capacities and on the dynamics within the learning group, which functions as a 'living book', in effect replacing a textbook. As Dufeu (1983a) has stated, it is a question of 'learning through experiencing'. Within a teaching situation, we aim at communication via a relational mode that is as genuine as possible, attempting to build and offer structures orientated towards the participants and taking into account both the current status and the evolution of the group. A pedagogic activity should be based on relational and interactional dynamics: the linguistic activity is focused on the participant and the group. The process of learning moves towards a *relational progression*, that is, towards the wishes and expressional needs of the participants of a given group in a particular situation defined by the *here-and-now*. The teaching of linguistic structures and correction of errors does not determine the learning situation but is rather embedded in the group's expressional needs and their realisation *in situ*. The relational and interactional dynamics find support in the dramaturgic catalyst. These two elements form the pillars of relational dramaturgy for language learning, which can be thought of as a kind of psychodramatic pedagogy (Springer, 1995), or pedagogy with a Morenian orientation. Moreno, in his book *The Theater of Spontaneity*, insists that

> [t]he reproductive process of learning must move into second place; first emphasis should be given to the productive spontaneous-creative process of learning. The exercises [sic] and training of spontaneity is the chief subject of the school of the future. (Moreno, 1973: 81)

## Relational Dramaturgy in Language Learning

Relational dramaturgy involves learners actively in the process and progress of the course; they experience the language and determine the linguistic content of their learning themselves; they are actors instead of consumers. The work is organised around the group or around a theme to which the group responds favourably. The learning itself is holistic: body, pose, gesture, movement, feelings, emotions and voice are all considered to be supportive instruments of choice as well as the constituent elements of a humanistic 'pedagogy of being' (Dufeu, 1994). In relational dramaturgy, situations and themes are transferred to and performed in a specific space and time, in a scene that channels and catalyses the energy, attention and concentration of the individuals and the group. To support his/her activities, the instructor may employ psychodramatic and psychodramaturgic procedures, such as the techniques of doubling, the mirror and role reversal (Dufeu, 1994, 2003) instead of focusing on gaps in knowledge of vocabulary and linguistic structures as with the customary learning material. If systematisation in the learning process occurs, instead of pattern drills, the mechanisms of communication are established: an atmosphere of 'stimulation and not simulation' (Dufeu, 1992). The dramaturgic dynamic allows redundant but creative learning situations to occur, creating many variations in transforming themes, situations, moments and scenes. Each time, in each new situation, the language and its paralinguistic elements are approached and considered from very different perspectives. This ensures both linguistic and relational deepening: they go hand in hand. Linguistic learning grows in tandem with the dynamics of the group. In a spontaneous, playful situation, the sensory and emotional memory can work as a mnemotechnical mechanism (Rellstab, 1976: 36).

## Inclusive learning and teaching

In addition to language acquisition, the practices associated with relational dramaturgy can bring much benefit to students as a contribution to:

- situations of personal evolution
- sensitisation of the perception of Self and Other
- development of potential and of relational faculties

Analogous to the psychodramatic model, the teaching process should follow three stages:

- warm-up and sensitisation
- elaboration and deepening
- conclusion

The first step is the basis for the quality of the later encounter and exchange in preparing the group's subsequent learning atmosphere, receptivity and spirit of collaboration. Therefore, every teaching sequence starts with a *warm-up and sensitisation* stage. Directed by the teacher, the exercises begin with the non-verbal and then move to the verbal. They promote the initial contact with individuals and with the group as a whole. The structured development of these exercises leads to the themes and sensitises the participants for the transposition to the stage and the performance. They offer the opportunity for 'warming up' to being in the group, to the language and to the theme of the session. In the *elaboration and deepening stage*, the situations and themes are transformed into spontaneous play. The language is experienced directly in the identification of the 'actor-students' with their roles. Speaking as a means of communication occurs in the here-and-now situation. The participants learn to control paralinguistic elements in the action, as well as to find their spontaneity and perception supported by communication. The situations can be played out on a real, an imaginary or a symbolic level. The realisation of the spontaneous play takes place in a creative sphere of dramaturgic and relational tension that represents a 'potential space' as a particularly fruitful place for cultural and linguistic production (Winnicott, 1989: 116). In the final stage, or *conclusion*, feedback is an essential element. In articulating the situations they have enacted, the students reflect on how they experienced the roles and how they identified with the roles or the actions.

Feedback is also important in building up intercultural awareness. It requires the use of interdisciplinary approaches which aim to increase awareness of the complexity of the field being tackled and to integrate the affective and intersubjective dimension in experiential-type practices. Interdisciplinary approaches that integrate the psychodramatic approach and specific theatrical forms are called for (Feldhendler, 1990a, 1990b, 1999b): specifically, those that can be used as tools for analysis, intervention and change. Such approaches act as cultural and social mirrors, as relational indicators and as catalysts for participants involved in intercultural communication. Collectively, these and other methods of intervention can be termed 'techniques of involvement' (Demorgon & Lipiansky, 1999).

In the different phases of learning, a didactically meaningful progression of increasing sensitivity to cross-cultural relations can be discerned. We distinguish:

- work on representations supported by images and photo techniques, along with recourse to imagology (dynamics of self-representations and representations of others)
- work on metacommunication (perception of the implicit and of intersubjectivity)
- mediation as an approach to proxemia, ambiguity, polarity, tensions and conflict resolution
- work on lived experience

## The application of relational dramaturgy in a university context

From 1976 to 2014, I taught and organised courses based on the principles of relational dramaturgy at Goethe University's Institute of Romance Languages and Literatures. These courses differed in type and level:

(a) Training courses in oral expression aimed at developing the students' skills in global and personal expression in a foreign language (French). These involved training in expression by:
  - the use of interaction exercises and role-play
  - a dynamic approach using the press and other media (dramatisation of information using the *Théâtre Journal Vivant*, or Living Newspaper Theatre methodology) (Feldhendler, 1988a, 1989)
  - the dramaturgic adaptation of creative work (poems, songs, short stories, novels, tales and myths)

- the development of activities based on creativity
- specific advanced theatre workshops (image theatre workshops, forum theatre, playback theatre)

(b) Seminars in the didactics of French as a foreign language aimed at the application of dramaturgic and relational procedures for language acquisition and learning. These seminars integrated practical approaches, research and theoretical work and reflections on their application in teaching situations, and dealt with the following subjects:
- activation of the participants of a learning group by dramaturgic and relational procedures
- application of dramaturgic models (Boal, 1989; Fox, 1994, 1999) in the teaching of languages
- perception of phenomena of interaction and communication in a language-learning situation (approaches using psychodramatic and sociodramatic methods)
- development of a didactic method to tackle intercultural phenomena in the French-German context (work on the images and representations of the Other using dramaturgic and psychodramatic procedures)

(c) Interdisciplinary seminars as intensive weekend courses with a focus on language dramaturgy and pedagogy in cooperation with other institutions.

From 1987 on, we regularly invited francophone contributors who were specialists in the field of expression and communication and the didactics of drama-based activities. The various guest speakers brought their ideas to life for the students and other participants, such as language teachers from adult education, the *Institutes Français* or high schools and colleges (Feldhendler, 1988b).

## Enacting Life: Playback Theatre as Method

The intention of the original playback theatre dramaturgy is to recreate and transform events, experiences and lived situations told as stories by audience members – immediately and respectfully brought to stage as short scenes, acted out in an abbreviated form and, so to speak, 'played back'. A fixed structure, which functions as a kind of ritual, serves as a frame to hold, encourage and enable people to recount their personal stories. A part of the room is designated as the stage, where the actors sit facing the audience. A musician sits to the right, with an array of musical instruments. On the left are two chairs, one for the director (conductor) and the other for the person telling a story (teller).

A first exchange of the conductor with the audience about their present mood and perceptions leads to the spontaneous mirroring of these using short dramatic forms (e.g. a 'fluid sculpture'). After this, a teller is invited to tell his/her experience (story), which is structured by questions and prompts from the conductor. After this interview, the conductor passes the story to the actors and musician on stage. Expressively, using movement, words, pieces of cloth as props and with accompanying music, the story is portrayed in such a way that its essence is vividly experienced.

After the scene, the teller's 'ownership' of the story is acknowledged by giving it back to him/her with respectful regard, while the teller comments on the spontaneous re-enactment. Normally, the first story told stimulates further tellers, each story linking to the others. Personal and individual experiences become a collective event happening *in situ*, whereby the common dialogue is supported by speech, music, dramatic metaphor and a range of dramaturgical forms, e.g. 'pairs', 'chorus', 'tableau' (Salas, 1993).

Playback theatre operates as a model of constructive social dialogue. The sharing of biographical moments in a narrative form and the immediate transformation into a dynamic mirroring incorporates the experience and builds up the resources for self-knowledge or perception of oneself and others. The method is also a medium of communication between the individual and the group – both magnifying glass and megaphone at the same time and allowing a kind of mindfulness to arise. The dialogical value emerges in the sharing of one's own experiences and in the cooperation with others, allowing the stories on the stage to touch everyone.

In a learning situation, participants are by turns actors or spectators, engaged in a process of dialogue and communication through telling and enacting the stories of their lived experience, expressing their feelings and emotions. Individuals are revealed in word and image, in the constant reflections sent back by the intersubjective mirror. Voicing one's own story means discovering one's story anew as well as being seen and heard.

The philosophy of playback theatre is embodied in the challenge it sets itself: to translate the essence of what the teller/narrator has expressed in images, in a condensed and metaphorical form. The 'receiver' must comprehend the literal and figurative meaning and the connotations of the story told and re-enact it meaningfully, respecting the original narrative and treating it empathetically, to allow the 'sender' of the story to receive it in turn. The process is very demanding, but the rewards are obvious: the development of reciprocal listening and reflexive communication.

There is an implicit connection to the philosophical hermeneutics of Paul Ricœur, whose work is guided by a central tenet: the shortest path from Self to Self is the word of the Other through the dynamic and reflexive sharing of our own life stories. It is shown to be an important tool for identity work, enabling and promoting as it does the formation of a 'narrative identity' (Ricœur, 1985, 1990). We see Ricœur's concept in application in playback theatre. There, the story told is the basis for an enactment which re-establishes the productive value of the story, re-presenting (*mimesis*) the action, and transforming it by conferring order, meaning and complexity (Pineau & Le Grand, 1993: 79). Moreover, the notion of narrative identity proves its fecundity in so far as it applies to the community as well as to the individual (Ricoeur, 1985); it is the identity which the human subject attains through the narrative function. Specular performative mediation (performance-as-mirror), as found in Fox's method, adds an appreciable dialectic to these considerations.

## Playback Theatre and Life History

Playback theatre as an oral form of storytelling is similar to life story approaches and bears potential for reflexivity and participatory action research, especially in social and educational fields, e.g. in the interdisciplinary study of lifelong learning processes defined as a biographical approach to life history (Feldhendler, 2008).

Life history has been given many meanings in several scientific fields. Biographical research refers to a variety of methods used for conducting qualitative narrative interviews. Since the 'biographic turn' in the 1970s – which harks back to the Chicago School of sociology of the 1920s – it has advanced from the periphery to the centre of scientific adult education, bringing a new educational debate about life paths, biography and lifelong learning. Some approaches to lifelong learning are conceptually close to the idea of reflexivity, which has become a central preoccupation of mainstream social science. The consciousness of one's own biography and developing reflexivity as an act of historicity (cf. concept of 'biographity' in Alheit, 2003) is considered by some sociologists to be a survival necessity in a more individualised, perpetually changing, paradoxical and risk-inducing culture. Using biographical and life history approaches in the study of adult and lifelong learning opens up new perspectives in the development of Europe in a globalised world (West *et al.*, 2007).

By way of example, in 2011, I taught in an intensive residential programme entitled 'Lives and History: A Comprehensive Course on Biographies and Society', run during the Summer Academy at the University of Coimbra (Portugal). The purpose was to offer a comprehensive study of human experiences of the social world, drawing from a combined theoretical axis of analysis, an anthropological understanding of lives and history and an experiential approach. I conducted a workshop to present and deepen the potential of playback theatre for action research in the field of life histories ('Theatre for Social Change: Enacting Life – Encountering the Other'). Playback theatre as an approach to personal stories contains the potential for a 'Theatre for Social Dialogue and Social Change in a World in Upheaval' (the title of the IPTN Conference 2011, Frankfurt). In order to bridge the gaps between different academic worlds, I proposed 'key words' as a way to connect playback theatre, life history and biographical research in their ongoing mutual influence:

> [...] life history and biography as narrative; story telling and enactment as mediation through symbolic interaction; art as holistic knowledge and as place of multiple mediation; identity building through narratives; to be and become actor and protagonist as subject of one's own story/history; life stories and histories as mirror of societies (micro-macrocosm); to develop a culture of remembrance, collective and multiple intelligence; to develop diversity and participation, reciprocity and reflexivity in lifelong learning processes for democratic education; to promote transitive dialog for an active democracy in a world of globalization; to share and care values and ethics of mindfulness and acceptance in a fragmented world; radical social encounter through mutual acknowledgment as creative response to alienation. (Feldhendler, 2014: 7)

In March 2014, I presented at a conference of the European Society for Research on the Education of Adults (ESREA) and its Life History and Biography Network, held at the University of Magdeburg, Germany, entitled, 'Before, Beside and After (Beyond the Biographical Narrative)'. The conference focused on professional lives, family and identity, on facing loss and on narratives of creativity and art. My presentation, 'Enacting Life as Social Mediation', exemplified new trends in this field of action research. The ESREA Life History and Biography Network first met in Geneva in 1994 and has inspired diverse and influential publications as well as major collaborative research projects and many other forms of collaboration. ESREA comprises seven networks, including the Life History and Biographical Research Network (founded 1991) and promotes and disseminates theoretical and empirical research on the education of adults and adult learning in Europe through research networks, conferences and publications (http://www.esrea.org/). It is connected with many other international networks, such as the French *Association Internationale des Histoires de Vie en Formation* (ASIHVIF), also founded in 1991 (http://www.asihvif.com/). As a member of this association, I have kept members informed of developments in the Enacting Life approach since 1998, through publications, lectures and workshops at international conferences.

In 2013–2014, Muriel Molinié (University of Sorbonne Nouvelle, Paris) and Hugues Pouyé (Municipal Courses for Adults, Paris), in partnership with other associations such as ASIHVIF, proposed a cycle of action-research programmes entitled 'Accompany and Enhance the Experience of Mobility and Migration in the City: New Challenges for Research,

Innovation and Training'. Favouring a multidisciplinary approach in the social sciences, they refer in particular to biographical research in education and educational approaches focusing on the multilingual and multicultural experience of the language learners, who are envisaged as *citizen-actors* in the city, on the move and in their life-paths in international migration. Arts and clinical disciplines that artists and actors bring with their specific practices (visual artists, arts therapists, psychologists, actors in the social field, researchers) converge in the need to take into account multilingualism and experiences of mobility and migration, through multimodal mediations, arts and culture such as theatre, image, collage, photography or text. Whether aimed at facilitators/teachers or learners/migrants, these approaches draw strongly on their relationship to *Otherness*, knowledge, languages, cultures. Action research focuses firstly on the historicity of a theoretical corpus that underpins these unconventional practices and secondly on its renewal process in recent decades in France, in Europe and in the world. The processes relate to the fact that these approaches are located at the intersections of various disciplines such as language didactics, social intervention and creation, in the tension between local and international challenges (Molinié, 2014).

It is important to mention here that Molinié (2006, 2015) belongs to an international network of mainstream francophone researchers who develop the multimodal potentialities of language biographies and portfolios in foreign and second language acquisition. I refer to their considerations in my specific approaches.

## Applications in Intercultural Education

Playback theatre has been an element in my courses in the French language since 1990. As an integrated, practical form, it functions as a tool for innovation in alternative teaching and learning methods, whether in beginning or advanced language studies, and can be employed in training teachers in the theory and practice of foreign language instruction. Further developments and integrative models have also been offered in teacher refresher courses (schools and adult education). In this pedagogical context, playback theatre actively trains the skill of reflection as a mode of enhanced perception of the self and others in communication. These skills are of great significance in verbal and non-verbal communication: active listening, hermeneutically deepened understanding of a message, transposing through a variety of modes of expression (body, voice etc.), learning of appropriate verbal and non-verbal interactive responses, dealing with feelings, learning as a transformative process and deepening of awareness, adoption of integrative feedback methods, building a pool of shared experience through process analysis and perception of interpersonal and thematic connections. Playback theatre offers useful tools for mediation and sensitisation for multicultural situations and encourages reflexive communication. It integrates different phases: listening, understanding, expression, action, interaction, retroaction and sharing, and it encourages the emergence of relational attitudes between 'sender' and 'receiver'. My practical experience in the university environment and in professional development for teachers confirms this hypothesis (Feldhendler, 2005). Its specific forms foster a capacity for listening and understanding, receptivity and expressiveness, spontaneity in speech and action, making an adequate response, using other registers to convey a message, integration of verbal and non-verbal expression, expression of affectivity and emotions, perception of the self and others, openness to new situations. Through workshops and seminars which I have led, not only in the academic language acquisition context, but also in continuing teacher training and adult education in Germany, in international summer schools and other projects in Europe and Canada, I have discovered that the dramatic enactment of personal stories and life histories brings a new dimension to intercultural communication.

Since 1997, I have undertaken experimental and action research in the university framework in order to contribute to the emergence of the 'subject' and the 'narrative identity' by combining the elements of writing of personal stories with dramatic enactment (Feldhendler, 1997, 2007, 2009). These workshops have been presented under headings such as: Enacting Life, Autobiography, Writing about the Self or Life Dramaturgies. They offer students training in writing and enactment of personal stories and life histories. The biographical approach is understood as a dynamic training process based on writing a personal diary of stories and histories to encourage emergence of a 'narrative identity' and enactment of fragments of lived experience using theatrical processes. The workshops encourage students to write about the 'I' by keeping a diary or log book, to look for the 'We' by identifying thematic and collective connections and to undertake joint work on the texts written by participants using dynamic processes (creating images, modes of stage representation, theatrical and relational work).

Working with these groups of students, we establish a thematic web, bringing together individual and group experiences. Examples of themes which appear are:

- my life as a student and how I became a student
- my awareness of my language biography
- my underlying motivation in studying the French language
- my transgenerational influences in the choice of my studies
- my experiences of socialisation at school
- my first intercultural experience
- my experiences of the *Other* in cross-cultural encounters

At a summer school at Caen University in 1999, organised by the French language department of the CIEP (Centre International d'Études Pédagogiques, Paris), our module entitled 'Dramaturgy, Personal Stories and Intercultural Relations' focused on topics such as:

- forms and principles of the enacting life approach
- experiential approach to personal stories
- exploration of lived experiences in intercultural situations
- integrating writing: keeping a diary of intercultural stories
- practical arrangements for using enacting life in the classroom

With teachers of French from all over the world attending, complex multicultural encounters were on hand, demonstrating the need for active listening structures based on reciprocity and for connections between individual experiences. The degree of personal expression this particular workshop engendered can be seen in these examples of the themes which arose:

- homesickness; travelling for the first time without family members; arriving alone
- being a foreigner; being confronted with racism or latent rejection
- being well or badly received; being frustrated by certain aspects of the welcome given
- feeling protected; being able to express one's real feelings such as sadness, stress and tiredness, fear, attraction
- recounting one's intercultural story; experiencing acknowledgement and respect of the Other
- discovering the culture of one's native country; gender roles in one's native culture

The greater the affective involvement of participants, the greater the need for carefully structuring and containing the setting. The trainer possibly needs new skills: flexibility, professional competence and relational know-how in order to facilitate and support the flow of words and narratives being released. Keeping a log book or journal is very often the only tool which allows the trainer's attitude to be monitored adequately during training. The practice of writing a log book or journal is an effective method of self-training in its focus on deliberate self-reflection. It encourages the trainer to be more aware of his/her own level of involvement, while creating the distance necessary and promoting measured reflection. After carrying out field work, engaging in individual or group supervision as professional follow-up gives the trainer the requisite tools to analyse his/her own practice and continue to progress in the future (Buer, 1999).

## A Field of Participatory Action Research

The dramaturgic potential of personal stories has opened up a broad field of investigation for performative approaches in language learning and teaching. Playback theatre increasingly demonstrates its value as a tool for dynamic learning and for cultural anthropological exploration. This approach serves to promote attitudes conducive to peaceful coexistence by enhancing fundamental interpersonal skills and communicative attitudes: empathic listening; mindfulness of oneself and of others; physical awareness; intuition; intellectual, affective and emotional openness; taking appropriate action; adequate perception of oneself and of others; flexibility in adopting roles; acceptance of responsibility; creative spontaneity.

Mirroring through the scenes enacted on stage works as the fundamental dynamic, catalysing hermeneutical learning born of aesthetic interpretation. The process of deepened understanding opens up dimensions of the collective consciousness and collective unconsciousness between individuals and society. Playback theatre becomes a venue for intersubjective dialogue, 'remembrance rooms' and historical awareness, for the opportunity to be the author of one's own story as well as of oneself and for developing a collective identity (Feldhendler, 2005; Rowe, 2007; Salas, 2007).

## The Necessity of Ongoing Professional Development for Teachers

Reflecting on my own path to enacting life, I recall the beginnings in the 1970s. At that time, I was becoming increasingly aware that many language teachers were not open to unconventional or interdisciplinary teaching methods. They frequently blamed their students for what was in fact their own resistance to new methods, failing to scrutinise their own practice. But I saw that the primary reason why new methods in foreign language instruction did not meet with wider acceptance from teachers was that there was no practical training in their application; they were uncharted territory. The teachers' resistance arose from their lack of hands-on experience and the absence of reliable information, which led many of them to avoid exploring these new ideas (Feldhendler, 1993). Indeed, appropriate training and professional development opportunities were often simply not available, though experimental work being done in professional development for teachers at universities or in adult education did show a need for teachers to become familiar with new, active and activating methods of teaching and learning (Feldhendler, 1988b, 1990b, 1999a). Professional development training that uses experience-oriented procedures often leads subjects to rethink and question traditional teaching methods and pedagogical theory. In addition, ongoing training and professional development promotes new insights into modes of behaviour in interpersonal relations. As Dufeu has stated:

> When teaching focuses directly on the learner, the teacher has increasingly to develop self-examination, and to improve his or her knowledge of communication structures and types of relationship. There must be an awareness of transfers and counter-transfers, projections, worries, fears, and personal vulnerabilities in teaching situations. There must be strong and purposeful contact with their pedagogical intentions, hopes and dreams; that is, with the deep conscious and unconscious aims underlying the task of teaching. (Dufeu, 1994: 167)

## The Need for Respect and a Code of Ethics

Not an afterthought, but a thread running through all teaching practice where learners share biographical information is the need to abide by a code of conduct which fully respects the sensitivity of the shared information. As an example of how practitioners of these methods respond to this challenge, the Centre for Playback Theatre (New York, http://www.playbackcentre.org/) has developed a code of ethics for education and further training for playback theatre practitioners. Important elements which pertain to intercultural awareness are:

> Respect
>
> *'We interact with our audiences, students, tellers, company members, and colleagues with respect at all times [...]'*
>
> Inclusiveness
>
> *'We are open to any story and also ready to engage with ethical complexities within a story. We seek to include voices that are often unheard in our communities'.*
>
> Competence
>
> *'We commit to ensuring that we have sufficient training and supervision for any Playback Theatre project that we undertake, acquiring further training as needed [...]'*
>
> Human Rights
>
> *'We promote the human rights of all those present and not present. When necessary we take appropriate action to address prejudice that may be expressed consciously or unconsciously by a teller or workshop participant'.* (Centre for Playback Theatre (New York, http://www.playbackcentre.org/)

At the beginning of the 21st century, the challenge for institutions and for initiators of change still remains to develop meaningful, progressive and continuous opportunities in education and to put them into practice.

## Acknowledgement

Special thanks to Janet Salas and Hildegard de Byl for their very professional proof-reading.

## References

Alheit, P. (2003) Identität oder Biographizität? Beiträge der neueren sozial- und erziehungswissenschaftlichen Biographieforschung zu einem Konzept der Identitäts-entwicklung. In H.G. Petzold (ed.) *Lebensgeschichten erzählen* (pp. 6–25). Paderborn: Junfermann.

Barret, G. (1989) *Essai sur la Pédagogie de la Situation en Expression Dramatique et en Éducation*. Québec: Editions Recherche en expression.

Blatner, H.A. (1973) *Acting-In*. New York: Springer.

Boal, A. (1980) *Stop! C'est Magique*. Paris: Hachette 1980.

Boal, A. (1989) *Theater der Unterdrückten*. Frankfurt: Suhrkamp.

Boal, A. (1990) *Méthode Boal de Théâtre et de Thérapie*. Paris: Ramsay.

Buer, F. (1999) *Lehrbuch der Supervision*. Münster: Votum.

Demorgon, J. and Lipiansky, E.M. (1999) *Guide de l'Interculturel en Formation*. Paris: Retz.

Dufeu, B. (1982) Vers une Pédagogie de l'Etre: la Pédagogie Relationnelle. *Die Neueren Sprachen* 81 (3), 267–289.

Dufeu, B. (1983a) La Psychodramaturgie Linguistique. *Le Français dans le Monde* 175, 36–44.

Dufeu, B. (1983b) Haben und Sein im Fremdsprachenunterricht. In A. Prengel (ed.) *Gestaltpädagogik* (pp. 197–217). Weinheim: Beltz.

Dufeu, B. (1986) Rythme et Expression. *Le Français dans le Monde* 205, 62–70.

Dufeu, B. (1990) Psychodrama, Dramaturgie oder Pädagogik: Die Psychodramaturgie. In R. Batz and W. Bufe (eds) *Moderne Sprachlehrmethoden* (pp. 372–387). Darmstadt: Wissenschaftliche Buchgesellschaft.

Dufeu, B. (1992) *Sur les Chemins d'une Pédagogie de l'Etre*. Mainz: Centre de Psychodramaturgie.

Dufeu, B. (1994) *Teaching Myself*. Oxford: Oxford University Press.

Dufeu, B. (1996) *Les Approches non conventionnelles des Langues étrangères*. Paris: Hachette.

Dufeu, B. (2003) *Wege zu einer Pädagogik des Seins*. Mainz: Centre de Psychodramaturgie.

Feldhendler, D. (1983) Expression dramaturgique. *Le Français dans le Monde* 176, 45–51.

Feldhendler, D. (1988a) Le Théâtre Journal Vivant. *Le Français dans le Monde* 220, 56–61.

Feldhendler, D. (1988b) Formation des Formateurs: Dramaturgies et Pédagogies des langues. *Zielsprache Französisch* 2, 74–79.

Feldhendler, D. (1989) Das lebendige Zeitungstheater: Teilnehmeraktivierung im Fremdsprachenunterricht durch relationelle und dramaturgische Arbeitsformen. In A. Addison and K. Vogel (eds) *Gesprochene Fremdsprache* (pp. 119–140) (Fremdsprachen in Lehre und Forschung 7). Bochum: AKS-Verlag.

Feldhendler, D. (1990a) Comment activer les participants d'un cours de langue? Expériences de Formation. *Zielsprache Französisch* 2, 94–102.

Feldhendler, D. (1990b) Dramaturgie et Interculturel. *Le Français dans le Monde* 234, 50–60.

Feldhendler, D. (1992) *Psychodrama und Theater der Unterdrückten*. Frankfurt: Wilfried Nold.

Feldhendler, D. (1993) Enacting life, proposals for a relational dramaturgy for teaching and learning a foreign language. In M. Schewe and P. Shaw (eds) *Towards Drama as a Method in the Foreign Language* (pp. 170–191). Frankfurt am Main: Peter Lang.

Feldhendler, D. (1997) Mise en Scène d'Histoires de Vie. *Le Français dans le Monde* 290, 39–52.

Feldhendler, D. (1999a) La Dramaturgie Relationnelle. *Le Français dans le Monde. Recherches et applications* 125–133.

Feldhendler, D. (1999b) Formation à la Relation Interculturelle par des Approches psychodramatiques et dramaturgiques. In C. Allemann-Ghionda (ed.) *Education et Diversité socioculturelle* (pp. 249–264). Paris: L'Harmattan.

Feldhendler, D. (2005) *Théâtre en Miroirs, l'Histoire de Vie Mise en Scène*. Paris: Téraèdre.

Feldhendler, D. (2007) Playback theatre: A method for intercultural dialogue. *Scenario* 2, 48–57.

Feldhendler, D. (2008) Playback theatre, life history and biographical research. In H. Dauber (ed.) *Wo Geschichten sich begegnen – Gathering Voices* (pp. 117–131) (Kasseler Beiträge zur Erziehungswissenschaft, Band 3). Kassel: Kassel University Press.

Feldhendler, D. (2009) Das Leben in Szene setzen: Wege zu einer Sprachdramaturgie. *Scenario* 1, 54–66.

Feldhendler, D. (2014) Playback theatre: Education for tomorrow. *Interplay* XIX (1/2), 1, 5–8.

Fox, J. (1987) *The Essential Moreno: Writings on Psychodrama, Group Method, and Spontaneity*. New York: Springer.

Fox, J. (1994) *Acts of Service*. New Paltz, NY: Tusitala Publishing.

Fox, J. (2015) *Beyond Theatre: A Playback Theatre Memoir*. New Paltz, NY: Tusitala Publishing.

Fox, J. and Dauber, H. (1999) *Gathering Voices*. New Paltz, NY: Tusitala Publishing.

Leutz, G.A. (1974) *Psychodrama*. Berlin: Springer.

Molinié, M. (2006) Biographie Langagière et Apprentissage plurilingue. *Le Français dans le Monde. Recherches et applications* 39, 6–10.

Molinié, M. (2014) (Se) Représenter les Mobilités: Dynamiques plurilingues et relations altéritaires dans les espaces mondialisés. *Glottopol*, Revue de sociolinguistique en ligne 24. See http://glottopol.univ-rouen.fr/numero_24.html (accessed 9 October 2016).

Molinié, M. (2015) *Recherche Biographique en Contexte Plurilingue*. Paris: Riveneuve.

Moreno, J.L. (1923) *Das Stegreiftheater*. Potsdam: Gustav Kiepenheuer.

Moreno, J.L. (1973) *The Theater of Spontaneity*. New York: Beacon House.

Moreno, J.L. (1974) *Die Grundlagen der Soziometrie*. Opladen: Westdeutscher Verlag.

Moreno, J.L. (1988) *Gruppenpsychotherapie und Psychodrama*. Stuttgart: Georg Thieme.

Pineau, G. and Le Grand, L. (1993) *Les Histoires de Vie*. Paris: Presses Universitaires de France.

Rellstab, F. (1976) *Stanislawski Buch*. Wädenswil: Stutz & Co.

Ricœur, P. (1985) *Temps et Récit III*. Paris: Editions du Seuil.

Ricœur, P. (1990) *Soi-même comme un Autre*. Paris: Editions du Seuil.

Rowe, N. (2007) *Playing the Other*. London: Jessica Kingsley Publishers.

Ryngaert, J.P. (1985) *Jouer, Représenter*. Paris: Cedic.

Salas, J. (1993) *Improvising Real Life*. Dubuque, IA: Kendall/Hunt Publishing Company.

Salas, J. (2007) *Half of My Heart*. New York: Hudson River Playback Theatre.

Schützenberger, A.A. (1970) *Précis de Psychodrame*. Paris: Editions universitaires.

Sheleen, L. (1987) *Maske und Individuation*. Paderborn: Junfermann.

Souriau, E. (1950) *Les Deux Cent Mille Situations Dramatiques*. Paris: Flammarion.

Springer, R. (1995) *Grundlagen einer Psychodramapädagogik. Köln: inScenario Verlag.*

Stanislavski, K.S. (1988) *Die Arbeit des Schauspielers an sich selbst* (Vol. 1 & 2). Berlin: Das europäische Buch.

West, L., Merrill, B., Alheit, P., Siigs Andersen, A. and Merrill, B. (2007) *Using Biographical and Life History Approaches in the Study of Adult and Lifelong Learning: European Perspectives.* Frankfurt am Main: Peter Lang.

Winnicott, D.W. (1989) *Vom Spiel zur Kreativität.* Stuttgart: Klett-Cotta.

# 11 Suitcase of Survival: Performance, Biography and Intercultural Education

Jane Arnfield

## Introduction

This chapter will present a case study of a performance (*The Tin Ring*) and a curriculum project (*Suitcase of Survival*) in order to explore issues associated with the use of biography and autobiography in teaching, the nature of performance and intercultural (language) education. Although the project was not specifically focused on foreign language teaching, the fact that the play works across cultures and addresses language and the importance of language learning makes it relevant and adaptable to this context. The play has been performed in English to international audiences who have often had English as their second language. Surtitles in Romanian were used for the Bucharest International Theatre Platform #1 *The Future is Feminine* (November 2014, by invitation of the British Council). It has been performed twice at Lodz University, The Marek Edelman Centre for Dialogue, in Lodz, where it received an invitation to be part of the 75th Commemoration of the Deportation of Western Jews to the Litzmannstadt Ghetto.[1] The memoir upon which the play was based originally appeared in Czech under the title *Lucky Star*, and the edited version was published in English in 2010 by Northumbria University Press (now McNidder & Grace). There is therefore considerable potential for placing the project in the context of foreign language education.

The play *The Tin Ring* was based on a memoir by Zdenka Fantlová (2001, 2013), one of a handful of Holocaust survivors still alive today. It was adapted for the stage by Mike Alfreds and the author of this chapter and performed by the author as a solo performance. Running in tandem with this production, *Suitcase of Survival* was developed as a participatory programme which explores human rights, human resilience and well-being. In what follows, I will describe the production itself and its origins in Fantlová's writings and interviews, highlighting in particular the way in which the experience of others, witnessed through the act of performance, is heard, reheard and transformed. The chapter will then go on to examine three examples of *Suitcase of Survival* used in different contexts and to lay out the general pedagogical implications. The discussion will draw on the preceding description to explore the links with interculturalism and the concept of intercultural performance, highlighting the concept of archetypes.

The type of work described in the performance and accompanying programme has similarities with theatre in education, forum theatre and playback theatre, but is not identical to any of these formats. Whereas theatre in education more often includes audience involvement directly in interaction with the actors during the performance (Jackson, 1993), *The Tin Ring* stands as a performance in its own right. Similarly, it does not include direct audience intervention (i.e. stopping the action and coming on stage to enact alternate ideas) associated with the forum theatre of Boal (1992). It shares elements of playback theatre in that it does deal with personal stories, but these are not improvised by actors in the same way (Rowe, 2007). The project described here, on the surface, takes the more traditional approach of a stand-alone theatre piece with accompanying workshop, but at a more general level it has in common with these approaches a commitment to active spectatorship and the transformational potential of theatre.

## The Tin Ring

Zdenka Fantlová was born in former Czechoslovakia and was 17 when the Second World War began. She became part of the war when her family was classified by the Nazis as Jewish. As the author says in the play and in her book, she lived in a small town where faiths intertwined and religious celebrations were shared among families without prejudice. As she commented in one interview:

> [M]y father kept the main Jewish holidays. I think more out of respect for his parents from what I can remember. It always had to do with food – either there was too much food or there was not enough. I really didn't pay much attention to it. We lived in relative peace in a very democratic country not much different from yours in England. (Fantlová, 2013: 27)

The ring of the title was given to her by Arno, her first love. Zdenka kept it with her as a symbol of truth and hope as she survived six camps and two death marches between 1942 and 1945. In one interview, Zdenka describes her memoir as 'a document of history', of experiences lived and witnessed. In turn, the document becomes a marker of one serving the memory of many, for example, her family and those who did not survive the Holocaust. In performance, Zdenka's memoir becomes a working, living document.

The play, based on her autobiography and interviews, premiered in 2012 at The Lowry in Salford, Greater Manchester, and has been performed internationally in schools, libraries, universities, theatres, galleries, museums, as part of international arts and literature festivals, in research centres, cultural centres, lecture theatres, the internment camp Terezin, staterooms and sitting rooms.

The importance of language emerges near the start of the play. As a young woman, Zdenka seeks a way of continuing her studies. After being expelled from school because of the Nuremberg Laws, she is finally allowed by her father to leave her town of Rokycany in former Czechoslovakia and to stay with her grandparents in Prague to study at the English Institute for one year (from 1939 to 1940). Zdenka has three reasons to learn English: to continue her studies; because she is enthralled by the English language itself after hearing the song 'You Are My Lucky Star' on a record of songs from the Hollywood musical *Broadway Melody* (1936); and finally, because her instinct is driving her to learn this language. She has a gut reaction or a 'premonition' which could be interpreted as a primal need, as a deeply known yet unconscious feeling that the action of learning English could be a tool which in the future she may need to draw on. This indeed turns out to be the case. While in Belsen in 1945, Zdenka communicates in English with a British medical officer, who goes against his orders, secretly evacuates Zdenka from the camp where she is dying and takes her to a British Army hospital in Bergen. This act enables her to recover.

The performance can be described as a potential contribution to intercultural education in different ways. As a testimony, it provides interaction between cultures, defined in the more conventional sense of different national or ethnic groups. This is the concept of cultural education embodied in the original UNESCO (2007: 8) constitution, which refers to the 'wide diffusion of culture and the education of humanity for justice and liberty and peace', and commits to the development of 'the means of communication between their peoples' and to employing these means 'for the purposes of mutual understanding and a truer, more perfect knowledge of each other's lives'. Zdenka's very survival depends on her ability to communicate effectively across cultures. The playing out of the material in performance and the reactions of the recipients of the performance demonstrate an intercultural exchange as well as showing and sharing the influence of a multitude of cultures and the impact these different cultures have had on Zdenka herself.

In terms of a broader definition of interculturality as extending to the 'experience of otherness' (Alred *et al.*, 2003), the use of witness testimony is a powerful vehicle because of the transformation process that takes place. Performance as an action seeks to present opportunities for both performer and spectator to de-centre from their respective selves, cultivating ways of seeing from the perspective of others and developing a flow of critical, cultural awareness. The original encounter is shaped through different phases: first-hand testimony is transferred from the host (Fantlová) to the first surrogate (the performer) and transmitted onto the group surrogate (the audience). The use of the word 'surrogate' is key here in the sense of ownership and of 'deputizing', of someone being appointed to act or bear witness for another (this concept was also employed in the follow-up workshops, as will be discussed in the next section). From an intercultural perspective, it is a process of de-centring, of seeing things from other perspectives, not in a purely cognitive sense but at a more holistic, emotional level where the surrogate 'inhabits' the original testimony.

In the course of the performance, a forum is created for spectators to experience and re-experience how to live, how we live and how we have lived. An open dialogue of learning can emerge, interchanging and interplaying the role of host and surrogate between performer and spectator through active or performed listening. In the case of performances in schools, the active role of the spectators is encouraged through the pre-performance activities facilitated by the teachers. The experiences of others, witnessed through the act of performance, are heard and reheard. Performance provokes individual spectators (while viewing performed material) to play out a series of private, personal performances in parallel with the imported/external performance being viewed by all. These private views, internal personal performances, are initiated within the individual audience member, sourced from his/her own mind and body. This is additional biographical material layered onto and into the collective viewing of the performance. Material from living memory is activated by the individual audience member but sourced from his/her personal memory bank, held in his/her physical archives, his/her muscle memory. This intellectual, spiritual, memory matter/material originates from the spectator's internal and external knowledge of the world. Additionally, a third layer is blended simultaneously with the existing two layers: the layer of the imagination. By incorporating imaginings and the action of imagining, perceiving, projection and projecting, combinations can occur of experiencing multiple selves while one is an audience member. Spectators can see others/characters as projected within the play's narrative and their imagined self, or how they might see themselves as the character and choices they might make within this process of viewing a play. The performance, due to its economy of means, reinforces an audience's ability to empathise, to recognise, to remember and to imagine – nothing gets in the way between performer and spectator.

## *Suitcase of Survival*

*Suitcase of Survival* (SOS) is a participatory programme which was designed to run in tandem with the theatre production of *The Tin Ring* and to explore human rights, human resilience and well-being. It was developed by The Forge and the theatre company Human Remain. It is a flexible programme that has been adapted for different contexts. To date it has included theatre making with young people, a creative resilience training programme, workshops in schools led by Northumbria Performing Arts students, panel-led discussions, film screenings and public engagement events. Three examples of SOS will be discussed in what follows. They all took place in schools in the North East of England: a primary school (working with Year 6 children aged between 10 and 11 who will transition to secondary school), a secondary school (working with Year 9 and also sixth form) and a specialist science college (caring for secondary-aged pupils who have a range of social, emotional and behavioural difficulties). At the core of all three projects are the principles of how humans cope with crisis: looking at what has gone before, what happens during and what happens afterwards.

SOS takes *The Tin Ring* as a point of entry for both students and teachers (although in the primary school example the play itself was not performed). Preparatory work is undertaken in advance by the school before the performance is shown, and the Second World War is examined in cross-curricular teaching, for example in history, geography and modern languages.

In the first case study, Performing Arts students in their final undergraduate degree year devised a series of workshops over several weeks which explored Zdenka's biography and used the pupils' knowledge of that period of history from their curriculum studies. This was the only situation where the play was not performed; however, Zdenka herself met the children and talked directly about her experiences and answered their questions. Over the following weeks, the children shared their own biographical details, examining in particular what the word 'crisis' means, how they might cope with a crisis, how humans more generally recover from crisis (if they do) and what enables that recovery to take place. The work culminated in each child constructing his/her own physical 'suitcase of survival' using a small generic cardboard box. Each child narrated his/her own stories of celebration and challenge and interwove their stories with those from history, including Zdenka's experience. The children used Zdenka as a bridge to see her situation in relation to their own and critically to see the situation of others from that period of history and also from subsequent periods of crisis and catastrophe in the world. Zdenka's story served as a marker for the children, an entry point to view one life, many lives and their own life. Although the children had not witnessed the performance, a number of the staff had and were able to bring their experience of the performance into the classroom during this project.

The second case study developed from the first and this time began by introducing two performances, one to mark the start and another to conclude the SOS project. This work took place over a week, with a return visit after a break of several weeks for the final performance. The first performance was presented for staff and students. The final performance included parents in the audience and invited guests who were supporters of the school. The opening performance was shown to a number of year-groups ranging from Year 9 to sixth form with staff from a number of specific areas: English, History and Religious Education. Staff had prepared and included the incoming performance within their teaching curricula for their designated subject area. Working with a Performing Arts graduate fellow who had also been part of the primary school workshop, I devised a structure whereby the workshop was experienced and taught to the sixth-form students, who then taught the workshop to the Year 9 students the following day. The project aimed to create 'ambassadors' who could experience, learn and sustain the workshop activity and any emerging dialogues long after the performer and facilitators had left the school. The workshop comprised a series of structured games and actions, using stimuli that included text and visual material, aiming to encourage physical participation and interaction. All students made an actual 'suitcase of survival' to conclude the workshop, using a small cardboard box to represent, present, reveal and conceal items which included family photographs; objects received as gifts from family and friends such as jewellery, letters/emails; found objects seen as reminders of important places and times such as stones, dried leaves and flowers; small items of clothing like a glove and soft toys; items denoting biographical details and shared with those of others. Items also included text, maps, photographs and historical information appropriate to their subject areas and their received curriculum teaching.

The last case study took place over a day and involved only myself as both performer and facilitator, working with a small number of students in the SOS workshop at the start of the day, where they discussed their perceptions of their own biographical details in relation to others. Once again, preparatory work had been sent and carried out by the teachers prior to the performance and SOS workshop, enabling the students to have a familiarity with the content and encouraging an engagement with the exercises and structured games of SOS. Students were invited to listen to their own and others' biographical stories and truths, which focused on the themes of survival and need. The performance was then offered to the whole school after lunch, followed by a discussion with students who had participated in the SOS workshop.

A central element of the SOS project is performing the biography and autobiography of the participants and then of passing narratives on to another to perform. Experiencing and re-experiencing the original biography through someone else is at the centre of the practice. For the host of the biography, an opportunity opens up allowing the host to listen to his/her own story through another, a surrogate. As Alfreds (2013) points out, the need to tell stories is a part of our make-up as human beings:

> The need to tell and be told stories seems as essential to our existence as breathing. Stories transcend time and space, travelling down generations and across borders, cutting through the otherness of cultures and languages. Prehistory pieces together whatever evidence it can find to tell us possible stories about our earliest selves. (Alfreds, 2013: 5)

For young people who are constantly assessing and reassessing who they are, a physical space emerges in SOS where they can view themselves through another, by others speaking their biographies. An intelligent observation can be experienced and forums created in order to observe one's self, and therefore commentary on one's self is permitted. An example is an exercise of text analysis and excavation, where young people are invited to write a short biographical monologue and to rehearse and present this as a performance to others. This exercise can take place over a period of weeks or within a day.

In collaboration with Carol Martin, professor of Drama at NYU Abu Dhabi, and her students, a further methodology is being developed to support an enquiry into the understanding and observation of the self. Professor Martin's teaching module is called 'Staging the Self-Biography, Autobiography and Performance as part of the Core Curriculum'. Students from a variety of disciplines, including Engineering, Psychology, Economics and Statistics (i.e. not just the Performing Arts) are introduced to the ways in which how we perform ourselves comprises a major component of 21st-century literacy. The course explores autobiography and biography as literary expression, social redress and cross-cultural communication. The informing questions of the course include: What are the ways in which performances of self and others (personal, communal and political) are constructed and interpreted? How is individual experience represented in specific mediums? Can individual experience portray collective historical reality and/or complex social relations? Are Erving Goffman's ideas about the presentation of self in everyday life[2] relevant to the identities represented in social media?

SOS has engaged with young people who have experienced behavioural difficulties, as demonstrated in the last case study. The workshop and performance of *The Tin Ring* have stimulated students to consider exercises of biographical writing. An extended exercise of handing over the biographical stories to others to perform focuses the material for the host and invites the host to become a spectator and surrogate of his/her own story. Working with students and teachers, the preparatory work uses a series of questions to consider while writing, performing and hearing the monologues:

1. What is your story about?
   Consider the narrative of your story. What appears interesting to you may not be of interest to others, how can you engage others in your story? Narratives do not have to be linear, but the narrative of your monologue needs to be dramatic. Your performed narrative requires dramatic action or a series of dramatic actions or simply the story being shared needs action embedded within it. It is the dramatic arc that will drive your story towards and for others, enabling others to listen to your story and encouraging joint ownership. The experiences of the individual within the narrative do not have to be shared, but the experience of performing the monologue has to be a shared one, providing a combined experience between performer and receiver/audience – a shared experience.
2. Who is your story for?
   The story is for others. Otherwise you would not share it, as you would be its only keeper.
3. Why share your story?
   For the pleasure of recounting, reclaiming, reimagining, reinventing for the present, for the memory and to impact on future memories, yours and others.
4. How did your story originate?
   Even if not fully disclosed through the material, all stories have a sense of time, place and a sequence of activity – of doing, of actions leading to other actions, reactions, thoughts, memories, revelations.
5. When (past, present, future) did your story take place?
   Your story is likely to have taken place in the past but you might also consider present and future possibilities.

In order to analyse any impact these exercises have on pupils and teachers or patterns and trends denoting a reconnection with memory, personal history, diversity, human rights, empathy, identity and interdependence, attention is focused on the actions of the host and the surrogates in the workshop. Developing host testimony as performance, performed by surrogates, provides another avenue within which the host can connect to the original material, and to that of *The Tin Ring* and Zdenka Fantlová. This is one example of exploring how the impact of biography resonates with the self. It is the act of performance that demonstrates how a host testimony can continue to have a living presence through the body of another.

One of the outputs of SOS is that a series of surrogates (as addressed in the opening section of this chapter) is created through the action of performance. Audience or second surrogates emerge through the first surrogate hosting the original testimony, demonstrating how the host can re-receive his/her testimony through the body of another. The second surrogates or audience (which the host can also be part of) both come into contact at times with a testimony that belongs to another and, for the host, also into contact with a testimony which belongs to the self-performed by another. An experience of re-viewing, re-seeing, re-hearing occurs as all involved participate in an act of re-engaging with a living memory or series of lived memories. The event can be explained as a live witness testimony performed by another who is outside the host but who also operates at times as both surrogate and host – surrogate for the original host and host for the second surrogate, the audience. Sacks (1985) has pointed out that we observe or recall details about someone but miss the actual person in the process:

> To restore the human subject as the centre - the suffering, afflicted, fighting human subject - we must deepen a case history to a narrative or tale; only then do we have a 'who' as well as a 'what', a real person. (Sacks, 1985: viii)

This is another core component of the work of SOS to provide routes and tracings of narratives that can be shared through creating a personal passport of stories. SOS is focused on developing cognitive behaviour and promoting an understanding of actions, advocating for an exploration and development where those involved are encouraged to problem solve and take action, rather than to be consumed with feeling and expression. Feeling arises through action – by placing the body in action. The principals of hope, aspiration, resilience and the capacity of the arts and humanities to unlock these tools of survival underpin the performance and workshop action of the SOS programme.

## Intercultural Education

Houghton *et al.* (2013: 1) rightly point out that 'as teachers of foreign languages and/or intercultural communication attempt to facilitate communication across cultural barriers in a rapidly globalizing world, one of the most challenging barriers to be overcome is the stereotype'. There have been criticisms of the tendency to see culture only in terms of national cultures and of essentialism and stereotyping in some of the intercultural literature. For example, Hofstede's (1981) framework has been criticised by McSweeney (2002) on the grounds of the methods used for working with too many generalities rather than particulars. The tendency to essentialise culture has also been identified by Holliday (2012). One of the problems is that forming generalisations and making connections are indispensable parts of developing understanding, even though there are risks involved because these generalisations so often take a negative form.

In developing this project, the concept of 'archetype' as opposed to 'stereotype' was useful. These terms are sometimes used interchangeably, but they can be distinguished. Whereas a stereotype is an oversimplified, reductive generalisation, an archetype is a concrete particular that serves as a model or prototype against which comparisons are made. According to Snowden (2001: 3), '[t]he archetype can help a group articulate understandings that have previously remained beneath the surface'. While both archetypes and stereotypes can be seen as forms of generalisation, the archetype always emerges from a concrete, particular instance rather than taking the generalisation as the starting point. Commenting on the nature of 'skill', Murray (2015) suggests that it is necessary

> to re-model skill so as to blur and confuse its apparent soft and hard qualities, to reconcile skill acquisition with the fruitfully generative embrace of failure, to understand and practise skill as a dispositional and relational quality whose muscles need as much training and exercise as our vocal chords, breath or spine. (Murray, 2015: 54)

These blurrings can serve to support the distinction and differentiation between the stereotype and the archetype, highlighting elements of learning which help to separate out these two concepts. If stereotyping is used to demonstrate actions of learning in the product or content of a performance, then ultimately specifics or the trace of the individual are lost. If, however, the audience members are allowed to engage with and co-construct the performance, then the performance absorbs any process – past, present or future – and is defined simply as initiating a dynamic interaction between performer and spectator to make the performance together. This relationship between performer and spectator also alleviates tendencies to stereotype or essentialise, as the roles of performer and spectator become interchangeable, blending intercultural experiences together to transform one action into a series of actions as defined by the original narrative, story or biographical detail.

In the work of *The Tin Ring* and SOS project, the demonstration of performed characters taken from testimonials comprises a series of archetypes. The performer demonstrates archetypal behaviour sourced from within the biographical testimony and narratives, producing a narrative of the real and avoiding stories of generalisation or narratives of the non-specific. These co-constructed narrative truths produced by the two initiators (performer and audience as active spectator) are particularly visible when working with memoirs/testimony/living memory/oral history.

Developing active spectators is an important part of the project and a key ingredient of the work when seen as a form of intercultural education. Performance has the potential to create opportunities for interactive experiences or encounters of integrity for the audience. This in turn encourages active spectators, as the audience members have to acquire skills to participate in the performance. The result is an on-going exchange and acquisition of skills between performer and spectator, and thus a need for both the audience and performers to acquire skills together while experiencing the performance. These skills include listening, imagining, reacting and blending the story of the play with the stories of each spectator in their own private worlds. The development of empathy from the spectator in a skilled performance is one form of de-centring – the ability to see things from the other's perspective – which is an essential element in the development of intercultural competence (Byram, 1997).

## Examples

1. Audience as spectators see the performed biographical self on stage and see other performed selves on stage sourced from the host testimony's life performed by the first surrogate actor.
2. Audience as spectators see their own self in relation to the selves being performed on stage becoming a second surrogate for the performed host testimony; the host is the original testimonial holder.
3. Audience as spectators see imagined selves relating to their own biographical narratives and those relating to the self and selves of the host within the performed biography on stage.

This empowers the audience as spectators to take a central and/or supporting active role within the presented performed experience. A co-construction occurs between the performer and the audience as active spectators. This active participation exists as an oscillation. The audience as active spectators take ownership of their participation, viewing the original sourced play/biographical narrative externally as presented to them by the actor/first surrogate, and at the same time, the audience also embodies multiple roles of performer, director, scriptwriter/dramaturge, set designer, lighting designer, composer, choreographer and spectator internally while spectating.

Performance witnessing and performance collaboration are places to reassemble data from our past, present and our imagined future. The act of performance creates a space where our biographical details and the biographical data of others can be shared, examined and edited. An opportunity to observe the self as well as the selves of others can be triggered during and after the performance and also shared at a later date if a discussion is activated, demonstrating the impact of the performance and signifying its legacy or sustainability. This intercultural and primal action of ascribing value to our own and others' biographical details through performative acts could be perceived as permitting value to the self/our self and the selves of others. If observations and the act of observing through intercultural connections can be further experienced through the encounter of performance, an empathetic space emerges, sanctioning the ability to comment (verbal, physical and visual) on one's self and on the selves of others. Schechner (2015: 42) substantiates the need for a constant enquiry into the action of collective engagement with performance because the action of performance contributes to public knowledge of and reflection on experiences of communities learning and living together: 'The theory feeds the practice; the practice feeds the theory'.

## Conclusion

There is an established tradition of using autobiography in education (Abbs, 1974; Graham, 1989). As Bates and Lewis (2009: 6) point out, 'The writing of an autobiography can be a cathartic experience that enables us to make sense of our disjointed experience and decipher patterns'. They go on to note that there are criticisms of the use of autobiography in education, with some suggesting that it can be rather self-indulgent and overly subjective. That depends, however, on the way it is handled in the classroom. One of the arguments of this chapter is that autobiography will contribute more effectively to intercultural education if it is not used in isolation but in relation to the biographies of others. Looking at our own lives in relation to others is potentially a first step in a process of de-centring that is an essential part of developing intercultural competence.

There are clearly challenges involved in importing external performances into schools. They may serve as a welcome distraction from day-to-day work, but may be experienced in a superficial way and have no impact on learning or legacy. The performance may have high production values and demonstrate excellent acting skills, but may exist in isolation and critically remain separate from the audience. In a climate where teachers are placed under extreme pressure to teach to targets, an external event may be even less likely to have a real impact. In this chapter, I have advocated for what can be described as a series of 'meeting points': points where the play and the curriculum can collide in order to produce conversation, interaction between teacher and student and debate centred on the impact of live performance working in tandem with intercultural education. An example of this occurred at Furrowfield School, where a teacher took the theme of resilience and survival as embodied in Zdenka's story and discussed being an observer and not a victim. This was then incorporated into Home Economics, where students developed recipes of resilience, and Geography, where students studied journeys of resilience and places in the world engaging or exhibiting resilience. This evidence, compiled collectively concerning the co-construction of the performed event by all parties, performer and spectator, is an example of the performance integrating into, and being sustained within, the curriculum in the school. By using this initial sign posting to guide all parties to meet (within the overall experience of witnessing a performance within a school), it is an aim to encourage a deeper level of intercultural understanding through performance, creating a new experience which is impactful, has legacy and is enriching for all participants, teacher, pupil, student and performer. By using performance effectively immersed within a curriculum, we are actually able to unlearn or relearn behavioural patterns and therefore to demonstrate flexibility by continuing to repeat actions with spontaneity and to apply acquired skills only where and when required.

## Notes

(1) See cf. http://www.centrumdialogu.com/en/about-us (accessed 23 June 2016).
(2) See cf. Goffman's widely available *The Presentation of Self in Everyday Life*.

## References

Abbs, P. (ed.) (1974) *Autobiography in Education*. London: Heinemann.
Alfreds, M. (2013) *Then What Happens?* London: Nick Hern Books Limited.
Alred, G., Byram, M. and Fleming, M. (eds) (2003) *Intercultural Experience and Education*. Clevedon: Multilingual Matters.
Bates, J. and Lewis, S. (2009) *The Study of Education: An Introduction*. London: Continuum.
Boal, A. (1992) *Games for Actors and Non-Actors* (trans. A. Jackson). London: Routledge.
Byram, M. (1997) *Teaching and Assessing Intercultural Communicative Competence*. Clevedon: Multilingual Matters.
Fantlová, Z. (2001) *My Lucky Star*. New York: Herodias.
Fantlová, Z. (2013) *The Tin Ring*. Northumberland: Northumbria Press.
Goffman, E. (1956) The Presentation of Self in Everyday Life. Edinburgh: University of Edinburgh.
Graham, R. (1989) Autobiography and education. *The Journal of Educational Thought* 23 (2), 92–105.
Hofstede, G. (1981) Culture and organisations. *International Studies of Management and Organisations* 10 (4), 15–41.
Holliday, A. (2012) Culture, communication, context and power. In J. Jackson (ed.) *The Routledge Handbook of Language and Intercultural Communication* (pp. 37–51). London: Routledge.
Houghton, S., Furumura, Y., Lebedko, M. and Li, S. (eds) (2013) *Critical Cultural Awareness: Managing Stereotypes Through Intercultural (Language) Education*. Newcastle: Cambridge Scholars Publishing.
Jackson, A. (1993) Learning Through Theatre: New Perspectives on Theatre in Education. London: Routledge.

McSweeney, B. (2002) Hofstede's model of national culture differences and their consequences: Performance assessment in organisations. *Work Study* 51 (6), 314–319.
Murray, S. (2015) Keywords in performer training. *Theatre, Dance and Performance Training* 6 (1), 46–58.
Rowe, N. (2007) *Playing the Other: Dramatizing Personal Narrative in Playback Theatre.* London: Jessica Kingsley.
Sacks, O. (1985) *The Man Who Mistook His Wife for a Hat and Other Tales.* London: Duckworth.
Schechner, R. (2015) *Performed Imaginaries.* Abingdon/New York: Routledge.
Snowden, D. (2001) Archetypes as an instrument of narrative patterning. *Knowledge Management* (Story Special Edition, November 2001). See http://www.anecdote.com/pdfs/papers/Snowden2001Archetypes.pdf (accessed 15 December 2015).
UNESCO (2007) *UNESCO Guidelines on Intercultural Education.* Paris: UNESCO.

# Part 6

# Performative Approaches to Intercultural Education: A Culture-Specific Perspective

# 12 The Intercultural Journey: Drama-Based Practitioners in JFL in North America, and in JSL and EFL in Japan

Eucharia Donnery

## Introduction

This chapter highlights several practitioners who are using performative approaches in the field of second language acquisition (SLA) for the purpose of developing intercultural communicative competence (ICC) in Japanese as a foreign and second language (JFL and JSL, respectively) and in English as a foreign language (EFL) in Japan. This is the first and very general attempt at giving an overview of these three areas of SLA, and cannot possibly do full justice to what each practitioner has developed.[1] However, the Japanese/Asian context within performative approaches to SLA has been featured relatively little in scholarly debate, and therefore the aim is merely to introduce some key figures whose work is gaining recognition in these three areas of SLA.

Using performative approaches to SLA is a form of content language integrated learning (CLIL), and this is described before emphasizing that the successful acquisition of a second/ foreign language also incorporates and develops factors in ICC. This introduces how Japanese and English language educators are using performative approaches in the worlds of JFL in North America and of JSL and EFL in Japan. In response to an open-ended questionnaire (see Appendix A), various educators explain their teaching philosophies regarding the use of performative approaches in second language education as CLIL, pertaining to changes in ICC in particular. One key finding is that, while the use of performative approaches is vibrant in JFL in North America, within the field of EFL in Japan there are far fewer advocates for a number of reasons, including lack of confidence and sufficient class-time from the perspective of the teachers, as well as perceived cultural tendencies toward uncertainty avoidance and shyness on the part of the students. Within the Japanese EFL educational system, however, the skills that many students identify as important in needs-analysis testing are those of oral communication and ICC (Nakano *et al.*, 2009: 48, 50). CLIL-driven performative approaches can help learners to develop these skills simultaneously, and by emphasizing experiential learning, they offer a new and dynamic way for Japanese EFL learners to engage with innovative pedagogies used in English-language educational systems. This facilitates a change from instrumental motivation, what Ushioda (2013: 5) terms 'grammar-focused "English for exams" *juken eigo,* with minimal attention paid to the development of communication skills', to integrative motivation, allowing a sense of ownership over English while developing ICC.

## Useful Terminology

### Second language acquisition

In the field of SLA, it is important to differentiate between SLA and foreign language acquisition (FLA). According to Ellis (1994), in

> second language acquisition, the language plays an institutional role in the community. For example, English as a second language is learnt in the United States, United Kingdom and countries in Africa such as Nigeria and Zambia. In contrast, foreign language learning takes place in settings where the language plays no major role in the community and is primarily learned in the classroom. (Ellis, 1994: 11–12)

Therefore, non-Japanese students study JFL outside Japan or JSL in Japan, while Japanese learners study EFL in Japan.

### Intercultural communicative competence

> [S]uccessful 'communication' is not judged solely in terms of efficiency of information exchange. It is focused on establishing and maintaining relationships. In this sense, the efficacy of communication depends upon using language to demonstrate one's willingness to relate, which often involves the indirectness of politeness rather than the direct and 'efficient' choice of language full of information. (Byram, 1997: 3)

Throughout this chapter, ICC is interpreted as a motivational shift in attitude from instrumentally motivated language study for test-taking purposes to the more integrative motivated language learning for communicative competencies, pertaining to grammatical, sociocultural, strategic and discourse-related skills. The focus is on how SLA educators are using performative approaches to influence Japanese and English language learners with respect to Byram's (1997: 34) five *savoirs* in ICC (see Figure 12.1): attitudes, knowledge, skills of interpretation and relating, skills of discovery, and education.

| | | |
|---|---|---|
| | **3. Skills:** Interpret and Relate | |
| **2. Knowledge:** of the Self and Other; of interaction; of individual and society | **5. Critical Cultural Awareness (Education):** Political Education | **1. Attitudes:** Relativizing Self Valuing Other |
| | **4. Skills:** Discover and/or Interact | |

**Figure 12.1** Byram's intercultural component chart

In 2001, Byram *et al.* (2001) updated their previous work to further refine intercultural attitudes as 'curiosity and openness, readiness to suspend disbelief about other cultures and belief about one's own', which they regarded as the most important ICC component. To move toward ICC, which Byram *et al.* (2002: 10) conceive as the 'ability to ensure a shared understanding by people of different social identities' and the 'ability to interact with people as complex human beings with multiple identities and their own individuality', the average SLA learner has to undertake a psychological journey, moving toward a more inclusive attitude regarding the target language and its cultural norms and mores. According to Gardner (2001), becoming a competent communicator in another language involves a certain degree of integrative motivation, a desire stemming from a genuine interest in gaining psychological closeness to speakers of the target language.

## Content and language integrated learning: Overview

Although the term was coined as recently as 1994 by David Marsh (1994), CLIL itself has long been established within the European language context in the immersive system of education, such as in the Gaelscoils in Ireland, where various subjects are taught through the medium of the Irish language. Indeed, Mehisto *et al.* (2008: 9) argue that 'the first CLIL-type programme dates back 5000 years to what is now modern-day Iraq'. Whether new or old, CLIL is extremely adaptable to learner needs. Instead of studying the language *as* the target, language learners are learning *through* the target language, simultaneously developing their language and learning skills while attaining deeper insight into their chosen field of specialization.

According to the European Commission as cited by Bernause *et al.* (2011:15), CLIL's multifaceted approach can offer a variety of benefits because it:

- builds *intercultural knowledge and understanding* (emphasis by ED);
- develops *intercultural communication skills* (emphasis by ED);
- improves language competence and oral communication skills;

- develops multilingual interests and attitudes;
- provides opportunities to study content through different perspectives;
- allows learners more contact with the target language;
- does not require extra teaching hours;
- complements other subjects rather than competes with them;
- diversifies methods and forms of classroom practice;
- increases learners' motivation and confidence in both the language and the subject being taught.

In addition to these benefits, for the individual student, CLIL is a way to maximize the learning process by facilitating Gardner's (2001: 3) motivational move from the 'instrumental' short-term accuracy target such as studying to pass an exam, to the 'integrative' fluency-model for lifelong learning. CLIL also provides a way to deconstruct Self and Other dichotomies as expressed in stereotypes that highlight difference, in favor of a more holistic, accepting and balanced worldview: the very essence of ICC.

For any SLA educator, there can be a number of challenges within each teaching context, for example age, gender, language and cultural background. As CLIL is highly learner centered, it offers a way of bridging these gaps, making content more accessible to the students and allowing the balance of power to shift from the teacher to the students. At Sophia University, one of Japan's leading universities, Makoto Ikeda, Chantal Hemmi and Richard Pinner have implemented a CLIL approach at the Center of Language Education Research to encourage educators to teach about their chosen fields of research *through* English rather than *for* English. In this way, CLIL allows the students to engage with the content and take ownership of their own language learning skills. It is optimal for the teacher to have a deep understanding of the students' cultural and linguistic backgrounds. Better still, the teacher should be able to communicate in the students' language in order to appreciate the struggle involved in SLA/FLA and the enormity of the task that the students face.

According to the 4Cs curriculum, the successful CLIL lesson should combine elements of the following: 'content (subject matter), communication (language), cognition (thinking/learning), and culture (intercultural communication, including awareness of self and *otherness*)' (Coyle, 2008). Cognitive development happens through the process of collaborative learning and through research and self-reflection, while ICC increases throughout, as learners encounter new ideas and cultural values in tandem with language skills. As Marsh (2002) notes, using a CLIL approach is more challenging, but more motivating for the students and teacher alike.

## Setting the Scene: Japanese and English SLA

### Japanese language and culture

Within the fields of JFL and JSL, performative approaches are being adopted in the classroom as a tool for understanding the myriad of nuance and meaning within Japanese language and culture by practitioners in Canada, the US and Japan. Many aspects of drama-based pedagogies have been utilized in JFL and JSL to help learners develop ICC. This is important, because in Japanese what is said does not always express the actual meaning. In fact, words are often seen as devaluing the richness of the meaning, while the epitome of successful communication is non-verbal, such that sometimes the very act of trying to understand is like trying to maintain one's balance on constantly shifting sands. Understanding *tatemae*, the Outside/Other face one wears in public, and *honne*, the private Self behind the face, can be difficult for people from cultures which are more 'direct'. For this reason, as well as adding authenticity of linguistic communication, performative approaches help learners to understand the more complex nuances of ICC.

An example of a Japanese cultural norm regarding *tatemae* and *honne* is that, in the highly implicit nature of the Japanese language, once the subject has been mentioned once and has been understood by both sender and receiver of the message, it is unnecessary to state it again. Thus, in a conversation in Japanese, the pronoun 'I' will not be repeated if the subsequent conversation continues to be about the speaker, and to repeat 'I' would seem unnecessarily forceful. From this perspective, the explicit nature of English, where the subject is stated repeatedly by both sender and receiver of information, can seem rather uncouth to Japanese sensibilities. This heightened sensitivity, or tacit understanding, is an essential part of Japanese culture, and one in which most Japanese take pride.

This implicit nature of the Japanese language means that it is important to be able to *kuki wo yomeru*, literally to 'read the air', rather than take the meaning at face value. Therefore, in Japanese, there is considerable attention paid to non-verbal cues and/or clues. Through performative approaches in JFL and JSL classes, these complex cultural norms and mores can be highlighted, resulting in the development of ICC skills of attitudes, knowledge, interpretation and discovery *through* interaction as well as critical cultural awareness and political education. Because of the relatively explicit nature of many other languages, the responsibility for the success or failure of communication lies with the speaker, whereas in Japanese, the onus for this same success or failure in communication is on the listener. This means that, in Japanese, active listening is very important, and this is signaled by verbal 'back-channeling'[2] called *aizuchi* and clarification. As Kita and Ide (2007) point out:

> Japanese conversation is noteworthy with respect to *aizuchi* ... Japanese speakers use 2.6 times more *aizuchis* per unit of time than American English speakers. (Kita & Ide, 2007: 1243)

This, and other cultural nuances that are difficult to teach in more traditional ways, are made explicit when more performative approaches such as role play and improvisation are employed.

## EFL in Japan: The average first-year university student

There are three important considerations when describing the average Japanese university student in an EFL context: previous educational experience, cultural background and socio-economic circumstances. Firstly, the average Japanese student has good test-taking skills and excels in the grammar and grammar-translation sections in particular, as these areas have been the focus of the six-year English language educational system throughout the junior and senior high school levels. Unsurprisingly, the repetitive nature of this type of learning has left many Japanese students demotivated and jaded toward this type of English language acquisition, taught as if it consisted of complicated mathematical formulae. When language is taught as a scientific equation in which there is no room for creativity and/or ambiguity but only for correct or incorrect answers, Japanese students react in different ways, but generally adhere to cultural norms: from polite passive-aggressive disinterest to open hostility. Japan, as a predominantly monolingual and homogenous culture, is by no means unique in its production of citizens who are disinterested in other languages because of deficits in the educational system.

A second issue in understanding the average Japanese student is the concept of *hitomishiri*, or 'shyness' within Japanese society. This concept of shyness, which can manifest as a fear of others, combined with what renowned and influential psychiatrist Doi (1971:105) in his book titled *The Anatomy of Dependence*, terms 'the anatomy of dependence', means that shyness is not seen in a negative light. Psychologists Craighead and Nemeroff (2001: 1522) reported that 57% of Japanese university students describe themselves as 'shy', as opposed to a mere 31% of their Israeli counterparts. They attribute this to differences between collectivistic and individualistic cultures; however, in addition to Doi's theory of dependence, there are other complex cultural reasons why Japanese society should formulate shyness as a part of self-image. In Japan, if a child is successful, then praise is given to the parents, the teachers, Japanese society as a whole and, traditionally, to the Buddha. However, should that same child fail, he/she fails alone. Even Japanese adults are not immune to debilitating bouts of shyness, especially when meeting foreign languages and cultures face-to-face. Given these circumstances, the average modern Japanese student is, understandably enough, reluctant to draw attention to himself/herself, and shuns the limelight for fear of failure, which is a solo burden to bear.

A third useful factor in drawing up a mental image of the average Japanese university student is that of socio-economic circumstances. If there has been sufficient disposable income when a child is young, the possibility that he/she will have had some private English conversational classes, either in the home or at a private English conversation school, is high. However, like the 'cram school' and textbook industries in Japan, these private English classes and schools are wholly unregulated, and there is a corresponding lack of consistency when it comes to standards of English. These can vary from superb to woefully unprofessional, taught by university students who have absolutely no teacher training and low English language skills themselves. It can be down to luck as to how valuable these lessons have been for the individual student.

## The Arguments for Performative Approaches and ICC

The social and holistic qualities of performative approaches to SLA mean that every student can make a contribution, regardless of linguistic abilities. Although writing with process drama in mind, Kao and O'Neill (1998: 16) argue that performative approaches to SLA seek to increase 'the fluency and confidence of students' speech, to create authentic communicative contexts, and to generate new classroom relationships', which parallels Byram's five *savoir* skills. In performative approaches to SLA, activities can be individual (for reflection and writing-in-role), paired, in small groups for research and role plays or in a class group. As Kramsch (1998: 3) argues, 'language expresses cultural reality', and thus performative approaches in SLA can help learners begin to see and understand what lies beneath language while simultaneously promoting change. An example of this is the phrase *o-tsukare sama desu* in Japanese, which, when literally translated to English means 'you must be tired'. However, it is a cultural sign of appreciation and serves as a greeting between people in a work or study environment. It is difficult to know when to use it initially, therefore more performative approaches such as situational role play can demonstrate clearly and succinctly when the phrase is to be used.

The primary data in this chapter was collected through an open-ended questionnaire (see Appendix A) in English and Japanese, both by paper-format and electronically, from members of two different professional groups: The International Association of Performing Language (IAPL) and Speech Drama Debate (SDD). The origins and aims of both groups are described in the following section, as are the ways that these particular language educators are using performative approaches, such as analyzing and acting-out play scripts and film scripts, role play, performance theater, docu-drama, readers' theater, boxing for debate and picture-story theater.

Other sources of information include personal emails and secondary sources.

## Performative Approaches to Second/Foreign Language Education

### Performative approaches in JFL: The International Association of Performing Languages (IAPL)

In 2006, three colleagues at the University of Victoria, Canada, organized a conference entitled 'Performing Language: An International Conference on Drama and Theatre in Second Language Education'. From this auspicious start, the IAPL emerged with the express goal of bringing together practitioners who utilize aspects of performance to teach language and communication from a diverse range of theoretical and practical perspectives. The current president is Cody Poulton. He, along with his colleagues Hewgill and Noro, has found that using *Tokyo Notes*, a work by playwright and JSL educator Oriza Hirata, 'shows learners of Japanese how native Japanese people actually communicate in a real setting, including linguistic, paralinguistic and non-verbal elements'. These three educators further note that

> in spoken Japanese, utterances of two interlocutors often overlap … Viewing *Tokyo Notes* and acting out skits based on this play are activities that provide the students with opportunities to analyze Japanese linguistics and cultural patterns as well as reflect on their own cultural and linguistic habits. (Hewgill *et al.*, 2004: 237)

This shows that, through reading and acting out the play script, students can develop skills of ICC, particularly in the areas of attitude and knowledge.

Poulton's colleague and co-founder of IAPL is Hiroko Noro, whose research interests include sociolinguistics, sociology of language, Japanese linguistics, intercultural communication and second language pedagogy. She has written extensively in Japanese about using performative approaches in JFL to highlight the cultural norms and mores of the Japanese language while encouraging students to reflect on their own culture and learn how to negotiate between cultures. Noro *et al.*'s (2012) most recent book, *Doramachikku Nihongo komyunike-shon* [*Dramatic Japanese Communication*], shows how educators can use performance in classes not as an isolated and random incident, but rather in terms of how language is influenced by culture, society and history. She is currently involved in a joint project, based on a modern Japanese play, to develop multimedia Japanese language teaching resources for advanced learners.

As mentioned above, playwright, JSL educator and teacher-trainer Oriza Hirata (2004) is an important figure in the worlds of performance, JFL and ICC. He develops his students' vocabulary and ICC through drama-based warm-ups, and examines differences in intercultural norms through the use of play scripts. Because of the validity of non-verbal communication in both drama and Japanese culture, Hirata allows the participants to creatively interpret the script in order to compel the participants to respond to the situation in a more natural way, rather than by merely remembering the lines. He himself uses this naturalistic technique in his own JFL classrooms, and this style of teaching has been adopted by some of the more progressive universities in Japan. For example, to show how various cultures have different ideas when it comes to behavior on public transportation, he asks the students in small groups to explain about each country's accepted norms, which they demonstrate through role play.

At one of the top four private universities in Japan, Waseda University, Yoshikazu Kawaguchi is a strong advocate of using drama-based pedagogy to build ICC skills, and has implemented it in his teaching praxis. In his novice-elementary level classes, he moves from a grammatical set phrase which the students develop into a natural conversation with appropriate body language, intonation and back-channeling, all vital parts of Japanese conversational style. In answer to the administered questionnaire, he summarizes his approach thus:

> Students in my class learn the usage of specific grammatical items or words and phrases in a natural conversation setting, through which their sense of learning newly introduced items through context will become sharper and more activated.

Nevertheless, he finds that students who are from cultures accustomed to a lot of meta-language and teacher-centered language classes initially find drama activities as well as the development of ICC quite daunting. As these students' discomfort subsides, however, they realize the importance of contextualization that these activities offer.

Another notable practitioner in the field of performative practices in JFL is Masako Beecken, who has been teaching Japanese at Colorado State University since 1988. She has won awards for her drama-based teaching praxis from the Colorado Congress of Foreign Language Teachers (CCFLT) as well as from the National Council of Japanese Language Teachers (NCJLT). She fuses creativity with traditional Japanese arts to produce student performances of Shakespeare's *A Midsummer Night's Dream* in Japanese.

Sakae Fujita wrote her doctoral dissertation at the University of California, Santa Cruz, in 2008, about how she uses *kyogen*, the comic dramatic interlude between acts in the staid Noh theater, to highlight

Japanese paralanguage and understand cultural nuances behind Japanese intonation. In her current position as lecturer in Japanese language, both her research and teaching are focused on the use of drama and theater techniques in the context of foreign language learning and ICC. She has also been a director and co-producer for the annual multilingual theater project, International Playhouse, at the University of California, Santa Cruz, for over a decade.

## Japan: Performative approaches in JSL

In Japan, language learners have the opportunity to use Japanese outside of the classroom, which brings both advantages and disadvantages to teaching practices. As some students struggle in various stages of culture shock, more performative approaches to teaching and learning can have both immediate and profound effects. Shingo Hashimoto at Gifu University uses role play to help his elementary and intermediate-level students, both Japanese and international, to understand the fuller cultural meaning behind the words, and this has benefits for both sets of needs: linguistic and cultural. The Japanese students' predisposition to shyness can be overcome through role play activities, while the linguistic and ICC benefits have immediate effects for the international students.

At Tokai University, Yukari Saiki utilizes a performative approach, which she terms 'docu-drama'. In this, students have a choice of five newspaper articles, which they read in groups, and then each group creates a mini-drama based on their chosen article. Other groups watch and decide which article the drama relates to. To extend this activity, Saiki advocates the use of online research for a written summary assignment. She encourages the students to insert as much of their own stories as possible to make the experience more authentic. While the students can initially be shy and in the throes of culture shock and withdrawal outside of class, these docu-dramas help build the students' confidence and support the process of acculturation by developing ICC skills.

## Japan: Performative approaches in EFL

As shown above, for many Japanese people, when it comes to FLA, English in particular can be seen as stepping outside of the Insider status, thereby negating the ability to read between *tatemae* and *honne.* This in turn has caused problems for many people – for example, Japanese students educated abroad who return to Japan, as well as non-Japanese – who are not able to differentiate between the two mindsets. On the other hand, the ability to communicate in English is, for some, seen in a more positive light, as a way to circumvent this gap between the public and private spheres. For others who have seen the country go from zero to near saturation of the internet market in the space of 10 years, the globalization and democratization of information have allowed individuals to think and explore in dynamic new ways. Consequently, there has been a growing sense of Japan within a global community, rather than the traditional image of a strong empire leading Asian and world markets with little or no need to accommodate others.

In contrast to these progressive attitudes to using performative approaches for the development of ICC in JFL and JSL, there seems to be reluctance in using drama-based pedagogy to develop various skills within English foreign language classes in Japan. Despite this rather perfunctory attitude, there are a growing number of EFL educators who are incorporating various performative approaches in English language teaching in order to develop ICC.

Yuka Kusanagi, a member of IAPL, is an advocate for using the Japanese traditional performing art called *gundoku*, a type of readers' theater, which is then interpreted into a dramatic role play. She has utilized this technique in her English classes in three universities in Japan to date, and has found that it is adaptable to all levels and abilities. Her observations with respect to the benefits of performative approaches to language teaching as a means to develop ICC from both the perspectives of teacher and workshop participant are insightful and reflect its suitability within the cultural context of Japan. In her email interview, she writes:

> Drama-based activities have a big impact on self-discovery, understanding others and connecting with others, discovering diversity among people, understanding humans (literature, culture), having a feeling of amusement or pleasure (as a result, reducing the anxiety in learning), having a feeling of accomplishment, and so on as well as learning a language. These elements can be well linked with holistic learning, experiential learning, cooperative learning, multiple intelligences, and intersubjectivity. As for language learning, students can learn the target language in a natural context. Thus, they can acquire nonverbal communication with words without difficulty. Perhaps they can learn the language with less cognitive load with supports of nonverbal information.

Influenced by the theories of Augusto Boal (1993) and Robert di Pietro (1987), as well as by the contributors to the annual conference of the Philippines Educational Theater Association (PETA), Yasuko Shiozawa of Bunkyo University utilizes performative approaches in her third- and fourth-year seminars. In these classes, which are limited to 10 students, she uses short one-act plays to explore differences between Japanese and English paralanguage and to develop ICC skills.

Maho Hidaka of Kyoto Women's University incorporates performative approaches in EFL in the form of role plays in her interpretation seminars, with the overt aim of improving tour guide skills in English, but also of developing ICC skills. (As Kyoto is the cultural capital of Japan, it attracts millions of tourists each year, both domestic and international.) She maximizes learner-centeredness by assigning the task of creating a role play for presentation in class mid- and end-semester. In her research seminars, she prepares the students for a theater performance on which their graduation thesis is based. Although her students have a variety of experiences and abilities, both linguistic and theatrical, they share one great asset, that of high motivation. In her former position at Seisen University in Tokyo, Hidaka was actively encouraged to utilize her background in performance drama in EFL. There, the courses in performance were compulsory, while the drama workshops were elective. In these courses, students worked on plays in English, which were performed during the university's annual Fringe Festival. Even if students were not initially enthusiastic about drama-based activities, Hidaka found, as did Kawaguchi at Waseda University, a marked change in attitude by the end:

> Again, it varies; however, generally, students' reactions are/were highly positive when the courses are/were elective. Even if their reaction was not very positive at the beginning of the course in compulsory classes, they mostly gain positive attitudes towards drama-based activities, once they get to learn the joy of drama activities, especially through experiencing performing and collaborating with classmates during their rehearsal and performance.

Because of her artistic background (an MA in Creative Arts from Western Australian Academy of Performing Arts at Edith Cowan University), Hidaka is quite unusual. She took an academic, yet performance-focused, route toward performance in her professional career, which inspired her to include performative approaches in her English language classes. She places great importance on flexibility and constantly analyzes her students' needs to make necessary changes to her basic syllabus.

The establishment of the SDD Special Interest Group (SIG) within the Japanese Association of Language Teachers (JALT) has been a relatively recent development. However, the group is a dynamic one, meeting to share ideas through workshops and presentations three times a year and also maintaining a vibrant online presence on Facebook. Within this group, there are EFL educators in Japan who use performative approaches with the aim of enriching the practice and development of ICC. Yoko Morimoto, for instance, uses role plays adapted from movies for advanced political science and economics majors in which the emphasis is placed on exaggerated gestures. Her unusual background as an amateur actor in a French theater group in Paris and her research areas of neuroscience and psychology have exerted an influence on her teaching praxis, particularly in the development of ICC skills. Similarly, David Kluge uses his background as a theater major to enliven as many classes as he can, incorporating performance through boxing into debate, dramatic readings of poetry and song lyrics, as well as role plays to heighten students' skills in ICC while they simultaneously forget that they are performing *through* the target language of English. Finally, Marian Hara's rationale for using performative approaches to EFL in a private all-girls junior high school is that it helps her students develop speaking skills, confidence and creativity. She uses situational role plays based on dilemmas faced by 12- to 15-year-old girls in Japan, before moving into role plays based on intercultural miscommunication in which students seek resolution.

Although there is an awareness in Japan of the benefits of performative approaches in EFL, and there is anecdotal evidence that these approaches are having positive effects on the students as outlined by the practitioners above, this is countered by the relatively few people who actively use them in the classroom and the relative lack of academic materials published by those who include them in their curricula.

## Conclusion

Within the fields of JFL, JSL and EFL in Japan, dedicated individual educators have quietly utilized performative approaches in their teaching for many years, either in class or as extra-curricular subjects. In the last 10 years, moreover, these professionals have been coming together to share knowledge and approaches in groups such as IAPL and SDD. Performative approaches in SLA have much to offer the learner, irrespective of age, not only in terms of language but also in the development of ICC. In essence, performative approaches in SLA offer the learner a chance to educate and to be educated, to entertain and to be entertained, while developing ICC and, in so doing, forgetting that this is being done *through* the target language.

By devolving teacher-centeredness, performative approaches shift the teacher into a more facilitative role, allowing and encouraging the learner in the development of agency and subjectivity. However, while language acquisition can be assimilative, ICC is based both on the conscious and unconscious acquirement of knowledge, meaning and understanding of another culture. Therefore, one of the main benefits of performative approaches in SLA lies in the development of ICC, when the learner reframes the cultural norms and realities of another language, while simultaneously developing new perspectives and depths in his/her own cultural reality in ways that are both dynamic and discursive. Nevertheless, a further, more coordinated and triangulated approach to this topic as a research methodology is necessary. But this chapter, as an initial descriptive sample on how educators are using performative approaches to help learners develop ICC skills in the worlds of JFL, JSL and EFL in Japan, is a start.

## Notes

(1) It would be desirable to compile more detailed profiles of practitioners in the years to come, perhaps similar to how Feldhendler gives a comprehensive overview of his own practice in Chapter 10 of this volume.

(2) Within a typical conversation structure, the term 'back-channeling' refers to secondary communication from the listener (such as 'I see' and 'Is that so?') to indicate that he/she is following the primary communication from the speaker.

## References

Bernause, M., Furlong, A., Jonckheere, S. and Kervan, M. (2011) *Plurilingualism and pluriculturism in content-based teaching: A training kit*. Austria: Council of Europe Publishing.

Boal, A. (1993) *Theater of the Oppressed*. New York: Theater Communications Group.

Byram, M. (1997) *Teaching and Assessing Intercultural Communicative Competence*. Clevedon: Multilingual Matters.

Byram, M., Nichols, A. and Stevens, D. (2001) *Developing Intercultural Competence in Practice*. Clevedon: Multilingual Matters.

Byram, M., Gribova, B. and Starkey, H. (2002) *Developing the Intercultural Dimension in Language Teaching*. Strasbourg: Council of Europe.

Coyle, D. (2008). CLIL: A pedagogical approach from the European perspective. In N.H. Hornberger (ed.) *Encyclopedia of Language and Education* (2nd edn; vol. 4; pp. 97–112). New York: Springer Science+Business Media.

Coyle, D., Hood, P. and Marsh, D. (2010) *CLIL: Content Language Integrated Learning*. Cambridge: Cambridge University Press.

Craighead, W. and Nemeroff, C. (eds) (2001) *The Corsini Encyclopedia of Psychology and Behavioral Science* (3rd edn). New York: Wiley.

di Pietro, R.J. (1987) *Strategic Interaction: Learning Languages through Scenarios*. Cambridge: Cambridge University Press.

Doi, T. (1971) *The Anatomy of Dependence*. New York: Kodansha International.

Ellis, R. (1994) *The Study of Second Language Acquisition*. Oxford: Oxford University Press.

Gardner, R. (2001) Integrative motivation and second language acquisition. In Z. Dörnyei and R. Schmidt (eds) *Motivation and Second Language Acquisition* (pp. 1–21). Honolulu, HI: University of Hawaii.

Hewgill, D., Noro, H. and Poulton, C. (2004) Exploring drama and theatre in teaching Japanese: Hirata Oriza's play, *Tokyo Notes*, in an advanced Japanese conversation course. *World Japanese Language Education* (14), 227–252.

Hirata, O. (2004) *Engi to Enshutsu* [*Drama and Performance*]. Tokyo: Kodansha.

Kao, S. and O'Neill, C. (1998) *Words into Words: Learning a Second Language Through Process Drama*. Greenwich, CT: Ablex.

Kita, S. and Ide, S. (2007) Nodding, *Aizuchi*, and final particles in Japanese conversation: How conversation reflects the ideology of communication and social relationships. *Journal of Pragmatics* (39), 1242–1254.

Kramsch, C. (1998) *Language and Culture*. Oxford: Oxford University Press.

Marsh, D. (1994) Bilingual education & content and language integrated learning. *International Association for Cross-Cultural Communication, Language Teaching in the Member States of the European Union (Lingua).* Paris: University of Sorbonne.
Marsh, D. (ed.) (2002) *CLIL/EMILE – The European Dimension: Actions, Trends and Foresight Potential.* Brussels: European Commission.
Mehisto, P., Marsh, D. and Frigols, M.J. (eds) (2008) *Uncovering CLIL: Content and Language Integrated Learning in Bilingual and Multilingual Education.* Oxford: Macmillan.
Nakano, Y., Gilbert, J.E. and Donnery, E. (2009) Needs analysis for the improvement of the English curriculum for the School of Human Welfare Studies: A preliminary study. *Kwansei Gakuin University Repository.* See *www.kwansei.ac.jp/s_hws/attached/0000085365.pdf* (accessed 12 June 2017).
Noro, H., Hirata, O., Kawaguchi, Y. and Hashimoto, S. (2012) *Doramachikku Nihongo komyunike-shon [Dramatic Japanese Communication].* Tokyo: Koko.
Ushioda, E. (2013) Foreign language motivation in Japan: An 'insider' perspective from outside Japan. In M.T. Apple, D. Da Silva and T. Fellner (eds) *Language Learning Motivation in Japan* (pp. 1–14). Bristol: Multilingual Matters.

# Appendix A

Dear drama-based practitioner in Japan,

As part of the series 'Languages for Intercultural Communication and Education' by Multilingual Matters, Dr. John Crutchfield and Prof. Manfred Schewe are editing a book called *Performative Approaches to Foreign and Second Language Education: Intercultural Contexts and Perspectives*. I have submitted an abstract, which has been accepted, for a chapter that describes how practitioners are using drama in SLA within the fields of JFL and EFL in North America and in the East Asian region. I have collected the data for practitioners in the fields of JFL; however, I need your help to describe accurately how you are using drama-based pedagogies in YOUR EFL classes. If you wish, you can either handwrite the answers, or I can send you an electronic version of this document.

**Drama in Second/Foreign Language Acquisition:**
**Views from within EFL/JSL in Japan and JFL in North America**

**Name:** ________________________________________
**Position:** ______________________________________
**Current University:** _____________________________
**Past Universities:** ______________________________

(1) Describe how you use drama-based pedagogy for second language acquisition in your current position. Please include class demographics, target language background and abilities, level of motivation and previous exposure to drama, if known.

(2) Describe how you used drama-based pedagogy for second language acquisition in your past positions.

(3) How is/was your students' reaction to drama-based activities?

(4) How do/did you evaluate students?

(5) In your professional career, what formal training or informal events influenced to the extent that you include drama-based pedagogies in your language classes?

(6) What philosophies and/or theories influenced your teaching practice with respect to drama-based pedagogy?

*Thank you very much for your cooperation!* ☺

第二言語・外国語習得におけるドラマ
―日本と北米における日英語教育―
(電子メールインタビュー調査)

氏名: ______________________
職名: ______________________
現勤務先: ______________________
前勤務先: ______________________

1. 現在行なっている第二言語もしくは外国語教育においてドラマ（または関連の活動）をどう教育に使っているのか説明して下さい。教育コンテキスト、学生の学習言語レベルと能力、学習動機レベル、ドラマの経験等の背景情報も含めて下さい。

2. 過去に行なった第二言語もしくは外国語教育においてドラマ（または関連の活動）をどう教育に使ったのか説明して下さい。教育コンテキスト、学生の学習言語レベルと能力、学習動機レベル、ドラマの経験等の背景情報も含めて下さい。

3. 学生（現在および過去）のドラマ（または関連の活動）に対する反応を教えて下さい。

4. ドラマの実践における評価について教えて下さい。

5. あなたの教員キャリアで、ドラマ（または関連の活動）を言語教育に含めるに至った正式なドラマの訓練、あるいは非正式なドラマに接した経験を教えて下さい。

6. あなたのドラマ（または関連の活動）を含めた教育実践に、影響を与えた教育哲学や理論はありますか。

ご協力ありがとうございました。ドネリ・ユーケリアまでお送り下さい。

# Index